THE **Building Christian English** SERIES

Building

Christian English

Following the Plan

Grade 5

Rod and Staff Publishers, Inc.
P.O. Box 3, Hwy. 172
Crockett, Kentucky 41413

Telephone: (606) 522-4348

Acknowledgments

We are indebted first and most of all to God, whose blessing made possible the writing and publishing of this book.

We express gratitude to each one who was involved in this work. The original edition was written by Lela Birky and Lucy Ann Conley, and the revision by Marion W. Leinbach. Marvin Eicher was the editor, H. Lynn Martin and various others were reviewers, and the artwork was done by Lester Miller and Timothy Conley. We are also indebted to the teachers who used the material on a laboratory basis in their classrooms, as well as to numerous people who assisted along the way by providing finances, by encouraging those directly involved in the work, and by interceding in prayer for the work.

Various reference books were consulted in accomplishing this task, such as English handbooks, other English textbooks, encyclopedias, and dictionaries. For these too we are grateful. We have chosen to favor the more conservative schools of thought that are considered authoritative in correct English usage.

—*The Publishers*

Table of Contents

(Stars indicate composition and oral English lessons.)

Chapter 1

Working With Sentences

Chapter 2

More About Sentences

Chapter 3

Nouns

Chapter 4

Verbs

Chapter 5

More About Verbs

Chapter 6

Pronouns

Chapter 7

Adjectives and Adverbs

Chapter 8

Punctuation

Chapter 9

Prepositions, Conjunctions, and Interjections

Chapter 10

Capitalization, Reference Books, and More Punctuation

Statement: Pauline is reading her Bible.

Question: Where did Peter find the coin?

Chapter 1
Working With Sentences

Command: Study diligently.

Exclamation: Look at this huge tree!

1. Introduction

God has given people the miraculous ability to communicate through speaking, listening, writing, and reading. Birds and animals communicate too, but their simple signals cannot be compared to communication between people. Our communication includes sharing information, expressing feelings, telling stories, giving directions, and much more. It is hard to imagine how we would live without communicating with each other.

Communication must first of all be clear and understandable. If you hope to communicate well in English, you must learn to speak and write according to the rules of English. Look at the following four sentences. They do **not** follow the rules!

It don't matter none what he seen.
There's four chickens drownded in the pond.
Them there busted windows gotta be fixed.
She musta knowed it was me and Paul.

We do not come to school with dirty, wrinkled clothes or with egg yolk smeared on our faces. We do not tease or insult our friends. And we do not use crude English as we see in the sentences above. We want to live a life that is courteous, neat, and pleasing to God and others. If we break the rules of standard English, people may suspect that we break other rules that do not suit us.

To do well in your study of English, you must have good work habits. One important habit is to have a clean, orderly desk, where you can always find things quickly when you want them. Another good habit is to use an assignment tablet, in which you carefully write every assignment as soon as it is given.

Yet another good habit is to keep each assignment paper where you can find it. You may have a certain place in your notebook for it, or you may keep it in your book at the lesson where you are working. Then you will know exactly where to look for your paper when the assignment is due.

Remember to prepare your paper in the same way every day. Use the pattern below, or follow the one that your teacher gives you.

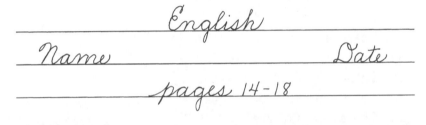

English

Name   *Date*

pages 14–18

> **Oral Drill**

A. Examine your book, and answer these questions.
   1. What is the title of your English book?
   2. What is the copyright date of your book?
   3. What company published your book? What is the address of the company?
   4. Look in the table of contents for answers to these questions.
      a. Which chapters teach about sentences?
      b. Which chapter teaches about pronouns?
      c. Which chapters teach about verbs?

5. Use the index to answer these questions.
   a. Which pages teach about proper nouns?
   b. Which pages teach how to use hyphens?
   c. Which pages teach about the verbs **may, might,** and **must**?
   d. Which pages teach nominative pronouns?
   e. Which pages tell about the articles **a, an,** and **the**?

B. Tell how to correct the following sentences.
   1. He sung to us.
   2. She don't know that song.
   3. Jesus dealt kindly with the sinful woman.
   4. Marla rung the bell this morning.
   5. The moon raises in the east.
   6. Lay down and rest.
   7. My bicycle sets in the driveway.
   8. Leave me catch the butterfly!
   9. Can I keep it?
   10. Learn me how to run this lawn mower.
   11. Aunt Lucy will read to she and I.
   12. Father and him fed the calves.
   13. I and you will feed the pigs.
   14. These here flowers are tall.
   15. Do your work good.

C. Write today's date in your assignment tablet, at the top of the page for today's assignments. Write your English assignment in the correct place, along with the date when it is due. Keep all your assignments in this tablet.

> Written Practice >

A. Prepare a paper according to the pattern shown in the lesson. Use it to do the following exercises.

B. Write the correct word for each definition by using the table of contents and the index for help.

noun   adjective   preposition
pronoun   adverb   conjunction
verb

1. A word that describes a verb by telling **how, when,** or **where.**
2. A word that shows action or being.
3. A word that names a person, place, or thing.
4. A word that describes a noun or a pronoun by telling **which, whose, how many,** or **what kind of.**
5. A word that takes the place of a noun.
6. A word that joins words or groups of words.
7. A connecting word that begins a phrase.

C. Write the correct word for each sentence. Use the table of contents or the index if you need help.

1. The children often (swang, swung) in the yard.
2. Mark (don't, doesn't) know the answer.
3. James (losed, lost) his new notebook.
4. Jerry (drank, drunk) all the juice.
5. Amanda was (raising, rising) her hand.
6. The water in the creek (raises, rises) after a heavy rain.
7. Please (lay, lie) the paper on my desk.
8. (Set, Sit) quietly during the church services.
9. (Let, Leave) me help you, Mother.
10. Do not go to church and (let, leave) your Bible behind.
11. (Can, May) you carry this heavy box?
12. (Can, May) I have a drink, please?
13. Will you (teach, learn) me how to hold a tiny baby?
14. In my science lesson, I (taught, learned) about the moon.
15. Give the book to (she, her).
16. My Sunday school teacher is (he, him).
17. Martha and (I, me) will gladly wash the dishes for you.

18. (Them, Those) pies smell delicious.
19. We should love the Lord (weller, better) than anyone else.
20. He pronounces his words (good, well).
21. Is Grandfather not feeling (good, well)?

D. Use the index if you need help in doing the following exercises. They will help you get ready to study sentences.
1. What is the definition of a verb?
2. List five action verbs.
3. What are the forms of the verb **be**?
4. What are the forms of the verb **have**?

E. Copy all the verbs in the following sentences. Watch for the helping verbs in verb phrases.
1. I am the Door.
2. Shepherds are watching their sheep.
3. He has a little lamb.
4. The sheep are in the fold.
5. The Martins have been shearing sheep all morning.
6. The Bensons had fifty sheep.

━━━━━━━━━━

2. Complete Sentences

Do you always speak in complete sentences? Often in conversation we use only parts of sentences because the other person knows the missing words.

What did you read in the Bible this morning?
A story.
Which one?
About Cain and Abel.

In writing we usually need to use complete sentences. The reader may not know what we are talking about if our sentences are incomplete. The reader cannot ask us questions. Read these complete sentences.

> What did you read in the Bible this morning?
> I read a story this morning.
> Which story did you read?
> I read the story about Cain and Abel.

A sentence is a group of words that expresses a complete thought. It has a **subject** that tells **who** or **what** the sentence is about, and a **predicate** that tells what the subject does or is.

The subject tells **who** or **what** the sentence is about. In the following sentences, the words in bold print are the subjects. A short vertical line divides each subject from the rest of the sentence.

> **The fear of the Lord** | is the beginning of wisdom.
> **Abraham** | obeyed the Lord.
> **Glenn and his sister** | picked the peas.
> **My little black dog** | is waiting for me.

The predicate tells what the subject does or is. The words in bold print in the following sentences are the predicates. A short vertical line divides each predicate from the rest of the sentence.

> The fear of the Lord | **is the beginning of wisdom.**
> Abraham | **obeyed the Lord.**
> Glenn and his sister | **picked the peas.**
> My little black dog | **is waiting for me.**

Every sentence begins with a capital letter and ends with a period or some other end punctuation.

> The Bible is God's Word.
> What did Jesus do?
> Jesus raised a dead man to life!

> **Remember:** A sentence is a group of words that expresses a
> complete thought. The subject and the predicate are the two main
> parts of a sentence.

> **Oral Drill** >

Tell whether each group of words is a **complete sentence,** a
subject, or a **predicate.** If it is only a subject or a predicate, add
words to make a complete sentence.
1. A large, uprooted tree.
2. Does not see the rabbit.
3. Harold can draw one for us.
4. Wearily climbed the long hill.
5. We shall find him soon.
6. The roof of the shed.
7. Has dug a hole in Mother's flower garden.

> **Written Practice** >

A. Match the subjects and predicates to make good sentences.
   Write each completed sentence correctly.
   1. great hailstones   was growing near the road
   2. brother mast and his son   fell on Israel's enemies
   3. a huge old oak tree   should obey their parents
   4. all children   laid concrete blocks rapidly

B. Copy each group of words. If it is not a complete sentence,
   add words to make it complete. Draw a short line between
   each subject and predicate.
   1. Was hurrying across the lawn.
   2. Several interesting pictures.

3. This boy wants to help us.
4. Blew furiously today.
5. The clean clothes.
6. Some trees are hundreds of years old.

—————————————

3. The Predicate of a Sentence

The predicate of a sentence tells what the subject does or is. The predicate of every sentence contains a verb. A verb is a word that shows action or being.

> **Examples of *action* verbs:** blow, learn, catch
> **Forms of the verb *be:***   am, is, are, was, were, be, been, being

The **complete predicate** contains the verb and all the other words that tell what the subject does or is. The verb is the **simple predicate** of the sentence. In the sentence below, the complete predicate is in bold print and is divided from the rest of the sentence by a short line. The simple predicate is underlined twice.

> Wise King Solomon | **<u>wrote</u> many proverbs.**

The simple predicate may be just one word, or it may be a **verb phrase.**

> The little bird | **<u>flew</u> rapidly away.**
> The drifting snow | **<u>was filling</u> the lane.**

A
soft answer
turneth
away wrath.

Proverbs 15:1

In a verb phrase, one or more **helping verbs** come first and the **main verb** comes last. Here are the helping verbs that you studied in grade 4. Be sure you know them all by memory.

> **Forms of *be*:** am, is, are, was, were, be, been, being
> ***H* triplets:**   have, has, had
> ***D* triplets:**   do, does, did
> ***M* triplets:**   may, might, must
> **Three sets of twins:**
> can—could, shall—should, will—would

Forms of **be, have,** and **do** can be main verbs or helping verbs.

I | **am** Alpha and Omega, the beginning and the end.
I | **am** rejoicing in the Lord.

Mother | **has** beautiful flowers.
This flower | **has** bloomed early.

Marcus | **did** all the chores.
We | **did** finish our work.

Remember: The complete predicate contains the verb and all the other words that tell what the subject does or is. The simple predicate is the verb or verb phrase in the predicate.

Be sure you know all the helping verbs so that you can recognize them instantly. They are as follows:

Forms of *be*: am, is, are, was, were, be, been, being
***H* triplets:** have, has, had
***D* triplets:** do, does, did
***M* triplets:** may, might, must
Three sets of twins: can—could, shall—should, will—would

> **Oral Drill** >

A. Give the main verb in each phrase.

   1. had gone   4. will have been

   2. will be coming   5. shall write

   3. were telling   6. have been singing

B. First read the complete predicate of each sentence. Then read the simple predicate.

   1. Christ died for us.

   2. We have a great High Priest.

   3. The Lord God planted a garden eastward in Eden.

   4. God has made everything beautiful.

   5. My God shall supply all your need.

   6. The Lord has done great things for us.

   7. The heavens declare the glory of God.

   8. Jesus healed the blind man.

> **Written Practice** >

A. Copy the complete predicate of each sentence. Draw two lines under the simple predicate.

Examples: a. My God shall supply all your need.

            b. I am the Bread of Life.

Answers: a. <u>shall supply</u> all your need

            b. <u>am</u> the Bread of Life

   1. Jesus called James and John.

   2. Our Saviour will come again someday.

   3. We shall see Him soon.

   4. Heaven is a place of eternal happiness.

   5. The apostle John saw many beautiful things in heaven.

B. Copy the simple predicate of each sentence. If the simple predicate is a verb phrase, write **H** above each helping verb.

Examples: a. Many people gathered around Absalom.

   b. Absalom was coming toward Jerusalem.

Answers: a. gathered

   b. was coming

1. David fled from Absalom.
2. Hushai was helping David.
3. He gave bad counsel to Absalom.
4. God was protecting David.
5. Jonathan and Ahimaaz carried a message from Hushai to David.
6. A lad had seen them.
7. The lad told David's enemies.
8. The young men hid in a well.
9. A woman covered the well.
10. Absalom's servants were searching for them.
11. The spies were soon there.
12. The young men escaped safely.
13. David's servants stayed with him.
14. God cared for King David.

Review and Practice

Follow the directions.

1. List five action verbs that are not used as examples in the lesson.
2. List all the forms of the verb **be.**
3. List ten helping verbs besides the forms of **be.**

4. The Subject of a Sentence

The complete subject of a sentence contains all the words that tell **who** or **what** the sentence is about. The complete subject usually has one main word that tells **who or what.** This word is usually a noun, and it is the simple subject of the sentence. The following sentence is divided between the complete subject and the complete predicate. The complete subject is in bold print, and the simple subject is underlined.

Twelve brave <u>Israelites</u> | spied out the land of Canaan.

The simple subject may be a noun or a noun phrase. A noun phrase is a group of words that name a person, place, or thing.

<u>Brother David Brown</u> | works here.
<u>North Dakota</u> | has large wheat fields.
The <u>Nile River</u> | is the longest river in the world.
A <u>mountain lion</u> | may reach a length of five feet.

The simple subject may be a pronoun. All the subject pronouns may be used as simple subjects. Do you remember them? They are listed here.

I, you, he, she, it, we, they

Here are some sentences with pronoun subjects.

She | is making apple pies.
We | like to eat them.

To find the simple subject, be sure to use the following steps.
a. First, find the simple predicate.
b. Ask **who** or **what** about the simple predicate.
c. Say the simple subject and the simple predicate together to see if they make sense.

Notice how these steps are used for the following sentences.

Uncle Dan strode briskly up the street.
>The simple predicate is **strode.**
>**Who** strode? Uncle Dan.
>**Uncle Dan strode** makes sense.
>The simple subject is **Uncle Dan.**

Your paint has spilled on the floor.
>The simple predicate is **has spilled.**
>**What** has spilled? Paint.
>**Paint has spilled** makes sense.
>The simple subject is **paint.**

Be careful! Not every noun in a sentence is the simple subject. The simple subject is only the noun that names who or what does or is something.

Our brown hen lays large brown eggs.
>Both **hen** and **eggs** are nouns. Which is the simple subject?
>The verb is **lays.**
>**What** lays? The hen lays, not the eggs lay.
>So the simple subject is **hen.**

Remember: The complete subject of a sentence contains all the words that tell **who** or **what** the sentence is about. The simple subject is the noun, noun phrase, or pronoun that tells **who** or **what** the sentence is about.

Use the following steps when finding the simple subject.
>a. First, find the simple predicate.
>b. Ask **who** or **what** about the simple predicate.
>c. Say the simple subject and the simple predicate together to see if they make sense.

Oral Drill

Read the complete subject of each sentence. Then tell which word or phrase is the simple subject.

1. Billowy white clouds drifted across the sky.
2. Brother Alvin Groff led the singing last night.
3. She was baking cookies today.
4. The other book may have better definitions.
5. They will build a new shed tomorrow.
6. A merry heart doeth good like a medicine.
7. Lynn Canal is in Alaska.
8. The lofty Mount Mansfield is found in the Green Mountains of Vermont.
9. The dump truck unloaded the gravel.

Written Practice

Copy each complete subject, and underline the simple subject.

1. I will pour out My Spirit upon you.
2. The Suda Bay is an inlet of the Aegean Sea.
3. Yellowstone National Park is in Wyoming.
4. A soft, kind answer will turn away wrath.
5. Sugar Loaf Mountain looks like a cone of sugar.

© Corel

6. We must work hard.

7. Mother will bring us some lemonade.

8. Ice cream is a favorite treat.

9. Our faithful God shall bring it to pass.

10. He shall bring forth thy righteousness as the light.

11. Noah was a faithful, godly man.

12. One happy leper was grateful to the Saviour.

13. Wise Solomon built the temple in Jerusalem.

> ### Review and Practice

Copy the simple subject and the simple predicate of each sentence. Draw one line under the simple subject and two lines under the simple predicate.

1. The princes cast Jeremiah into a dungeon.

2. Ebed-melech told the king.

3. Jeremiah was drawn by cords out of the dungeon.

4. Ebed-melech was blessed for his kindness.

5. God delivered Jeremiah from death.

6. The stones were laid for the temple.

7. The temple was built by willing men.

8. The trumpet sounded loud and long.

9. Abigail gave good advice to David.

10. David lived at Bethlehem.

5. Writing About a Personal Experience

Do you ever have trouble knowing what to write about when you start a letter or a composition? There are many things to write about. One thing you can always write about is something that happened to you. Many interesting things happen to you that do not happen to anyone else.

Once there was a blind girl named Helen. She wrote an interesting story and had it printed, but then she found out that someone else had written about the same thing. The other writer was displeased because he thought Helen had copied from his story. Helen felt discouraged. She said, "I am afraid to write stories. How can I know someone else did not write one like it before me?"

One person gave Helen a good answer. He said, "Write about yourself. Tell about things that happened to you and how you felt about them. Then you will know that no one else wrote that story before you did."

Helen followed his advice. She began writing about the struggles that blind people have. Many people still receive encouragement from her writings.

All of us have stories to tell. We may write about some important experience like a storm, fire, trip, sickness, accident, or flood. Or we may write about a more common event, like when we made and flew a kite or when we found baby kittens in the barn. A well-told story about something common can be just as interesting as a story about something unusual.

We may not think that many interesting things happen to us. But when something happens, we are probably not noticing details that make it interesting. We need to ask ourselves questions like **who, what, when, where, why,** and **how.** The problem is not that we lack interesting experiences but that we fail to notice what makes them interesting.

Here is a story that tells very little. The questions following the story could be used to find details that would make the story much more interesting.

Last summer our barn burned down. It happened at night. Our neighbors helped to build it again.

1. Were you sleeping when it happened?
2. Who saw it first? Did you?

3. Who or what woke you?
4. How much was burned before someone saw it?
5. Who called the fire department?
6. Was your whole family out watching it?
7. Was anyone hurt in the fire?
8. Were you frightened?
9. How long did it take for the fire engines to come?
10. Did you ever find out what started the fire?
11. Where did the firemen get water to fight the fire?
12. How much was the cost of the damage?
13. How many people came to help rebuild the barn?
14. How long did it take to rebuild the barn?

When you write about a personal experience, be sure you know the details well. You must keep things in their proper order, with first things first and last things last. Include all the important information, but leave out unnecessary details. Give the story a good beginning and a good ending. And remember to use good grammar, correct spelling, and neat handwriting.

Remember: Learn to ask questions about personal happenings so that you can think of interesting details.

Oral Drill

A. Think of questions you could ask for details to make the following story more interesting.

One time a tornado came near our house. It tore out a tree just behind our house. My mother heard the noise, and she was scared.

B. Give some questions you should answer in writing stories about the following topics.
1. The Big Blizzard at School
2. Saving the Injured Bird
3. Special Visitors at School
4. An Unusual Birthday Gift
5. When My Sister Fixed the Table Lamp
6. The Day We Cleaned the Attic

C. Tell which details are unnecessary in this story.

Our family was building a new house. My little brother was upstairs watching the workmen. The one workman's name was Isaac. Everyone liked him because he talked a lot. Isaac showed us where he once cut his finger in a saw on another job. The floor of the upstairs was not yet finished, but the plasterboard was nailed on for the ceiling downstairs. My little brother didn't know this was not the real floor. He stepped off the joists and down onto the plasterboard. Before anyone knew what had happened, he landed on the floor of the kitchen down below. My mother, who was painting nearby, didn't know what was suddenly coming down beside her. She was painting the woodwork. There was a lot of woodwork to paint, and it took a long time. Up above was a gaping hole in the plasterboard where my brother had just come through. We were thankful that he was not seriously hurt.

Follow these steps to write a story about a personal experience.

1. Write down an idea for your story.
2. Write a list of questions you could ask to help you think of interesting details. Put the questions in proper order, with first things first.
3. Write your story, answering the questions you wrote.

6. Statements and Questions

Why did God make sentences? He chose this way of giving His knowledge to us. He used one kind of sentence to tell something, and another kind to ask something. He gave us the ability to understand His sentences and to communicate with Him and with one another in the same way.

A sentence that states a fact or gives information is a **statement.** A sentence that asks for information is a **question.** A statement ends with a period, and a question ends with a question mark.

> **Statement:** Blessed are the pure in heart.
> **Question:**   Adam, where art thou?

There are different kinds of questions. Some questions can be answered with **yes** or **no.**

> Is the bear sitting on a large rock?

Some questions begin with **wh** words: **who, whose, whom, what, which, when, where,** and **why.**

Where is the bear sitting?
What is the bear sitting on?

Almost all questions have a helping verb before the subject. In each question below, the subject is underlined once and the verbs are underlined twice. The helping verbs are in bold print.

Where **has** the old yellow cat hidden her kittens?
Will your neighbor raise cotton and peanuts?
Was the house near the bridge struck by lightning?

Remember: A statement states a fact or gives information. It ends with a period. A question asks for information. It ends with a question mark.

Oral Drill

Tell whether each group of words is a **statement** or a **question.** Tell what end punctuation each should have.

1. Leeuwenhoek (lā´· vən· hük) looked through his microscope
2. He was surprised to see little creatures in the water
3. They were swimming about like tadpoles in a pool
4. Were they little animals
5. He found them in every drop of water
6. Which ones live in milk
7. Where did the little animals come from
8. How had Leeuwenhoek discovered bacteria
9. Did anyone imagine that these creatures might be dangerous
10. No one worried about the tiny creatures until about two hundred years later
11. Louis Pasteur realized that they are among the most important things in the world

> Written Practice >

A. Write **S** or **Q** to tell whether each sentence is a statement or a question. Also write the correct end punctuation for each sentence.

1. Louis Pasteur studied the little animals
2. Louis showed dairymen how to kill the creatures so that milk would not turn sour
3. What did he call the tiny creatures
4. He called them microbes
5. Doctors began to realize that the microbes cause many diseases
6. Which diseases are caused by microbes
7. How can the diseases be cured
8. God made every creature, great and small
9. He has made everything good
10. What has brought diseases into the world
11. Sin has brought sickness and sorrow

B. Rewrite each statement as a question that can be answered with **yes** or **no.**

Example: Brian mowed the lawn.
Answer: Did Brian mow the lawn?

1. Father bought a calf for me to raise.
2. The calf can drink out of a bucket.

C. For each of the following statements, write three **wh** questions that the statement will answer.

Example: Carl's horse galloped swiftly down the road.
Answer: What galloped swiftly down the road?
              Whose horse galloped down the road?
              Where did the horse gallop swiftly?

1. The brown cow eats alfalfa in the morning.
2. In the Garden, Jesus prayed earnestly to His Father.

Review and Practice

A. List the seven subject pronouns.

B. Write four noun phrases. Two should name people, and two should name places.

Challenge Exercise

A. For each sentence, write a question that can be answered with **yes** or **no.** Write a negative answer for each question.

Example: We have seen him.
Answer: Have we seen him?
　　　　　No, we have not seen him.

1. Wilbur has fed the chickens.
2. She has forgotten the address.
3. He will recognize us.

B. For each sentence, write a question that can be answered with **yes** or **no.** You will need to change the verb form and use the helping verb **did.** Write a negative answer for each question.

Example: She wrote the letter.
Answer: Did she write the letter?
　　　　　No, she did not write the letter.

1. He caught a fish.
2. The raccoon stole a chicken.
3. Galen pulled weeds.

7. Commands and Exclamations

God uses a certain kind of sentence to tell us what to do and what not to do. In the New Testament, Jesus said, "Do not steal." Jesus gave a command. A **command** tells someone to do something. It may give instructions, or it may make a request. A command ends with a period.

The subject of a command is always **you,** but it is usually not stated in the sentence. When it is not given, we say that the subject **you** is understood.

> Write your name on your paper. **(You)** write.
> Have another apple. **(You)** have.
> You tell your sister to come. **You** tell.

The verb is usually the first word in a command, but sometimes it comes after a word like **please, always,** or **never.**

> Always sign your name. **(You)** sign.

A statement, question, or command that expresses strong feeling is an **exclamation.** An exclamation ends with an exclamation mark. Read the following sentences that are used as exclamations.

> **Statement:** The cows are out in the road!
> **Question:**   How could you do such a thing!
> **Command:** Watch that child!

Some exclamations have their own special word order.

What a pleasant surprise that was!
How he laughed!
If only I had known earlier!

Remember: A command tells or requests you to do something. It ends with a period. An exclamation shows strong feeling. It ends with an exclamation mark.

> **Oral Drill**

A. Tell whether each group of words is a **statement, question,** or **command.** Tell what end punctuation should be used.
   1. These jars can hold two quarts
   2. Please tell your parents the news
   3. When did the ice melt off the pond
   4. Can a mosquito hear
   5. Always practice good posture
   6. Strive diligently to enter in at the strait gate, which leads to life

B. Tell what kind of sentence each would be if it were not an exclamation.
   1. Thank God for His plan of salvation!
   2. How hard it is for those who trust in riches to enter the kingdom of God!
   3. How mighty is our God!
   4. Be courteous!
   5. What is that obstacle ahead of us!
   6. How did the steer get into the cellar!

> Written Practice >

A. Write **S, Q,** or **C** to tell whether each sentence is a statement, question, or command. Also write the correct end punctuation.
   1. By what authority did Jesus teach and heal others
   2. Jesus rode triumphantly into Jerusalem on a colt
   3. To what did Jesus liken the kingdom of God
   4. Go into all the world, and preach the Gospel
   5. What book are you reading
   6. You will have much joy and gladness
   7. A good tree cannot bring forth evil fruit
   8. The twelve disciples marveled at Jesus' authority
   9. Come now, and let us reason together
   10. Will the Lord correct those He loves
   11. Search me, O God, and see if there is any wicked way in me
   12. Praise the Name of God with a song

B. Write **statement, question,** or **command** to tell what kind of sentence each of these would be if it were not an exclamation.
   1. The whole earth is full of God's glory!
   2. Praise ye the Lord!
   3. He has made everything beautiful!
   4. Can one go upon hot coals and his feet not be burned!
   5. Go and preach to Nineveh!
   6. What would have happened if the people had not repented!

C. Write a statement, a question, a command, and an exclamation of your own. Punctuate each one correctly.

> **Review and Practice**

Copy the simple subject and the simple predicate of each sentence. Draw one line under the simple subject and two lines under the simple predicate.

1. We shall go to church tomorrow.
2. Brother John will bring the message.
3. Toward the south many geese flew.
4. The whippoorwill was heard each evening.
5. The squirrels have hidden all their nuts.
6. Mother has made two dresses.
7. I do see the geese in the sky.
8. The Jordan River runs into the Dead Sea.
9. The Sea of Galilee is located north of the Dead Sea.
10. They learned their verses yesterday.

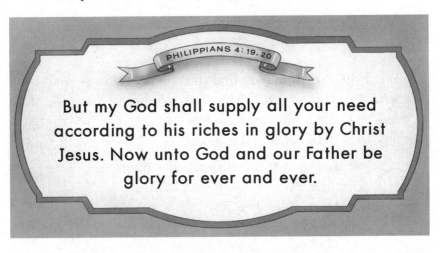

PHILIPPIANS 4:19, 20

But my God shall supply all your need according to his riches in glory by Christ Jesus. Now unto God and our Father be glory for ever and ever.

8. Diagraming Sentence Skeletons

Drawing a diagram or picture of something helps us to see the different parts better. Diagraming sentences helps to show us the work of each word in a sentence.

The simple subject and the simple predicate (or verb) form the **skeleton** of a sentence. The simple subject is put on the left half of a sentence diagram, and the simple predicate (or verb) is put on the right half. A line separates the subject from the predicate.

The young boy gave his lunch to Jesus.

boy	gave

He was sharing.

He	was sharing

To find the skeleton, first find the simple predicate and then ask **who** or **what** about it. The word or phrase that tells **who** or **what** is the simple subject. Check by saying the two parts together to be sure they make sense.

A slow, steady rain was falling that morning.
> The simple predicate is **was falling.**
> **What** was falling? Rain.
> **Rain was falling** makes sense, so it is the skeleton.

If the simple subject is a noun phrase, be sure to write the whole phrase on the left half of the diagram.

Mount Mitchell is the highest peak in the Appalachians.

Mount Mitchell	is

A polar bear weighs less than two pounds at birth.

| polar bear | weighs |

If the simple predicate is a verb phrase, be sure to write the whole phrase on the right half of the diagram. In many questions, the verb phrase is split. Part of it comes before the subject, and part of it comes after. Study the following examples.

Statement: Pauline **is reading** her Bible.

| Pauline | is reading |

Question: Where **did** Peter **find** the coins?

| Peter | did find |

Many questions are easier to diagram if you put the words in normal order before you diagram them. Study the following question and its diagram.

Inverted order: Will you memorize these verses?
Normal order: (you Will memorize these verses)

| you | Will memorize |

Remember that **you** is understood in most commands. When you diagram such a command, write **you** in parentheses for the simple subject. Do not use parentheses if **you** is stated.

Consider the work of God.

| (you) | Consider |

You do your homework.

You	do

Remember: Use the following steps to find the skeleton of a sentence.
1. First, find the simple predicate.
2. Ask **who** or **what** about the simple predicate.
3. Say the simple subject and the simple predicate together to see if they make sense.

> Oral Drill >

Give the skeleton of each sentence, and diagram it on the chalkboard.
1. The Susquehanna River flows through Pennsylvania.
2. You bring your book the next time.
3. Was your older sister baking pies?
4. He had taken the last doughnut.
5. Never molest a sleeping dog!
6. Has any rain fallen this month?
7. Teach me Thy way.
8. Where have you been?
9. Jeremiah's book was burned.

❯ Written Practice ❯

Diagram the sentence skeletons.
1. Prepare the Passover.
2. Where shall we prepare it?
3. Go to the large upper room.
4. A lad came to the field with Jonathan.
5. You go after the arrows.
6. Are they beyond you?
7. Carry them to the city.
8. Sail to the other side of the lake.
9. A fierce windstorm came up!
10. Jesus was sleeping in the ship.
11. Be still!
12. The disciples feared greatly.
13. He commanded the wind and water.
14. They will obey Him.
15. Lake Louise shimmers in the sunlight.
16. Is Mount Everest the highest mountain in the world?
17. Will you read the story to us?
18. The chain saw can cut the large tree.

❯ Review and Practice ❯

A. Write **S, Q,** or **C** to tell whether each sentence is a statement, question, or command. Also write the correct end punctuation.
1. Be sure to observe the beauty of nature
2. Leaves have been falling from the trees
3. Are the geese flying south already
4. They fly in a **V** formation
5. Thank the Lord for His goodness to us

B. Write **statement, question,** or **command** to tell what kind of sentence each of these would be if it were not an exclamation.

1. Look at all those geese!
2. How wonderful God has made them!
3. Did you see that!
4. Help me pull it out!
5. How big it was!

> Challenge Exercise >

Diagram all the words in these sentences. See how much you remember from grade 4.

Example: That big book on the table was printed in Germany.

Answer:

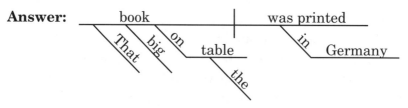

1. A boy with red hair came down the road.
2. James waited near the door for his little brother.
3. The cookies in the bag are for your friends.
4. Eleven faithful disciples were following Jesus to the Garden.
5. Shirley and her new friend are still working hard.

9. Using Exact Words

The English language contains hundreds of useful and inter-esting words. You probably know thousands of them already! By continuing to read and write, you will learn more and more words as you grow older.

Take time to choose exact words when you write. Some words describe a thought more precisely than others. The more words you know, the better you will be able to choose just the right word. Learn new words so that you can select the best word to suit your purpose.

Suppose you are to write a paragraph describing a flower. You could write about the **sections** of the blossoms, the **little things** in the middle, and the **small parts** underneath. But your para-graph will be much better if you use exact terms. Study the diagram below. What exact words could you use in writing about the different parts of a flower?

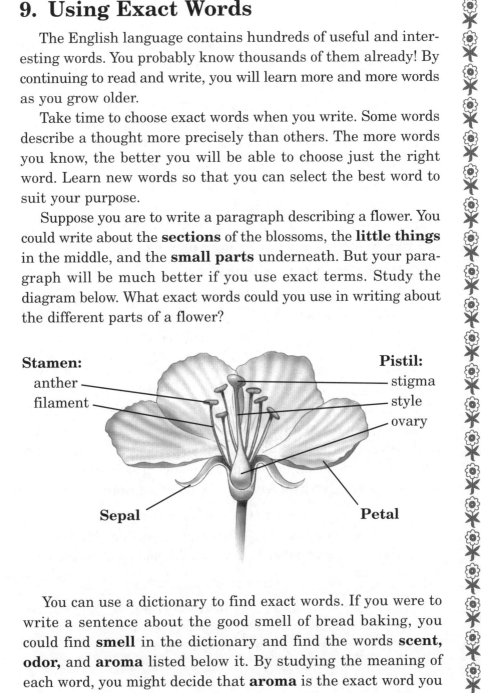

Stamen:
anther
filament

Pistil:
stigma
style
ovary

Sepal

Petal

You can use a dictionary to find exact words. If you were to write a sentence about the good smell of bread baking, you could find **smell** in the dictionary and find the words **scent, odor,** and **aroma** listed below it. By studying the meaning of each word, you might decide that **aroma** is the exact word you need to tell about the **smell** of the bread.

Some words are so broad in meaning that they do not say much. One example is the word **bad.** If you say "He was a **bad** boy," do you mean he was just **disagreeable,** a little **mischievous,** or downright **disobedient**? When you say "He did a **bad** job," do you mean he did a **faulty** job that is still good enough? Or did he do such an **unacceptable** job that the result is totally **worthless**? There usually are several words that are more exact than the first word that comes to your mind.

Your words should be exact, but they should not be bigger than necessary. For example, **desire** means much the same as **want. Manner** means much the same as **way.** Which of the following sentences are more simple and natural?

Do you **want** to go with me?
Do you **desire** to go with me?

The boy walked in the same **manner** as his father.
The boy walked in the same **way** as his father.

Do not use a big word when a short, simple word will express the meaning just as well. Do not use big words to show off your vocabulary. The best writing has words that are clear and exact, but also as simple and natural as possible.

Modifying words must not be overused. They should be left out if they add little meaning. Read the following sentences as they are, and then read them without the boldface words.

The morning was **a little** cool but **pretty** pleasant.
He had a **very** long list of **rather** important things to do.
There was a **terribly** heavy snowfall and an **awfully** brisk wind.

A dictionary will help you to choose exact words. A dictionary usually gives synonyms. By comparing their meanings, you should be able to choose exactly the word you need.

> **Remember:** A good writer uses exact words. A dictionary is helpful for choosing the best word to suit your purpose.

Oral Drill

A. Replace each boldface word with one that is more expressive. Use your dictionary for help.
1. The boys found a **funny** turtle.
2. We saw a **big** tree.
3. The calf **squashed** the **little** flower.

B. Use a dictionary to find three synonyms for each of these words, and use them in brief sentences.
   1. hard   3. pretty
   2. fast   4. break

C. Give five words that name various shades of red.

Written Practice

A. Write a more expressive word to replace each boldface word. Use a dictionary for help.
1. A **bright** star was overhead.
2. The weather was **nice.**
3. Our hosts served **good** meals.

B. For each word, write two synonyms and two short sentences in which you use the synonyms. Use a dictionary to help you find synonyms.
   1. nice
   2. little
   3. good
   4. funny

C. Write six short sentences that name animals and tell what sounds they make.

Example: Horses neigh.

D. List six words that tell what the wind does.

> **Review and Practice**

Answer these questions.

1. What is one thing you can always write about that will give you many interesting topics?
2. What questions should you ask to help you notice interesting details?
3. What three rules should you remember when writing a story?
4. What tool will help you find exact words to use in writing?

10. Chapter 1 Review

> **Oral Drill**

A. Answer the following questions.

1. Why should we study English?
2. Why must communication be clear, orderly, and attractive?
3. Why are good work habits helpful?
4. What must you know well to write about a personal experience?
5. In what order should the facts of your experience be given?

B. Answer the following questions about verbs.
1. What is the definition of a verb?
2. What are the forms of the verb **be**?
3. What are the forms of the verb **have**?
4. What other helping verbs did you study in this chapter?

C. Give the complete predicate and the simple predicate of each sentence. Tell which is the main verb in each verb phrase.
1. Abraham entertained strangers very kindly.
2. Clean water was given to them for their feet.
3. Sarah had a meal ready.
4. God will destroy Sodom.
5. I am a jealous God.
6. He shall come someday.
7. The diligent shepherds are building sheepfolds.

D. Give the complete subject and the simple subject of each sentence.
1. Mr. Joseph Bailey was the mayor.
2. I am the Good Shepherd.
3. The Gulf of Mexico receives the water from all the rivers in Louisiana.
4. White-tailed deer roam in wooded swamps.
5. Six brown pelicans built nests by the water.

E. Tell what kind of sentence each would be if it were not an exclamation.
1. Oh, how I love Thy law!
2. Study diligently!
3. This is a valuable lesson!
4. I heard a loud noise!
5. What was that!
6. Take care!

> **Written Practice** >

A. Copy each group of words. If it is not a complete sentence, add words to make it complete. Draw a short line between each subject and predicate.
   1. Mary loved the Bible.
   2. Visited her neighbors every Saturday.
   3. Studied her Sunday school lesson there.
   4. The diligent girl.
   5. She traveled many miles on foot.
   6. Mary Jones walked alone.
   7. Bibles were very scarce.
   8. Cried heartbrokenly.
   9. Sympathetic Mr. Charles.
   10. The happy girl carried her Bible home.

B. Write the correct word to match each definition.
   1. It tells you to do something.   statement
   2. It asks for information.   question
   3. It gives information.   command
   4. It shows strong feeling.   exclamation

C. Write **S, Q,** or **C** to tell whether each sentence is a statement, question, or command. Also write the correct end punctuation.
   1. Penguins can swim well
   2. Do penguins live in colonies
   3. Look at them
   4. Watch the ones in the water
   5. The feathers on their backs are bluish black
   6. Does the male penguin hatch the eggs
   7. What is a rookery
   8. It is a colony of penguins
   9. Find it in the encyclopedia
   10. Feed them now

D. Diagram the skeleton of each sentence.
1. This colorful shell is from an abalone.
2. They are found in most mild seas.
3. Have you found one?
4. New Zealand has many of them.
5. Try abalone steak.
6. The snail's muscular foot is made into steak.
7. Put your ear to this shell.
8. Can you hear the ocean?

E. For each boldface word, write a more exact word that could be used to replace it.
1. This is a **pretty** scarf you made.
2. That carpenter did an **awful** job.
3. It was a **great** day for a picnic.
4. You have written a **fine** poem.

Compound Subject:
   Paul and Silas were not sleeping in the prison.

Compound Predicate:
   Zacchaeus ran and climbed a tree.

Chapter 2
More About Sentences

Compound Subject and Predicate:
Joan and Judy washed and dried the dishes.

Compound Sentence:
The sun was shining, and the flowers were blooming.

11. The Paragraph

You have learned about complete sentences. Now you can learn to write a group of sentences that work together in a meaningful way. A group of sentences working together makes a paragraph.

A paragraph is a group of sentences that develop a single **topic** (main idea). A paragraph usually has one sentence that tells what the topic is. This sentence is the **topic sentence,** and it usually comes first in the paragraph. All the other sentences should explain or add to the topic of the paragraph. Sentences that tell about other topics must be left out or used in other paragraphs.

A paragraph follows a certain pattern. The first sentence is indented about half an inch. The other sentences come one after the other, filling up the lines as there is room. The left margin is kept straight, and the right margin is kept as straight as possible.

In the following paragraph, the topic sentence is underlined. The other sentences have variety in length and word order so that the paragraph is interesting and easy to understand.

> <u>The snapping turtle is true to his name.</u> He has no teeth, but his jaws are very sharp. An old turtle can snap off the head of a baby turtle. When a baby turtle is hatching and is only half out of the shell, he will snap at your finger or a twig that is held in front of him. God has given the turtle this means of protecting himself.

The topic of this paragraph is the snapping turtle's nature to snap. The first sentence expresses this main idea, and all the other sentences tell about the same topic.

Remember: A paragraph tells about only one topic. The topic sentence gives the topic of a paragraph.

> Oral Drill >

A. Read this paragraph, and answer the questions below.

Mother elephants take good care of their babies. If a baby elephant wanders away into tall grass where there is danger, the mother spanks him soundly. Lions spank their cubs too. When a little elephant is spanked, he cries like a child. But the mother elephant knows that is the way he must be trained to obey.

1. Which is the topic sentence?
2. Which sentence does not belong?

B. Choose the best topic sentence for the following paragraph.

Topic sentences:
1. Amsterdam is a city of canals and bridges.
2. Amsterdam is a busy place.
3. Amsterdam is a city of canals.

The city is drained by more than one hundred canals, and the canals have hundreds of bridges over them. The people of Amsterdam have added a new ring of canals every time the city has needed more land. The canals as well as the bridges are used for transportation. In the summer, boats and barges travel on the canals. In the winter, people skate on the ice. This city of canals and bridges is a busy place.

Written Practice

A. Use the following sentences to write a paragraph in proper form. Choose the best topic sentence, and leave out the sentences that do not belong.

Topic sentences:
   a. Many interesting birds live in Antarctica.
   b. Penguins are among God's most unusual creatures.
   c. Penguins look like little people.

1. They have feathers like other birds, but they swim and dive like fish.
2. They are well equipped for life in the frozen regions of snow and ice around the South Pole.
3. Seals, fish, and gulls also live in that frozen land.
4. Although penguins have wings, they cannot fly.
5. Their wings are used as oars for swimming and as legs for running.
6. I have never seen a penguin.
7. Penguins look like little people dressed in neat suits of black and white.

B. Use one of these topic sentences to begin a paragraph of your own. Complete the paragraph with sentences that tell more about the topic.

1. Saturday is a busy day at our house.
2. We use milk in many forms.
3. Some signs of rainy weather are easy to recognize.
4. Owning a dog brings certain responsibilities.

> **Review and Practice**

Choose and write the correct words in parentheses.
1. The best experiences to write about are the ones that have happened to (you, others).
2. Asking **who, what, when, where, why,** and **how** helps you think of (the main idea, details) for a story.
3. A paragraph is a group of sentences that develop (a single topic, several main ideas).
4. In a paragraph, the (left, right) margin is kept straight except for the first line. The (left, right) margin is kept as straight as possible.

12. Compound Subjects and Predicates

If two sentences have the same simple predicate but different simple subjects, the word **and** can be used to join them into one sentence. The new sentence then has a **compound subject.** Notice how this is done in the following sentences.

Father | will help us learn valuable lessons.
Mother | will help us learn valuable lessons.
Father **and** Mother | will help us learn valuable lessons.

Marcus | is my brother.
Jason | is my brother.
Marcus **and** Jason | are my brothers.

If two sentences have the same simple subject but different simple predicates, they can be joined into one sentence that has a **compound predicate.**

> Abraham | <u>loved</u> Ishmael.
> Abraham | <u>sent</u> him away.
> Abraham | <u>loved</u> Ishmael **but** <u>sent</u> him away.

The conjunctions **and, but,** and **or** can be used to join simple subjects or simple predicates.

Compound subjects and compound predicates are diagramed as shown here.

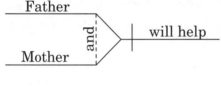

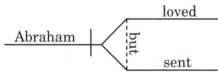

The word **not** is an adverb. Do not diagram it as part of the sentence skeleton.

Jane and Sarah are **not** coming.

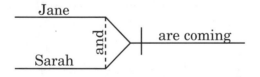

Remember: The conjunctions **and, but,** and **or** can be used to combine simple subjects or simple predicates.

 Oral Drill

A. Combine these sentences, using the conjunctions in parentheses.
1. Martha is coming later. Eileen is coming later. (or)
2. Chickens were feeding in the barnyard. Ducks were feeding in the barnyard. (and)
3. Flies buzzed around. Mosquitoes buzzed around. (or)
4. We searched everywhere. We found nothing. (but)
5. The otters swam. The otters played. (and)

B. On the chalkboard, diagram the sentence skeletons.
1. The students read or studied quietly.
2. Saul prayed but received no answer.
3. Ananias and Sapphira did not obey.
4. Martha or Sarah dusted the room.
5. Not candy but fruit has vitamins.
6. The little kitten sprang and pranced around.

 Written Practice

A. Combine these sentences by making compound subjects or compound predicates. Use the conjunctions in parentheses.
1. Zacchaeus ran. Zacchaeus climbed a tree. (and)
2. Gehazi gained riches. Gehazi suffered for his greed. (but)
3. Ezra was a scribe. Baruch was a scribe. (and)
4. Ezra arose. Ezra read the Book of the Law. (and)
5. Oranges have vitamin C. Strawberries have vitamin C. (and)
6. The girl is standing near the road. Her brother is standing near the road. (or)

B. Diagram the skeleton of each sentence.
1. Lydia and the other Christians were worshiping the Lord.
2. Paul and Silas were not sleeping in the prison.
3. A widow came and cried to Elisha.
4. She and her two sons were in great trouble.
5. Elisha spoke and gave her comfort.
6. Not a few vessels but many vessels were gathered by the boys.
7. All the vessels were filled with oil.
8. The widow and her sons were saved.

C. Write three conjunctions that can be used to join simple subjects or simple predicates.

Review and Practice

Write **S, Q, C,** or **E** to tell whether each sentence is a statement, question, command, or exclamation. (Write **E** only two times.) Also write the correct end punctuation.
1. Is a lizard a reptile
2. Oh, get away from that snake
3. Terrapins are turtles that live in fresh water
4. Is a tortoise a kind of turtle
5. Tortoises are turtles that live on land
6. How slowly they move
7. Find out how many kinds of snakes there are
8. There are over 2,500 different kinds of snakes

13. More Compound Subjects and Predicates

You have learned that two sentences can sometimes be joined into one sentence that has a compound subject or a compound predicate. The conjunctions **and, but,** and **or** are used to join them. Now you are ready to learn more about compound subjects and compound predicates.

Sometimes a sentence has both a compound subject and a compound predicate.

Paul and Silas sang and prayed.

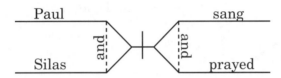

A sentence may even have three subjects or three verbs. When three or more parts are joined, a comma is placed after each item except the last one, which comes after **and.**

Faye, Freda, and Frances cleaned the desks, washed the windows, and changed the bulletin boards.

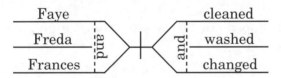

In sentences with compound parts, you may need to look carefully to find the subjects and verbs. Often there are nouns and other words that are not part of the skeleton. But if you always follow the rules for finding the skeleton, you will not have much trouble.

a. First, find the simple predicate. (There may be more than one verb.)

b. Ask **who** or **what** about the simple predicate. (There may be more than one simple subject.)

c. Say the simple subject and the simple predicate together to see if they make sense.

> Gideon and his men blew the trumpets and broke the pitchers.
> The verbs are **blew** and **broke.**
> **Who** blew and broke? Gideon and men.
> <u>Gideon</u> and <u>men</u> <u>blew</u> and <u>broke</u>.
> This makes sense, so it is the skeleton.
>> (Two other nouns are **trumpets** and **pitchers,** but these are not simple subjects.)

> **Oral Drill**

A. Combine these sentences, using the conjunctions in parentheses. Tell where commas are needed.

1. John saw Jesus. John baptized Jesus in the Jordan River. (and)

2. Carl will help with the chores. Joe will help with the chores. (or)

3. The teacher enjoyed the trip. Her pupils enjoyed the trip. (and)

4. The toad flipped out his tongue. The toad missed the fly. (but)

5. Janice brought cookies. James brought cookies. Jason brought cookies. Janice brought fruit. James brought fruit. Jason brought fruit. (and)

6. Melinda drew the flowers. Melody drew the flowers. Margaret drew the flowers. Melinda colored the posters. Melody colored the posters. Margaret colored the posters. Melinda hung the pictures on the wall. Melody hung the pictures on the wall. Margaret hung the pictures on the wall. (and)

B. On the chalkboard, diagram the sentence skeletons.
1. Saul threw a javelin, but missed David.
2. The boys and girls read stories or sang songs.
3. Matthew saw the fire and shouted for help.
4. Chickadees, nuthatches, and titmice do not migrate.
5. Birds eat weed seeds, destroy insects, and help farmers in many other ways.
6. Come here, look at this, and explain it to me.

> Written Practice >

A. Combine these sentences by making compound subjects and compound predicates. Remember to use commas when three or more parts are joined.
1. Ezra stood. Ezra opened the Book of the Law. Ezra read from it.
2. Jason raked a huge pile of leaves. Jason burned a huge pile of leaves.
3. The chipmunk picks up seeds. The chipmunk carries them in the pouches of his cheeks.
4. Robins were singing. Wrens were singing. Bluebirds were singing.
5. Nancy cut out the pictures. Naomi cut out the pictures. Nancy pasted them on the poster. Naomi pasted them on the poster.

B. Diagram the skeleton of each sentence.
1. Shadrach, Meshach, and Abednego did not bow.
2. The workers saw the truck and shouted at the dog.
3. Larry, Leonard, and Lewis saw it first.
4. They scraped off the old paint, sanded the wood, and put a fresh coat of paint on it.
5. The boys and girls worked and sang.
6. Repair the old shed, or tear it down.

7. Wolves and coyotes yapped and howled.
8. John picked up a nail and hammered it into the board.

> Review and Practice

Write the correct word for each description.

noun	predicate	command
verb	statement	exclamation
sentence	question	paragraph
subject		

1. It tells what the subject does or is.
2. It is a group of words that express a complete thought.
3. It shows strong feeling.
4. It states a fact or gives information.
5. It shows action or being.
6. It asks for information.
7. It tells you to do something.
8. It is a group of sentences that develop a single topic.
9. It names a person, place, or thing.
10. It tells **who** or **what** a sentence is about.

14. Compound Sentences

Often in speaking and writing, we join two short, closely related sentences into one sentence. Such a sentence is a **compound sentence.** A compound sentence is one sentence with two skeletons.

The <u>sun</u> | <u>was shining</u>. The <u>flowers</u> | <u>were blooming</u>.
The <u>sun</u> | <u>was shining</u>, **and** the <u>flowers</u> | <u>were blooming</u>.

The two skeletons in a compound sentence are joined with a comma and a conjunction. Three common conjunctions are **and, but,** and **or.**

> The <u>girls</u> <u>washed</u> windows, **and** the <u>boys</u> <u>raked</u> leaves.
> <u>We</u> <u>worked</u> inside, **but** <u>they</u> <u>worked</u> outside.
> <u>We</u> <u>must hurry</u>, **or** <u>we</u> <u>will</u> not <u>finish</u> today.

A compound sentence is diagramed as shown below. Notice the two skeletons in the diagram.

> The <u>lions</u> | <u>roared</u> loudly, but <u>God</u> | <u>spared</u> Daniel.

| lions | roared | but | God | spared |

Remember: A compound sentence is one sentence with two skeletons. The two parts of a compound sentence are joined by a comma and a conjunction. Three common conjunctions are **and, but,** and **or.** A comma is placed before the conjunction in a compound sentence.

> Oral Drill

A. Combine each pair into a compound sentence, using the best conjunction. Use **and, but,** and **or** at least once each. Tell where commas are needed.
   1. The sun shone. The breeze blew.
   2. Be careful. You will get hit.
   3. Karen ran. She missed the bus.
   4. He called. They answered.

B. On the chalkboard, diagram the sentence skeletons of these compound sentences.
1. Naaman was a mighty man, but he was a leper.
2. The Israelite maid cared about her master's trouble, and she told Naaman's wife about the prophet of God.
3. Naaman told the story to the king, and the king sent a letter and many gifts to Israel's king.
4. Israel's king read the letter, and he rent his clothes.
5. Naaman went to the prophet's house, but he did not see Elisha.
6. Naaman was angry, but later he obeyed the prophet.
7. He dipped into the Jordan seven times, and the leprosy vanished.

> Written Practice >

A. Combine each pair into a compound sentence, using the best conjunction. Use **and, but,** and **or** at least once each, and place commas where they are needed.
1. The birds pecked the berries. A chipmunk nibbled at them.
2. Carl fell off the roof. He was not hurt badly.
3. They expected her to be early. She was late.
4. She has forgotten the appointment. She is having car trouble.
5. He forgot to study. He failed the test.

B. Diagram the skeletons of these compound sentences. (**Prairie dog** is a noun phrase.)
1. Prairie dogs may bark, but they are rodents.
2. The sound was like the yapping of a hundred puppies, but it came from prairie dogs.
3. Prairie dogs eat many kinds of green plants, but they like grass best.

4. I walked toward their colony, and they popped instantly into their holes.
5. A curious baby popped up his head, but his mother pushed him in again.
6. Prairie dogs may be small, but they are very brave.
7. A wolf came, and they snapped at him.
8. They live in large colonies, and they are friendly and helpful to each other.

> **Review and Practice** >

These sentences have compound subjects or compound predicates. Diagram the skeleton of each one. (The noun phrases are in bold print.)

1. Birds and mammals are warm-blooded animals.
2. Most fish hatch from eggs and have scales.
3. The Brazilian **electric eel** can produce electricity in its body and can stun a man with its shock.
4. Frogs and toads are amphibians.
5. Frogs have smooth, moist skin and are usually green.
6. Toads have rough, warty skin and are usually brown.
7. Weed seeds, insect pests, and rodents are eaten by birds.
8. The penguin and the ostrich are unusual birds.
9. The **arctic tern** and the **golden plover** migrate many miles each year.
10. Birds are covered with feathers and breathe with lungs.

15. Writing Paragraphs With Unity and Order

You have learned much about sentences. Now you can use your knowledge of different kinds of sentences to write meaningful paragraphs.

If sentences are to make a good paragraph, they must fit together in at least two important ways. The sentences in a paragraph must have **unity,** and they must come in a proper **order.**

For paragraph unity, all the sentences must support and develop the topic sentence. Each sentence must stick to the main idea of the paragraph. Sentences that do not develop the main idea must be left out. This gives the paragraph unity, or oneness.

For paragraph order, the sentences must follow one another in a sensible way. One kind of order is the order of time. This kind is used in stories, where a paragraph tells what happened first, second, and so on. The order of time is also used in giving directions for doing something. Then a paragraph will tell what should be done first, second, and so on.

Order in a story:

> After the prodigal son had spent all his money, a great famine came to the land. Soon the son was in great need, and he began herding swine for a farmer. He became so hungry that he wished he could have the husks that the swine were eating. Finally one day the prodigal son came to himself.

Order in directions:

> To make popcorn, get a popper and put in enough cooking oil to cover the bottom. Add one-half cup popcorn kernels, turn a burner on high, and put the popper on the burner. Keep the popcorn moving by shaking or stirring it constantly so that it will not burn. When it has finished popping, empty the popcorn into a bowl and sprinkle salt over it.

Another kind of order is the order of importance. This order is used when a paragraph gives reasons for something. It may give the most important reason first and the least important one last. Or it may give the least important reason first and the most important one last.

Reasons from least important to most important:

There are several reasons for learning to read well. Reading brings enjoyment to ourselves as we read interesting things that people have written. By reading we can also share good things with others. Most important, we should learn to read well so that we can read and understand the Bible.

Whatever the order is, it should make the paragraph simple to read and understand. Sentences in a paragraph should not come in just any order, but they should work together to express one main idea in a clear, meaningful way.

Remember: A paragraph must have unity and order.

> **Oral Drill**

Tell in what order the following sentences should be written. Tell which sentence does not belong. The topic sentence is given.

Topic sentence: Men worked long and hard to learn how to make steel.

1. Iron makers knew steel was better and stronger than iron, but they did not know how to make large amounts of steel.
2. Finally a man named Henry Bessemer invented the blast furnace.

3. This man also invented gold paint and a new kind of pencil.

4. Now large quantities of steel could be made at less than half the price it had cost before.

5. In a blast furnace, hot air is blown through the iron ore as it is being melted.

6. Later some men were successful in making small amounts of steel in little pots called crucibles, but steel was still very costly.

7. At first, iron makers cut small amounts of steel from the tops of their cast-iron blocks.

8. This burns up the carbon that makes the iron weak.

> Written Practice >

A. Arrange the following sentences in proper order. Write them in paragraph form. Leave out the sentence that does not belong. The topic sentence is given first.

Topic sentence: It is easy to make toast with a modern toaster.

1. Wait until the toast pops up.

2. Next, put a slice of bread into each slot.

3. Long ago people made toast by laying slices of bread on a rack over a cookstove.

4. First, make sure the toaster is plugged into an electrical outlet.

5. Then remove the toast and serve it.

6. Adjust the knob that controls how light or dark the toast will be.

7. Press down the lever to lower the bread.

B. Write a paragraph about one of the following topics. Your topic sentence may be in question form as given.

1. Why did Columbus want to sail west?

2. Why did the *Titanic* sink?

3. Why did the Mennonites come to America?

4. How do you wash dishes (or clean a room)?

5. How do you make pancakes (or cookies)?

6. How do you make a kite (or a birdhouse)?

7. How do you wash a car (or a dog)?

16. Simple Sentences and Compound Sentences

You have learned that a sentence with two skeletons is a **compound sentence.** Its two parts are joined by a comma and the conjunction **and, but,** or **or.** The comma is placed before the conjunction.

Earl | <u>mowed</u> the lawn, **and** <u>Keith</u> | <u>raked</u> the grass.

| Earl | mowed | and | Keith | raked |

A sentence with only one subject and one verb is a **simple sentence.** A simple sentence may have a compound subject or a compound verb. It may even have both a compound subject and a compound verb. But it is still a simple sentence because it has only one skeleton.

All the following are simple sentences. Each has only one skeleton.

<u>Joan</u> | <u>washed</u> the dishes.

<u>Joan</u> | <u>washed</u> and <u>dried</u> the dishes.
(simple sentence with compound verb)

<u>Joan</u> and <u>Judy</u> | <u>washed</u> and <u>dried</u> the dishes.
(simple sentence with compound subject and compound verb)

A compound sentence has a skeleton on **each side** of the conjunction. Study the following sentences and the "addition problems" after them.

The <u>parrots</u> <u>talked</u> or <u>scolded</u>.
(subject | verb + verb = simple sentence)

The <u>parrots</u> and <u>parakeets</u> <u>talked</u>.
(subject + subject | verb = simple sentence)

<u>Parrots</u> and <u>parakeets</u> <u>chirped</u> and <u>talked</u>.
(subject + subject | verb + verb = simple sentence)

<u>Parrots</u> <u>talked</u>, and <u>monkeys</u> <u>chattered</u>.
(subject | verb + subject | verb = compound sentence)

The following diagrams also show the difference between simple and compound sentences. A simple sentence has **only one skeleton.** A compound sentence has **two skeletons.**

Simple:
Joan washed the dishes.

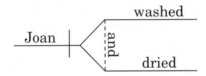

Simple:
Joan washed and dried the dishes.

Simple:
Joan and Judy washed and dried the dishes.

Compound:
Joan washed the dishes, and Judy dried them.

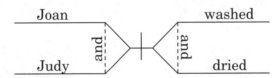

> **Remember:** A simple sentence has only one skeleton, but a compound sentence has two skeletons. In a compound sentence, there is a skeleton on each side of the conjunction.

Oral Drill

A. Tell whether each sentence is **simple** or **compound.** Tell where commas are needed. On the chalkboard, write the "addition problem" for each sentence, using **S** for simple subject and **V** for verb.

1. The dog bit me and the cat scratched me.
2. The dog and the cat hurt me.
3. Mother comforted me and she bandaged my sores.
4. Father spanked the dog and he scolded the cat.
5. The cat and the dog looked sad and ran away.
6. We will go to the store and get some bread.
7. The cook gathered the supplies and mixed the dough and the baker baked the bread.
8. Thomas pulled weeds and I mowed the lawn.

B. On the chalkboard, diagram the skeletons of sentences 1–5 in Part A.

> **Written Practice** >

A. Write the "addition problem" for each sentence, using **S** for simple subject and **V** for verb. Copy the words that should have commas after them, and add the missing commas.

1. Peter and John heard the women's report.
2. The two disciples ran toward the tomb but John outran Peter.
3. John stooped down and looked into the tomb.
4. Peter went in and he saw the linen clothes.
5. Then John also went in and saw the clothes.
6. Both men saw the empty tomb but they did not understand.
7. Later Jesus appeared to the disciples and then they understood.
8. Joy or fear filled their hearts.
9. Jesus spoke to them and showed them His hands and His side.

B. Diagram the sentence skeletons in Part A of Written Practice.

> **Review and Practice** >

Write the more exact word for each sentence.

1. The (pretty, fragrant) flower had large pink petals.
2. The teacher quieted the (loud, noisy) children.
3. A strong (smell, stench) hung in the air after the dog's encounter with the skunk.
4. George's pet monkey is quite (mischievous, bad) at times.
5. The two girls (walked, strolled) through the park.
6. The (little, tiny) bird flew to the trumpet vine.
7. Brother Glenn has a (big, generous) heart.
8. Charles Smith is a (nice, friendly) person.

17. Avoiding Comma Splices and Run-on Sentences

Do you know what a splice is? It is something used to join two ends together. Adhesive tape may be used as a splice for a broken cassette tape. A broken rope may be mended by splicing the ends together. The splice pictured here is known as the short splice.

It is important to use the right kind of splices to make strong connections. In a compound sentence, a comma and a conjunction act as a splice between two simple sentences. They make a strong connection between the two parts of a compound sentence.

Sometimes a compound sentence is written with only a comma to join its two parts. But a comma is not strong enough to hold two simple sentences together. Unless there is also a conjunction, the compound sentence may "come apart" and be hard to understand. The mistake of joining two sentences with only a comma is a **comma splice.**

Sometimes two simple sentences are written together without a conjunction or even a comma. This mistake is a **run-on sentence.** Study the following examples.

> Favor is deceitful, and beauty is vain. (correct)
> Favor is deceitful, beauty is vain. (comma splice)
> Favor is deceitful beauty is vain. (run-on sentence)

Another mistake is to write a group of words in the form of a sentence when the thought is not complete. This is a **sentence fragment.** Sentence fragments must be corrected by adding the missing words.

Fragment: The tall boy with dark hair.
Correct:　The tall boy with dark hair is my brother.

Fragment: Hoping to leave soon.
Correct:　We are hoping to leave soon.

Remember: The two parts of a compound sentence must be joined with a comma and a conjunction. A sentence must have a complete thought, or it is a sentence fragment.

> Oral Drill >

A. Tell whether each sentence is **correct,** has a **comma splice,** or is a **run-on sentence.**
 1. Abraham's servant prayed, God brought Rebekah to him.
 2. Mephibosheth's nurse picked him up and fled, but in her haste she dropped him.
 3. Jephthah went out to battle the Lord gave him victory.
 4. He went home in triumph a great disappointment awaited him.
 5. Jephthah kept his vow, and he gave his daughter to God.
 6. David sent for Mephibosheth, he came with respect.
 7. David showed kindness to Mephibosheth he was very thankful.

B. On the chalkboard, write each pair of sentences correctly as a compound sentence. Use the conjunction **and, but,** or **or,** and add a comma where it is needed.
 1. The people wanted lighter burdens. Rehoboam would not listen to them.
 2. Was Rehoboam wise? Was he foolish?
 3. Rehoboam ruled Judah. Jeroboam ruled Israel.

4. Some kings of Judah were godly. All the kings of Israel were evil.

5. Jonah was a prophet in Israel. Joel was a prophet in Judah.

6. The people needed to repent. They would be punished.

C. Add words to make complete sentences from these sentence fragments.

1. Lived in the Garden of Eden.

2. The fruit from one tree.

3. Satan in the form of a serpent.

4. Punished Adam and Eve for their sin.

5. A great promise to them.

6. Would bring salvation someday.

> Written Practice >

A. For each group of words, write **C** for correct, **CS** for comma splice, **RO** for run-on sentence, or **F** for fragment.

1. Hannah made a little coat, Dorcas made garments.

2. The circle is round, or I cannot see accurately.

3. The ram charged forward the ewes stayed behind.

4. A large animal with heavy wool and curved horns.

5. Thunder rumbled, or a jet flew overhead.

6. Thunder boomed I was not afraid.

7. So loudly that the windows rattled.

8. Lightning flashed, thunder crashed.

9. Larry sat still, but Lester squirmed.

10. Lucy wrote stories, Margaret wrote poems.

11. Martha hurried she was still late.

12. Get your work done, or you may not go along.

13. Jesus ate the Passover with His disciples.

14. A large upper room in the city.

B. Combine these sentences, using a different conjunction each time. Be sure to use commas correctly.
1. Hagar had to find water. Ishmael would die of thirst.
2. Hagar thought her son would die. God showed her a spring of water.
3. Isaac became the father of the Jews. Ishmael became the father of the Arabs.

> Review and Practice >

A. Write **S, Q,** or **C** to tell whether each sentence is a statement, question, or command. Also write the correct end punctuation.
1. Do you like the taste of olives
2. You would not like them right off the tree
3. Never pick olives and eat them right away
4. Why should they not be eaten then
5. The strong acid can upset your stomach
6. Treat them in lye and salt water first
7. How did people find out how to treat olives
8. Lye is even more dangerous than green olives
9. Is lye poisonous
10. The lye takes the strong acid out of the olives
11. The olives are soaked for three days
12. Test them several times
13. Rinse the olives
14. Soak them in salt water again
15. Would you like to eat some olives now

B. Write what you might say if you had just eaten a green olive right off a tree. Answer with two sentences that are exclamations.

18. Combining Choppy Sentences

You know that two sentences written incorrectly as one sentence make a run-on sentence. But you should also avoid too many short, choppy sentences. There are proper ways of combining sentences so that your writing is smooth and pleasant to read.

You have learned to combine sentences by making a compound subject or a compound verb. Sentences can also be combined by making other compound parts. See how the following sentences are combined.

Compound subject:
> Moses led the children of Israel.
> Aaron led the children of Israel.
> Moses and Aaron led the children of Israel.

Compound verb:
> Moses scolded the people.
> Moses struck the rock.
> Moses scolded the people and struck the rock.

Compound direct object:
> Mother instructed the boys.
> Mother instructed the girls.
> Mother instructed the boys and the girls.

Two short sentences can often be combined into one compound sentence. Remember to use a comma and a conjunction in a compound sentence.

> **Choppy:** We wanted to pull weeds. It was raining.
> **Better:**   We wanted to pull weeds, but it was raining.

Another way to combine sentences is to take adjectives and adverbs from one short sentence and put them in another sentence. Adjective and adverb phrases may be moved in the same way.

Choppy: A new flower bloomed this morning. It was red. It was in our garden.

Better: This morning a new red flower bloomed in our garden.

Choppy: The cat is mine. She is yellow. She likes to be petted.

Better: My yellow cat likes to be petted.

Choppy: The little boy sat down. The little boy cried. He was lost. He was hungry.

Better: The lost, hungry little boy sat down and cried.

Remember: Do not use many short, choppy sentences in your writing.

> Oral Drill >

A. Tell how to combine each group of sentences into one sentence.

1. Pharaoh's army was drowned in the Red Sea. Pharaoh's horses were drowned in the Red Sea.
2. Every pupil must have a pencil. Every pupil must have a tablet. They must have them for the test.
3. The woodchuck was alert. He whistled an alarm. He disappeared quickly. He went into his hole.
4. Father inspected the tractor. He did it last night. The tractor was old. The tractor was well kept.
5. The boy was pale. The boy was thin. He was eager to work.

B. Tell how to improve this paragraph.

> Henry is little. He is my brother. Sometimes he tries things. He tries things that get him into trouble. Henry needs to learn that there are limits. He must learn that he cannot do everything. Some things may hurt him. Some things are dangerous.

> Written Practice

A. Combine each set of sentences into one sentence. If you write a compound sentence, remember to use a comma before the conjunction.

1. Gerald is coming. His brother is coming with him. They are coming down the road.
2. The tea was cold. The tea was delicious. It quenched our thirst.
3. The foolish virgins wanted to go inside. The door was shut.
4. Last week I was collecting leaves. My sister was collecting them too. The leaves were colorful.
5. The clouds sailed across the blue sky. They were enormous. They were white.

6. Jesus went to a mountain. It was large. His disciples followed Him.

7. The children can sell melons. The children can sell squash. They can always sell them. They sell them at their stand.

8. We finally found the calf. It was wet. It was dirty. We found it this morning.

9. We dug potatoes. There were many of them. Father sold them. He sold them at a produce stand.

10. The morning was cold. The morning was windy. It was not fit for building.

B. Rewrite the paragraph in Oral Drill, Part B. Combine the choppy sentences.

> ➤ Review and Practice ➤

For each group of words, write **C** for correct, **CS** for comma splice, **RO** for run-on sentence, or **F** for fragment.

1. Reading a book.
2. Rushing water will frighten the timid sheep.
3. We waited quietly, soon three deer walked by.
4. The balloon burst suddenly I was startled.
5. Most of the children were surprised, but James was frightened.
6. The smiling, cheerful girl.
7. Everyone worked quickly the chores were soon finished.
8. The work was hard to do.
9. Jesus called Lazarus, and Lazarus came out of the grave.
10. Solomon's temple was built in silence, the stones had been shaped beforehand.

> Challenge Exercise >

A. Change the boldface words to **which** or **that,** and combine the sentences.

Examples:

Julia brought a chocolate cake. Mother had made **it.**

We all liked the story. The teacher read **it.**

The apples tasted sweet. Father had bought **them.**

Answers:

Julia brought a chocolate cake which Mother had made.

We all liked the story that the teacher read.

The apples that Father had bought tasted sweet.

1. Father bought the car. **It** had been in a flood.
2. The book was on the table. We had read **it.**
3. The oranges tasted delicious. Ruby had picked **them.**
4. We all admired the picture. Walter had painted **it.**
5. Nelson caught a catfish. **It** weighed over five pounds.

B. Change the boldface words to **who,** and combine the sentences.

1. Philip met a man. **He** was riding in a chariot.
2. We helped a lady. **She** was stuck in a ditch.
3. We asked for directions from two boys. **They** were walking by.
4. Jesus told a story about two men. **They** went into the temple to pray.

19. Sentence Variety in Paragraphs

You have learned about a variety of sentences. You know that there are four kinds of sentences. You have studied sentences with compound parts, and you have met compound sentences. Now you can use your knowledge to write better paragraphs.

Which of the following paragraphs is more interesting?

Rebekah came out to draw water from the well. She went down to the well. She filled her pitcher. Abraham's servant ran quickly to meet her. He said, "Please give me a drink." Rebekah gave him a drink from her pitcher. Then she drew water for his camels.

       *   *   *   *   *

Rebekah came out to draw water. She went down to the well and filled her pitcher. As she came up, who should come running to meet her but Abraham's servant! "Please, may I have a little drink?" he requested. Rebekah quickly gave him a drink from her pitcher, and then she drew water for his camels.

The second paragraph is more interesting because it has **sentence variety.** Reading becomes tiresome when all the sentences follow the same pattern.

Use a variety of sentence types. There are four main types of sentences: **statements, questions, commands,** and **exclamations.**

Varying the length of the sentences in a paragraph also adds interest. Make some sentences simple. Use compound parts in some sentences, and make some sentences compound. Can you see how this was done in the second paragraph about Rebekah?

Do not forget that every sentence in a paragraph must support the topic sentence and that sentences must be written in a logical order.

Remember: Use a variety of sentences in a paragraph.

> Oral Drill >

Follow the directions for changing the sentences below.
1. Change **a** and **b** to questions, and **c** to an exclamation.
   a. There was a person that David had missed.
   b. I do not know how it could have happened.
   c. Mephibosheth had a great surprise.
2. Combine each pair in the shortest way possible.
   a. Mephibosheth fell on his face. Mephibosheth honored King David.
   b. David called for Saul's servant Ziba. Ziba came to David.
   c. Ziba would work for Mephibosheth. Ziba's sons would work for Mephibosheth.

> Written Practice >

A. Think of a way to join each pair of sentences with the least words possible. Change sentence 5 to a question. Then write the sentences in proper form as two paragraphs.

Paragraph 1

1. King David wanted to show kindness to Mephibosheth. Mephibosheth was Jonathan's son.
2. He sent for Mephibosheth. He talked with him.
3. David said, "I will give you all the land of your grandfather Saul. You shall eat bread at my table."

Paragraph 2

4. Mephibosheth bowed his head. He said, "Behold, I am your servant."
5. "I don't know who I am that you should notice me."
6. David gave Mephibosheth all of Saul's land. David gave him plenty of food.

B. Write a paragraph of your own about something interesting that happened to you. Use a variety of sentences. Here is an example.

Last week I broke a window at school. Do you know how it happened? I threw a ball to John, and he missed it. It flew right through the window and shattered the glass! My father said, "You will have to help pay for it, and you must not play ball near a window again." It was an expensive lesson.

> **Review and Practice**

Write a word for each blank. You may find some answers in the "Remember" boxes in the lessons.

1. When you need a topic to write about, use ——— experiences.
2. To make a good story, you need to know many interesting ———.
3. A ——— is a good tool for finding exact words when writing.
4. When you write a story, do not add ——— details.
5. Be sure to write in ——— sentences when you write a story.

6. A paragraph is a group of sentences that develop a single ———.

7. The topic sentence gives the ——— ——— of a paragraph.

8. The sentences in a paragraph must have ——— and ———.

9. Use a ——— of sentences in a paragraph.

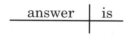

20. Sentences That Begin With *There Is* or *There Are*

Most sentences have the simple subject before the simple predicate. This is called normal word order.

The <u>answer</u> | <u>is</u> somewhere.

In a sentence that begins with **there,** the verb usually comes before the subject. This is called inverted word order.

There <u>is</u> an <u>answer</u> somewhere.

Remember that **there** is not the subject, even though it begins the sentence. Study the following diagrams.

Wrong:

There	is

Right:

answer	is

Be careful not to use **there is** or **there's** when the subject is plural.

Wrong:
>There is two men in that car.

Right:
>There **are** two men in that car.
>>(Skeleton: <u>men</u> | <u>are</u>)

Wrong:
>There's oranges and apples for your lunch.

Right:
>There **are** oranges and apples for your lunch.
>>(Skeleton: <u>oranges</u> and <u>apples</u> | <u>are</u>)

Sometimes a sentence that begins with **there** has a compound subject. Do not use **there is** or **there's** when the subject is compound.

>There <u>are</u> a <u>blue jay</u> and a <u>cardinal</u> on the feeder.

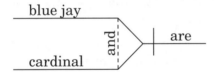

Usually it is better to write sentences in normal word order than to begin with **there.** Normal order is more simple and direct. So if a sentence begins with **there,** it is often better to change it to normal word order.

>There was a Bible on the shelf.
>A Bible was on the shelf.
>
>There came up a sudden storm.
>A sudden storm came up.

A few sentences, however, cannot be changed to normal word order. Here are two examples.

>There is one true God.
>There were twelve tribes of Israel.

> **Remember:** Many sentences beginning with **there** have inverted word order. Do not use **there is** or **there's** to begin a sentence that has a plural subject or a compound subject. Usually it is better to write sentences in normal word order than to begin with **there.**

Oral Drill

A. In each sentence, tell which word is the subject. Then choose the correct words in parentheses.
   1. (There is, There are) sixty-six books in the Bible.
   2. (There was, There were) men who copied the Bible by hand long ago.
   3. (There was, There were) a man who wrote more than twelve letters in the New Testament.
   4. (There is, There are) a boy and a girl on the playground.
   5. (There was, There were) more children earlier.
   6. (There's, There are) a watermelon and a cantaloupe in the car.

B. On the chalkboard, diagram each sentence skeleton in Part A.

C. Change each sentence to normal word order.
   1. There is someone coming in the lane.
   2. There is something in my eye.

Written Practice

A. Diagram each sentence skeleton.
   1. There are several eggs in the nest.
   2. There is a little calf in the barn.
   3. There is a new Bible verse on the chalkboard.
   4. There were seven kittens on the farm.

B. Write the simple subjects. Then write the correct words in parentheses.
1. (There is, There are) some books we should not read.
2. (There's, There are) a maple and a pine in the back yard.
3. (There's, There are) a nest in the maple tree.
4. (There is, There are) several high mountains in Palestine.
5. (There's, There are) a buck and a doe.
6. (There is, There are) a small trout in the pool.

C. Rewrite these sentences in normal word order.
1. There are some books on the table.
2. There is a worm in my apple!

> Review and Practice >

Diagram the sentence skeletons. Remember that **not** is not a verb, so do not diagram it with the verb.
1. Evil thoughts come from the heart.
2. I cried unto the Lord.
3. Jesus will be coming again soon.
4. John Mark was traveling with Paul and Barnabas.
5. David and Jonathan parted sadly.
6. I have not spoken in secret.
7. The title was written in Hebrew, Greek, and Latin.
8. Peter saw the waves, and he was afraid.
9. Jesus reached out and caught Peter.
10. Jesus healed the lepers, the blind, and the lame.
11. Is there no balm in Gilead?
12. There is a God.
13. Praise Him.
14. Where is the hiding place?

21. Chapter 2 Review

Oral Drill

A. Tell how to combine these sentences.
1. Alfred raked the leaves. Jason gathered them up.
2. The minister read from the Bible. The minister prayed.
3. David picked a song. Ruth picked a song.
4. Gerald built a birdhouse. Gerald built a doghouse.
5. Mother bought several oranges. She also bought one large melon.
6. The house is vacant. It is forlorn. It is in the woods. It has been purchased by a new family.
7. She sent them a reply. She sent it yesterday. It was short. It was friendly.
8. The fruit was fresh. The fruit was sweet. It was in the bowl. It tasted delicious.

B. On the chalkboard, diagram the sentence skeletons.
1. The queen and many other passengers rode swiftly through the night on an express train.
2. Hit the brakes, and stop the train now!
3. The train whistled and screeched to a grinding stop.
4. The engineer and the brakeman jumped off in a hurry.
5. A storm had raged all night, and the bridge was out.
6. An angry river roared and raged below.
7. The train had stopped only a few yards before the great chasm.

C. Give three conjunctions that can be used to join simple subjects, simple predicates, or simple sentences.

D. Say the forms of the verb **be.**

E. Tell which of the following are compound sentences. Tell where commas are needed in those sentences.

1. Frogs and toads have long hind legs.
2. Reptiles have scaly skin but amphibians have moist skin without scales.
3. Tadpoles wiggled and darted everywhere.
4. Frogs are green and toads are brown.
5. Amphibians begin their life in water but they spend most of their adult life on land.

F. Tell whether each sentence is **correct,** has a **comma splice,** is a **run-on sentence,** or is a **fragment.**
   1. Some turtles grunt other turtles bellow.
   2. Female turtles make hissing sounds, few people hear them.
   3. Tortoises are land turtles, and terrapins are freshwater turtles.
   4. A turtle with a domed shell and club-shaped feet.

G. Tell which sentence in this paragraph is the topic sentence. Tell which sentences do not belong.

   God had a good reason for giving the zebra a striped coat. Its black and cream-colored stripes are an excellent camouflage. A tiger's coat is striped too. The zebra must constantly be on guard against his chief enemy, the lion. Lions also eat antelopes, pigs, and young elephants. The zebra's striped coat blends well with light and shadows in his surroundings, making it easy for him to hide.

> Written Practice >

A. Combine each set of sentences into one sentence. If you write a compound sentence, remember to use a comma before the conjunction.
   1. Susan baked a cherry pie. It was eaten before the day was over.
   2. Mother bought milk. Mother bought eggs.

3. Anna made the supper. Martha set the table.
4. Mary Jane washed the dishes. Ida Ann washed the dishes.
5. The Assyrian officer called boastfully. He called to the men. They were on the wall.
6. A messenger brought it. It was a letter. Hezekiah spread it out. He spread it before the Lord.
7. Isaiah received a message. It was from God. It was for the king.
8. The Lord promised to defend the city. He would destroy the Assyrians.

B. Diagram the sentence skeletons.
   1. Why did they stop the train?
   2. The engineer had seen a strange black figure ahead.
   3. The black figure stood in the middle of the track and waved his arms.
   4. The fields and woods were searched for the kind person.
   5. The mysterious flagman was not found that night.
   6. The night was very foggy.
   7. A moth had been stuck to the headlight.
   8. They found the moth on the engine's headlight after a few days.
   9. Its shadow had been reflected by the fog.
   10. The queen and other passengers thanked and praised the Lord for a safe trip.

C. Copy each compound sentence, and add the missing comma.
   1. Amphibians live in moist places and lay their eggs in pools or puddles of water.
   2. Snakes and lizards are reptiles.
   3. Many people are afraid of snakes but snakes are really helpful to man.
   4. Some snakes are poisonous but snakes eat mice and other pests.
   5. Do not threaten or annoy a snake.

D. Write **C** for correct, **CS** for comma splice, **RO** for run-on sentence, and **F** for fragment.
1. A sea horse is a real fish, but it does not look like a fish.
2. A small fish with a head like that of a horse.
3. Sea horses are seen in warm months, they disappear in winter.
4. Eels are snakelike fish most eels live in the ocean.
5. Freshwater eels live in streams, but they lay their eggs in the sea.

E. Write the simple subjects. Then write the correct words in parentheses.
1. (There is, There are) a diamond mine in Arkansas.
2. (There is, There are) diamond mines in Africa too.
3. (There's, There are) plants almost everywhere in the world.
4. (There is, There are) plants without flowers or seeds.
5. (There's, There are) many tiny plants and animals in seawater.
6. (There was, There were) a cheetah in the zoo.
7. (There was, There were) a lion and a tiger too.
8. (There was, There were) three hawks flying near our house.

F. Copy the following sentences in proper paragraph form. Arrange them in order from the least thing to the greatest thing. Leave out the sentence that does not belong. The topic sentence is given.

Topic sentence: How fast can birds fly?
1. Homing pigeons can go 62 miles per hour, and canvasbacks can fly 72 miles per hour.
2. Fastest of all are the duck hawks, which may reach a speed of 180 miles per hour when they dive.
3. A cheetah is the fastest animal.
4. Robins can travel about 36 miles per hour.
5. Golden eagles soar at 120 miles per hour.

Nouns name . . .

Persons

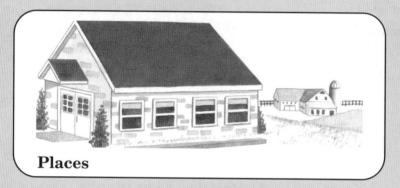

Places

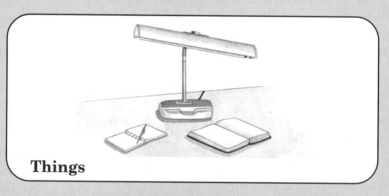

Things

Thoughts

Ideas

Chapter 3
Nouns

Singular   **Plural**

Singular
Possessive: baby's toy

Plural
Possessive: foxes' tracks

22. Nouns

You have learned that a noun names a person, place, or thing. It should be easy for you to recognize nouns such as **Ray, book, hospital, sister, rose,** and **New York.**

A noun may also name an **idea.** At first you may find it harder to recognize this kind of noun, for ideas cannot be seen or touched. But you can soon learn to recognize them, for all nouns **name.**

A noun is a word that names a person, place, thing, or idea.

Persons	Places	Things	Ideas
girl	home	plant	truth
brother	store	table	courage
fireman	church	Bible	meekness
Susan	country	air	honesty
baby	zoo	rock	salvation

A noun may be **concrete** or **abstract.** A concrete noun names something you can see or touch. So far in English, you have studied only concrete nouns.

An abstract noun names something you cannot see or touch. It names an idea. Most ideas are just as real as something you can hold in your hand. The main difference is that you cannot see or touch them.

Many words become abstract nouns when endings like **-ness, -ment, -ity,** and **-ion** are added. These suffixes can help you to recognize abstract nouns.

happy—happiness	pure—purity
excite—excitement	interrupt—interruption

Another help in recognizing nouns is to look for the words **a, an,** and **the.** These are called **noun markers** or **articles.** You may remember these from grades 3 and 4. **A, an,** and **the** are like markers that help you to pick out nouns.

In the following list, the words in bold print are abstract nouns. Noun markers can be used with them. Each word names something.

a **consideration**   an **honor**
a **belief**   the **politeness**
an **appointment**   the **goodness**

In the next list, the words in bold print are not nouns, because it does not sound right to use noun markers with them. They do not name things.

a **consider**   an **appoint**   the **polite**

Remember: A noun is a word that names a person, place, thing, or idea.

> Oral Drill >

A. Make nouns by adding the suffix **-ness, -ment, -ity,** or **-ion** to the following words.
   1. complete   4. promote
   2. great   5. atone
   3. odd   6. agree

B. Tell which words are nouns.
   1. The stranger asked the mailman about the location of the laundry.
   2. Selfishness is an evil disease.
   3. Paul was bound in chains in Rome.
   4. Those who deny freedom to other people do not deserve it for themselves.
   5. Godliness with contentment is great gain.
   6. The Israelites found themselves in a great predicament.

> Written Practice

A. Write the definition of a noun. Be sure to use the definition you learned in this lesson.

B. Change each word to a noun by adding the suffix **-ness, -ment, -ity,** or **-ion.** Check the dictionary if you are not sure of the spelling.
   1. real
   2. blessed
   3. announce
   4. attract
   5. direct
   6. wicked

C. Copy all the nouns in these sentences.
   1. God is our refuge and strength.
   2. Truth is the only safe ground to stand upon.
   3. By grace are ye saved through faith.
   4. The truth will give us freedom.
   5. Zebras and giraffes are interesting animals from the plains of Africa.
   6. The Israelites knew that God was with them when they saw the pillar of cloud and of fire.

D. List five nouns that name things one might see in a landscape picture.

   Examples: waterfall, cliff

E. List five nouns that name places one might see on a map.

   Examples: mountain, gulf

F. List five nouns that name ideas. Try to think of nouns that are not given anywhere in the lesson.

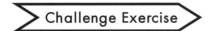

Copy several stanzas of a hymn that uses abstract nouns. Underline all the concrete nouns, and circle all the abstract nouns. A few suggestions are given.

1. Love at Home
2. God Is Love
3. Walk in the Light
4. Faith of Our Fathers
5. Faith Is a Living Power From Heaven

23. Common and Proper Nouns

Some nouns are **common nouns,** and some are **proper nouns.** A common noun is a name **common** to a group of persons, places, things, or ideas. A proper noun names a particular person, place, thing, or idea.

A common noun names any person, place, thing, or idea of a certain group. Common nouns are **ordinary, general** names of persons, places, things, and ideas. These are some common nouns.

girl	town	river
father	country	honesty

A proper noun is the name of **one particular** person, place, thing, or idea. Proper nouns are **specific, exact** names of persons, places, things, and ideas. These are some proper nouns.

Betty	Bethlehem	Ohio River
David	Switzerland	

The common name for one kind of animal that is milked is **cow.** But to tell exactly which cow, we use a proper noun such as **Bess, Pet, Heidi,** or **Buttercup.**

Cows   **Heidi**

Some kinds of proper nouns are listed in groups below. Notice that a proper noun always begins with a capital letter. Words like **uncle, city, street, river,** and **mount** are also capitalized when they are part of a proper noun phrase.

Names of persons:
    Matthew   Brother John   Mrs. Murphy

Calendar items:
    January   Sunday   Thanksgiving Day
      (but not the names of seasons: spring, autumn)

Names of things:
    New Testament   Proverbs   Liberty Bell

Geographical names:
    Africa   North America
    Pacific Ocean   Winnipeg
    Red Sea   Maryland
    Mount Carmel   Badlands National Park

Some proper noun phrases include little words like **a, an, the, and, in,** and **of.** Then you should follow the rules for capitalizing a title. Capitalize the first and last words and all other words except articles, conjunctions, and prepositions with less than four letters.

Gulf of Mexico   House of Representatives
Song of Solomon   Thompson's Feed and Seed
John the Baptist   The Declaration of Independence

Remember: A proper noun is the name of one particular person, place, thing, or idea. A proper noun must be capitalized.

> **Oral Drill** >

A. On the chalkboard, write three proper nouns for each common noun. Remember to capitalize your answers.

  1. boy   4. state   7. weekday
  2. city   5. country   8. month
  3. bay   6. ocean   9. holiday

B. Tell which words need capital letters.
  1. independence day in the united states is also called the fourth of july.
  2. The gettysburg national military park is in adams county, pennsylvania.
  3. egypt, libya, and algeria are in africa on the shores of the mediterranean sea.
  4. At columbia christian school, we use books from rod and staff publishers.

> **Written Practice** >

A. Copy and capitalize all the proper nouns.
  1. mr. benton and jack saw the liberty bell in philadelphia.
  2. uncle ivan lives in jackson, mississippi.
  3. The president lives in the white house in washington, d.c.
  4. seth was a son of adam and eve.

5. The men of judah found king adonibezek in bezek.
6. The fifth book of the new testament is called the acts of the apostles.
7. Chapter 5 was read by brother james.
8. jesus ascended to heaven from the mount of olives.
9. The Jewish day of worship is saturday.
10. The passover is a Jewish feast held in march or april.

B. Write a proper noun for each description.
1. the name of a newspaper or a periodical, such as a church paper
2. the name of a national park
3. the name of a hymn
4. the name of a person
5. the name of a holiday

Review and Practice

A. Write the definition of a noun.

B. Change the following words to nouns by adding the suffix **-ness, -ment, -ity,** or **-ion.** Check the dictionary if you need help with the correct spelling.
1. inspect   3. scarce   5. react
2. smooth   4. announce   6. personal

C. Write the correct words.
1. (There is, There are) many kinds of spiders.
2. (There's, There are) animals with ten legs.
3. (There's, There are) a nest in that stump.
4. (There is, There are) crabs and lobsters in this pond.
5. (There is, There are) an insect called an ant lion.

24. Singular and Plural Nouns

A **singular noun** names only one person, place, thing, or idea. A **plural noun** names more than one.

> **Singular:** girl, city, life, tomato
> **Plural:**   girls, cities, lives, tomatoes

The following rules tell how to form the plurals of nouns.

a. Make the plural form of most nouns by adding **-s.**

> lad—lads   book—books
> home—homes   farm—farms

b. If a noun ends with **s, sh, ch,** or **x,** make the plural form by adding **-es.**

> dress—dresses   ditch—ditches
> octopus—octopuses   peach—peaches
> bush—bushes   box—boxes

c. If a noun ends with **y** after a consonant, change the **y** to **i** and add **-es.** If the **y** comes after a vowel, simply add **-s.**

> baby—babies   boy—boys
> city—cities   monkey—monkeys
> enemy—enemies   Friday—Fridays

d. For some nouns ending with **f** or **fe,** change the **f** to **v** and add **-s** or **-es.** For other nouns ending with **f** or **fe,** simply add **-s.** A few may be spelled either way.

> calf—calves   chief—chiefs
> half—halves   roof—roofs
> knife—knives   hoof—hoofs or hooves

e. If a noun ends with **o** after a consonant, make the plural form by adding **-es.** But if it is a musical term, simply add **-s.**

potato—potatoes	alto—altos
domino—dominoes	soprano—sopranos
hero—heroes	piano—pianos

f. If a noun ends with **o** after a vowel, simply add **-s.**

patio—patios	kangaroo—kangaroos
trio—trios	

Check a dictionary whenever you are not sure about the spelling of a plural noun. If no plural form is shown, it is made in the usual way, by adding **-s** or **-es.**

Remember: A singular noun names only one. A plural noun names more than one. Check a dictionary when you need help with the spelling of a plural form.

> **Oral Drill**

A. Tell how to spell the plural form of each noun.

1. church	5. mystery	9. waitress
2. life	6. name	10. soprano
3. knife	7. chief	11. piano
4. roof	8. echo	12. tray

B. Write these sentences on the chalkboard, changing all the nouns to the plural form. Change other words to make your sentences sound right.
   1. The brush was in the glass on the shelf.
   2. The waitress peeled the potato with a knife.

> Written Practice >

A. Write the plural form of each noun.

1. switch	5. candy	9. valley
2. rash	6. alto	10. tax
3. leaf	7. potato	11. hobo
4. paper	8. patio	12. trio

B. Rewrite each sentence, changing all the nouns to the plural form. Change other words to make your sentences sound right.
   1. The chief struck the calf with the switch.
   2. The boy was baking a potato on the hot coal.
   3. The girl was selling candy in the city.

C. Write sentences of your own, using the plural forms of these nouns.

1. valley	2. roof	3. wolf

> Review and Practice >

Copy the nouns in these sentences. Write **C** after each common noun and **P** after each proper noun. The numbers in parentheses show how many nouns you should find.
   1. Did the Canary Islands get their name from the bird? (3)
   2. When explorers discovered the islands long ago, they found many fierce dogs there. (3)
   3. The islands were called *Canaria,* from the word for dogs in Latin. (5)
   4. Freedom is found in knowing truth. (2)
   5. True happiness is found in the way of the Bible. (3)
   6. Paul wrote about faith, hope, and charity. (4)

25. Developing Paragraphs by Giving Examples

All the sentences in a well-written paragraph help to develop and support the topic. The developing should be done in a definite way. One way is by giving examples. The following paragraph is developed in this way.

> Cereal grains produce hard kernels that are eaten by men and animals. In Europe and North America, the main cereal grain is wheat. Rice is important in China and other Asian countries, and in Latin America the chief grain is corn. People in India and Africa raise much millet and sorghum. Barley, rye, and oats are raised in cool, damp places where wheat does not grow well.

The topic sentence introduces the topic: cereal grains. The other sentences develop the paragraph with examples of different kinds of cereal grains.

Read the following paragraph. Its topic sentence is similar to that in the paragraph above, and it is also developed by giving examples. But the examples are different from those in the paragraph above.

> A cereal grain produces hard kernels that are eaten by men and animals. Wheat is one kind of cereal grain. We use wheat flour to make bread. We also use wheat in cakes, pies, doughnuts, cookies, and crackers. We eat much wheat in the form of hot or cold breakfast cereals. And for lunches or snacks, we have pretzels and other things made of wheat.

In the second paragraph, only one cereal grain is mentioned: wheat. This paragraph is developed by giving examples of the many ways that wheat is used.

Remember: One good way to develop a topic sentence is by giving examples.

> Oral Drill

A. Tell what examples you could use to develop these topic sentences.
   1. There are many signs that tell us spring is coming.
   2. Birds eat a great variety of foods.

B. Tell where you could find information to develop the following topic sentences by giving examples.
   1. Apples can be used in various ways.
   2. People around the world have different kinds of domestic animals.
   3. Electricity has many uses in our modern homes.
   4. A number of different flowers are commonly raised in flower gardens.

> Written Practice

Choose one of the topic sentences in Oral Drill, and write a paragraph about that topic. Use examples to develop your topic sentence.

Review and Practice

A. Copy the nouns in these sentences. Write **S** after each singular noun and **P** after each plural noun. The numbers in parentheses show how many nouns you should find.

1. The wild canary was found on the Canary Islands. (2)
2. The bird was named after the islands. (2)
3. People on the islands catch and train wild canaries and sell them all over the world. (4)
4. Aunt Martha has a canary that sings many cheerful songs. (3)
5. A tame canary sings more beautifully than a wild one. (2)

B. Diagram the skeletons of numbers 2, 4, and 5 in Part A.

26. More Plural Nouns

Some nouns have plural forms that are made in irregular ways. You will study a number of them in this lesson.

1. The plural forms of seven nouns are made by changing the vowels.

foot—feet   mouse—mice   man—men

goose—geese   louse—lice   woman—women

tooth—teeth

2. The plural forms of three nouns end with **-en** or **-ren.**

child—children   ox—oxen   brother—brethren

Brethren is an old plural form. Today we usually write **brothers** instead.

3. For some nouns, the plural form is the same as the singular form. Most of these are the names of animals.

sheep   salmon   trout
deer   moose

Remember: Some nouns have irregular plural forms.

> Oral Drill >

A. Tell which nouns are spelled incorrectly. Write them correctly on the chalkboard.
   1. Most of the mans had tired feets.
   2. Some deers may carry louses.
   3. The boies caught two trouts.
   4. The childs helped to catch salmons as they came upstream.
   5. The mouses were eating our cookys.
   6. How can those gooses stand to wade in that icy water with bare foots?
   7. Sharks have strong jawes and sharp tooths.
   8. The oxes pulled the covered wagons over mountains and through vallies.
   9. Pioneer men, womans, and childs had to work hard to make a living.

B. Read each sentence, changing all the nouns to the plural form. Change other words to make your sentences sound right.
   1. The boy takes care of a sheep and an ox on the farm.
   2. The leaf is falling off the tree.
   3. A mouse has a long tail and a sharp tooth.
   4. I found a knife, a fork, and a spoon in the drawer.

Written Practice

A. Write the plural form of each noun. Give two plurals for number 4.

1. woman	5. tooth	9. child
2. goose	6. ox	10. sheep
3. mouse	7. man	11. trout
4. brother	8. deer	12. louse

B. Rewrite each sentence, changing all the nouns to the plural form.
1. A sheep and a deer were feeding together in the valley.
2. The goose has a webbed foot.
3. The disciple tried to send the child away.
4. Let the child come to Me.
5. He also welcomed a man and a woman.

Review and Practice

A. Make a noun from each word by adding the suffix **-ness, -ment, -ity,** or **-ion.** Use the dictionary if you need help.

1. complete	3. acknowledge
2. stable	4. except

B. Find each word that should begin with a capital letter, and write it correctly.
1. manila is the capital of the philippines.
2. people of palestine used to call the mediterranean sea the great sea.
3. mr. white showed kindness to mr. shoemaker.
4. avik and omak were two boys from a tribe of inuit at coronation gulf.
5. "wouldn't it be odd if people went to new hampshire instead of california in search of gold?" remarked nancy.
6. james dulin went to boston to test the metal he had found at newburyport.

7. in the story "the sacrifice," mr. whitney was very impatient with ralph morely's pet calf named molly.

8. many icebergs from greenland reach major shipping routes in april, may, and june.

9. lito of the philippines loved miss naomi's stories from the bible.

10. the little mining village of greengairs was located halfway between edinburgh and glasgow in scotland.

> Challenge Exercise >

Write the plural forms of these nouns, using a dictionary for help. If two plural spellings are given, write both forms.

1. crisis
2. father-in-law
3. basis
4. index
5. focus

6. aquarium
7. spoonful
8. larva
9. cactus
10. stimulus

27. Possessive Nouns

A **possessive noun** shows ownership. It is often used as an adjective that tells **whose.** An apostrophe is used to form a possessive noun.

Whose lunch box is on the shelf?
Jerry's lunch box is on the shelf.

Whose new toy is this?
It is the **baby's** new toy.

Whose art pictures are on the wall?
The **students'** art pictures are on the wall.

The possessive form of a singular noun is made by adding an apostrophe and **-s** (**'s**).

girl—girl's   duck—duck's

The **girl's** purse is lost.
This **duck's** feet are orange.

If a plural noun ends with **-s,** the possessive form is made by adding only an apostrophe (**'**).

calves—calves'   days—days'

All the **calves'** ropes were cut.
The Good Samaritan's two pence were two **days'** wages.

If a plural noun does not end with **-s,** its possessive form is made by adding an apostrophe and **-s** (**'s**).

children—children's   men—men's

The **children's** toys were new.
The **men's** hats were on the shelf.

Remember: A possessive noun shows ownership. It is often used as an adjective. An apostrophe is used to form a possessive noun.

> Oral Drill >

A. Tell how to rewrite the following expressions, using possessive nouns.

Examples: a. the tracks of the fox
             b. the tracks of the foxes
Answers: a. the fox's tracks
             b. the foxes' tracks

1. the dish of the cat
2. the dish of the cats
3. the hole of the mouse
4. the hole of the mice
5. the pen of the sheep
6. the books of the child
7. the shoes of the boy
8. the dolls of the girls

B. Spell the possessive and plural forms of the following nouns. (The first three are done for you.) For numbers 9 and 10, give sentences using each form.

Singular	Singular Possessive	Plural	Plural Possessive
1. animal	animal's	animals	animals'
2. child	child's	children	children's
3. baby	baby's	babies	babies'
4. parent	———	———	———
5. year	———	———	———
6. home	———	———	———
7. fox	———	———	———
8. sheep	———	———	———
9. wolf	———	———	———
10. man	———	———	———

> Written Practice >

A. Rewrite the following expressions, using possessive nouns as in Oral Drill.
1. the tail of the monkey
2. the tails of the monkeys
3. the coats of the women
4. the purse of the woman
5. the gloves of the boys
6. the Bible of the lady
7. the work of the ladies

B. Make a chart like the one shown here. Copy each noun, and write its possessive and plural forms.

Singular	Singular Possessive	Plural	Plural Possessive
1. teacher	———	———	———
2. goose	———	———	———
3. waiter	———	———	———
4. coat	———	———	———
5. mouse	———	———	———
6. deer	———	———	———
7. brush	———	———	———
8. cherry	———	———	———
9. calf	———	———	———
10. box	———	———	———

C. Write sentences of your own, using the following words.
1. geese's
2. teacher's
3. mouse's
4. girls'

> Review and Practice

A. Write whether each sentence is **correct,** is a sentence **fragment,** is a **run-on** sentence, or has a **comma splice.**
1. The third largest land mammal is the rhinoceros.
2. The rhinoceros has a front horn that may be as much as 3 feet long poachers want this horn.
3. For a short distance can run as fast as a horse.
4. Wild rhinoceros live in Africa and Asia, some live in islands along the Atlantic coast.
5. The rhinoceros may be up to 6½ feet tall, and he may weigh 3 tons.

B. Combine each set of choppy sentences, using as few words as possible.

1. The skunk is a small animal. He is black and white.
2. The skunk can defend himself. He does this by shooting a spray. It is a spray that has a terrible smell.
3. First he stamps his front feet. He hisses or growls.
4. Then the skunk stands up. He stands on his front feet. He lifts his tail. He shoots the spray. It is a strong spray. It is a foul-smelling spray.
5. The skunk does not like the smell either. He sprays only if he must.

28. Appositives and Nouns of Direct Address

An **appositive** is a noun that comes right after another noun and gives more information about it. An appositive may be a noun standing alone, or it may be a noun modified by an adjective.

> This is my friend **David Nolt.**
>> The appositive **David Nolt** gives more information about the noun **friend.**

> Samuel anointed Saul, **the first king.**
>> The appositive **the first king** gives more information about the noun **Saul.**

If an appositive is a noun standing alone, it usually needs no comma. (See the first example above.) If an appositive is a noun modified by an adjective, it is set off by a comma. Two commas are used if the appositive comes in the middle of a sentence.

> Saul, **the first king,** was anointed by Samuel.

Sometimes we use a noun in a sentence to name the person to whom we are speaking. We may use his name or another noun that refers to him.

> **Mrs. Roland,** your chickens are in your garden.
> The ice is not safe, **my friend.**
> Be careful, **little girl,** when you cross the street.

Any noun or phrase that names the person to whom we are speaking is a **noun of direct address.** We **address** the person when we call him by a name as we talk to him.

When a noun of direct address is used, a comma sets it off from the rest of the sentence.

> **Sherry,** your friends have arrived.
> The calves have not been fed, **James.**

Two commas are used when a noun of direct address comes in the middle of a sentence.

> I'm sorry, **Mrs. Martin,** but we have no more eggs.

In a command, the subject is always **you.** The subject is **you,** even when the sentence begins with a noun of direct address. A noun of direct address is never the subject, and it must always be set off by a comma.

> Robert, feed the hogs.
> **Wrong:**

> **Right:**

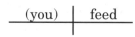

Janet, sweep the floor.
Wrong:

Janet	sweep

Right:

(you)	sweep

Remember: An appositive is a noun that comes right after another noun and gives more information about it. Appositives modified by adjectives are set off by commas.

A noun of direct address names the person to whom we are speaking. Nouns of direct address are set off by commas.

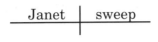 Oral Drill

A. Tell which words or phrases are appositives. Tell where commas are needed.
   1. James my oldest brother often brings us to school.
   2. My brother James is eighteen years old.
   3. That island is Greenland the world's largest island.
   4. Australia the smallest continent is south of the equator.
   5. We live on the planet Earth.
   6. Earth a beautiful planet travels around the sun in 365 days.
   7. The planet Mars looks reddish.

B. Tell which words are nouns of direct address. Tell where commas are needed.
   1. Patrick you may go now.
   2. This is what I brought for you Rachel.

3. The new book Timothy is for you.
4. Marie when will you study your lesson?
5. I will study it when Mother comes home Sandra.
6. Esther start with the mending.
7. This job Michael should be done soon.
8. Sarah share the work with Sally.

C. On the chalkboard, diagram the skeletons of numbers 5–8 in Part B.

▷ Written Practice ▷

A. These sentences have appositives. Copy the words that need commas after them, and add the missing commas.

Example: Joyce my youngest sister is three years old.
Answer: Joyce, sister,

1. On Sunday we invited Brother Alvin our deacon.
2. Those children my cousins also came to our house.
3. Today we will have art my favorite subject.
4. Solomon the wisest man was king after David his father.
5. Methuselah the oldest man lived 969 years.
6. Enoch his father was on the earth for 365 years.
7. Boaz married Ruth a widow.
8. The sun a medium-sized star shines steadily.
9. March the third month was named for the planet Mars.
10. Saturday was named for Saturn another planet.

B. These sentences have nouns of direct address. Copy the words that need commas after them, and add the missing commas.

1. I tell you Barry it will not be easy.
2. I know Martha that we must hurry.
3. This assignment Priscilla needs to be recopied.
4. Dennis you have forgotten your hat.
5. Children do your work well.

6. Please close the windows Marjorie.

7. Your response my boy has pleased me very much.

8. Mother said that you should mix the bread dough Joyce.

9. You have greatly cheered me faithful brother.

10. Roger wants the tractor over here Ronald.

C. Diagram the skeletons of numbers 4–7 in Part B.

D. Write sentences using these expressions as nouns of direct address. Use one at the beginning of a sentence, one at the end, and one in the middle. Use one in a command.

1. little brother

2. Mr. Sommers

3. Darlene

4. my friend

> Review and Practice >

Write **statement, question, command,** or **exclamation** to tell what kind of sentence each is. Also write the correct end punctuation.

1. How did you like the story "The Second Mile"

2. It is about a boy who lived in Palestine

3. Read it carefully, and think of ways that you could go the second mile for someone

4. How amazing it was that enemies became friends so quickly

> Challenge Exercise >

Sometimes two sentences with the same words can mean completely different things. It depends on where commas are placed in them. Study the following examples.

> Mr. Jones, my neighbor, would like to talk with you.
> **My neighbor** is an appositive.

> Mr. Jones, my neighbor would like to talk with you.
> **Mr. Jones** is a noun of direct address.

Write each sentence two times, using commas to give it different meanings. First, write it with an appositive, and then write it with a noun of direct address.

1. Charles your little brother is calling for you.
2. Aunt Beth our third grade teacher wrote this story.
3. Jake my black horse is too old to travel that far.

29. Developing Paragraphs by Using Steps

All the sentences in a well-written paragraph develop and support the topic in a definite way. You learned that one way to do this is by giving examples.

Another way to develop paragraphs is by using steps. When you tell how to do something, you should give the first step, then the second step, and so forth. When you describe something, you should tell about its parts in step-by-step order. You may describe from top to bottom, from left to right, from outside to inside, or from near to far. In any case, the steps must come in a sensible order. Then another person can read the paragraph and understand exactly what you mean.

The following paragraph uses steps in describing an insect's life. It tells about the changes that many insects go through as they develop from eggs to adults. The details are given in step-by-step order.

When you see a duckling, a calf, or a kitten, you know what it will be when it grows up. But many insects go through an amazing series of changes called metamorphosis. The insect starts out as an egg. Then the egg hatches, and out comes a tiny wormlike creature called a larva. The larva has a great appetite, and it eats and grows rapidly. Soon the larva stops eating and goes into a quiet, dormant state. This is called the pupa. The pupa is very plain, like a capsule. But inside, it changes each day, forming legs, wings, and other parts. Finally the insect comes out as a mature adult.

The next paragraph describes the parts of an insect. It begins with the head and ends with the abdomen.

Every insect has a separate head, thorax, and abdomen. The head is the front part, and it usually includes two compound eyes and a pair of antennae (feelers). The thorax is the middle part. Six jointed legs are attached to the thorax, and often there are one or two pairs of wings. The abdomen is the back part, and it contains various organs. Insects such as wasps and bees have a stinger at the tip of the abdomen.

When writing in steps, do not use the words **then** or **and then** too often. Use a variety of words, such as **first, second, soon, next, later, immediately,** and **afterward.**

> **Remember:** A paragraph can be developed by writing details step by step. The steps must be written in an orderly way.

Oral Drill

Discuss ways to develop the following topic sentences by using steps. Tell how you could give the steps in an orderly way.

1. Transplanting a flower is a simple job.
2. If you cut an apple in half, this is what you will see.
3. Do you know how to clean a chalkboard?
4. I help to prepare corn for the freezer every summer.

Written Practice

Choose two topic sentences from Oral Drill. Develop a paragraph from each one, using orderly steps.

Review and Practice

Write the correct words for these descriptions. You will not use all the answers.

unity	examples	steps
right	encyclopedia	left
paragraph	topic	order
dictionary		

1. A group of sentences that develop a single topic.
2. The main idea of a paragraph.
3. The margin of a paragraph that is kept completely straight.
4. What a paragraph has when all the sentences tell about the same topic.

5. A tool that is helpful for finding exact words.
6. What a paragraph has when the sentences follow one another in a sensible way.
7. Two ways in which a paragraph can be developed.

> Challenge Exercise >

Write the following sentences in paragraph form. Put the details in a sensible order, and leave out any sentences that do not belong. Underline the topic sentence.

How to Plant a Young Fruit Tree

1. Make the sides of your hole straight up and down, not sloped like a bowl.
2. Dig a hole about as big as a three-gallon bucket, about a foot wide and just a bit deeper.
3. Sweet cherry trees will not bear fruit unless two varieties are planted close together.
4. Put some loose topsoil in the bottom of the hole.
5. Now put in your tree, and begin filling the hole with soil.
6. Won't it be nice when you can pick peaches from this tree?
7. Following a few simple rules will give your young fruit tree a good start in the orchard.
8. When there is enough dirt in the hole to hold the tree upright, pour in half a bucket of water.
9. Finish by filling the hole with the rest of the soil.
10. The water will help to pack the soil around the roots and drive out air pockets.

30. Chapter 3 Review

> ▷ Oral Drill ▷

A. Give the definition of a noun.

B. Tell which words are nouns in the following sentences.
1. Ferdinand Magellan, an explorer from Spain, named the Pacific Ocean.
2. This ocean was peaceful when Magellan sailed on it.
3. Many times during the year, typhoons rage along the coast-lines of the Pacific.
4. Magellan did not know about these storms when he named the ocean.
5. The Atlantic Ocean got its name from the Atlas Mountains.
6. Long ago, people thought the Atlas Mountains were at the edge of the world.
7. Then they found a large ocean on the other side of the mountains, so they named it the Atlantic.
8. To have good friends, a person must show love and kind-ness.

C. Give a proper noun for each common noun, and write it correctly on the chalkboard.
1. pet   3. river   5. ocean
2. brother   4. city   6. book

D. Tell how to spell the following possessive and plural forms.

Singular	Singular Possessive	Plural	Plural Possessive
1. mother	———	———	———
2. canary	———	———	———
3. monkey	———	———	———
4. deer	———	———	———
5. fox	———	———	———

E. Tell whether each sentence has an **appositive** or a noun of **direct address.** Tell which words should have commas after them.

1. Joshua have you seen Crater Lake in Oregon?
2. No Julie I have only read about it.
3. Dover a town of England is located on the coast.
4. Have you ever seen a picture of the white cliffs of Dover Samuel?
5. The largest river is the Amazon a river in South America.

> Written Practice >

A. Write the definition of a noun.

B. Copy all the nouns in the following sentences.
1. Some travelers came to the Dead Sea many years ago.
2. This sea is between the countries of Israel and Jordan.
3. The Jordan River flows into the Dead Sea.
4. The travelers noticed that no birds flew over the Dead Sea, so they thought the air above the sea must be poisonous.
5. Birds can find little food there because no fish live in the salty water and few plants grow there.
6. The hills near the Red Sea are a reddish color.
7. The seaweed and other plants in the water are red too.
8. Can you see how this sea between Africa and Asia got its name?
9. Jesus gives true peace and joy.

C. Copy and capitalize all the proper nouns.
1. The pan american highway links north america, central america, and south america.
2. This highway runs through mexico, guatemala, el salvador, honduras, nicaragua, and costa rica.
3. It extends from the border between mexico and the united states to southern chile.

4. The hoover dam was built in the black canyon along the colorado river.
5. It is located on the border between arizona and nevada.
6. The concrete used in the dam was enough to build a road from new york to san francisco.
7. The pipe that was used was enough to reach from new york to chicago.
8. The blue nile and the white nile join at khartoum, sudan, to form the nile river.
9. The mouth of the nile river is at the mediterranean sea.
10. lake victoria is the source of the white nile, and lake tana in ethiopia is the source of the blue nile.

D. Write the possessive and plural forms of each noun listed.

Singular	Singular Possessive	Plural	Plural Possessive
1. ship	———	———	———
2. Monday	———	———	———
3. goose	———	———	———
4. knife	———	———	———
5. baby	———	———	———

E. Write **A** or **D** to tell whether each sentence has an appositive or a noun of direct address. Then copy the words that should have commas after them, and add the missing commas.
1. The cliffs of Dover Jerry are made of thick layers of chalk.
2. Chalk a kind of limestone is soft and fine-grained.
3. The chalk makes the cliffs look white Kevin.
4. Susan show the picture to Mary next.
5. Chalk is ground to make whiting a fine powder.
6. Whiting a useful substance is used to make paint and putty.
7. Sister Sarah where did the chalk come from?
8. No one really knows Mary except that God made them that way.

F. Write whether each paragraph below is developed by **giving examples** or by **using steps.**

Paragraph 1

Have you ever looked closely at an elephant? His trunk is like a cleaner hose between two fierce-looking tusks. His ears resemble two large fans, and his back is so broad that it would make a fine seat for riding through the jungle. His sturdy sides are covered with a wrinkly hide, and his legs are like strong pillars resting on round, flat feet. The elephant's tail resembles a rope with a bunch of long bristles at the end.

Paragraph 2

Latin America was named for the Latin-based languages that are spoken there. The most common language is Spanish, which developed from the Latin of people in Spain. People in Brazil speak Portuguese, which developed from the Latin used in Portugal. People in Haiti speak French, which developed from the Latin used in France. English and some other languages are also spoken in Latin America, but they are not nearly as common as the languages that developed from Latin.

Verbs show . . .

Future Tense

Present Tense

Past Tense

Chapter 4
Verbs

Verbs show . . .

Action

Being

31. Verbs

A verb is to a sentence much as an engine is to a car. A car without an engine will not run. The driver could sit in the seat, turn the steering wheel, and press the accelerator, but the car would not take him anywhere.

General Motors
Corporation

**A car without an engine
will not run.**

In the same way, a sentence without a verb cannot do its work. Every sentence must have a verb. A sentence cannot have a complete thought without a verb.

A verb is a word that shows action or being.

Action verbs include anything a person or thing can do, such as **talk, write, learn,** and **roll.** There are so many action verbs that we could not list them all.

Action verbs can show physical or mental action. Some verbs of physical action are **work, fly, jump,** and **scamper.** Some verbs of mental action are **study, think, love,** and **memorize.**

Have, has, and **had** are action verbs that show possession. They show that the subject of the sentence **owns** or **did own** something.

The verb **be** shows being instead of action. This verb has eight different forms. You will study the verb **be** in the next lesson.

Remember: A verb is a word that shows action or being.

 Oral Drill

A. Give the definition of a verb.

B. Give the verbs in these sentences. Tell whether each verb shows **physical action, mental action,** or **possession.**
1. The children had an enjoyable time at recess.
2. Bring your map tomorrow.
3. Study diligently and regularly.
4. God loved us and sent His only Son into the world.
5. Pray to God every morning and every evening.
6. We thank God for His great mercy to us.
7. We have many promises in the Word.
8. In winter the bears hibernate.
9. Watch the egg.
10. The shell cracks, and pieces fall off.
11. A small chick with wet feathers wriggles out.
12. The feathers dry in the air.
13. The chick walks about and looks for food.

 Written Practice

A. Write the definition of a verb.

B. Copy all the action verbs in each sentence.
1. The blind man heard Jesus and called to Him.
2. Trust in the Lord, and do good.
3. We love Him because He first loved us.
4. Read your Bible, and pray every day.
5. God created the universe.
6. We have two new calves in our barn.
7. A joey hops beside the mother kangaroo.
8. Opossum babies ride on their mother's back.
9. Otters dive, splash, and play in the water.
10. A mother bear brings her cubs out of the winter den.
11. The cubs eagerly explore their new world.

12. The mother carefully watches her inquisitive cubs.
13. The cubs snap, growl, and slap each other playfully.
14. Mother bears sometimes spank naughty cubs.
15. One afternoon a cub climbed a tree and slept on a branch.
16. They catch fish in the water and eat berries.

C. Follow the directions.
1. Write a sentence using an action verb that shows possession.
2. Write a sentence using a verb that shows physical action.
3. Write a sentence using a verb that shows mental action.

> Review and Practice >

Write the simple subjects. Then write the correct words in parentheses.
1. (There is, There are) a rhinoceros in the tall grass.
2. (There's, There are) zebras running in a herd.
3. (There's, There are) a mother and a baby in the kangaroo cage.
4. (There is, There are) its head sticking out of the pouch!
5. (There's, There are) a whale spouting in the distance.
6. (There was, There were) a dolphin and a porpoise in one large tank.
7. (There was, There were) monkeys swinging on the vines.
8. (There is, There are) a keeper feeding the seals.
9. (There was, There were) many buffaloes on the plains long ago.
10. (There's, There are) still some wild horses on the plains today.

32. The Verb *Be*

Most verbs show action, but the verb **be** does not. It gives meaning to a sentence by showing that something exists or has existed. It tells that something **is** or **was.**

The eight forms of **be** are **am, is, are, was, were, be, been,** and **being.** Memorize these forms if you do not know them.

See how the forms of **be** are used in the following sentences.

I **am** happy today.	They **were** in the kitchen.
She **is** at school.	He will **be** here soon.
You **are** in Ohio.	We have **been** there before.
He **was** here.	Are you **being** thankful?

Remember: The forms of the verb **be** are as follows: **am, is, are, was, were, be, been, being.**

> **Oral Drill**

A. Give the definition of a verb.

B. Give the correct form of each **be** in bold print.
1. The Lord **be** great.
2. I **be** ready to go.
3. Saul **be** the first king of Israel.
4. We **be** thankful for all the Lord has done.
5. Yesterday we **be** taking a test.
6. We are **be** diligent.

C. Tell which words are forms of **be.**
   1. Blessed is the man that feareth the Lord.
   2. Jesus said, "I am the door of the sheep."
   3. John wrote, "I was in the Spirit on the Lord's Day."
   4. John had been on the isle of Patmos.
   5. Jesus will be coming again.
   6. The students are being reverent.
   7. Some students were giving reports.

> Written Practice >

A. Write all the forms of the verb **be** in order.

B. Copy all the forms of **be** in these sentences.
   1. The Lord is good to all.
   2. We are being quiet.
   3. Blessings are upon the head of the just.
   4. Jesus said, "Before Abraham was, I am."
   5. We will be true to Him.
   6. The children have been working busily.

> Review and Practice >

A. Copy all the verbs in the following sentences. After each verb, write **A** for action or **B** for being.
   1. I am Alpha and Omega, the beginning and the ending.
   2. Read that story again, please.
   3. A fat black bear lumbered slowly into the woods.
   4. This book shows many colorful birds.
   5. Abraham staggered not at the promise of God.
   6. Moses was meek above all other men.
   7. Moses viewed the land from a mountaintop.
   8. The seed yielded much fruit.
   9. He marveled because of their unbelief.

10. John peered into the empty sepulcher.

11. Jesus' body was not there.

12. Jesus ascended into heaven from the Mount of Olives.

B. Write whether each sentence is **correct,** is a sentence **fragment,** is a **run-on** sentence, or has a **comma splice.**

1. Most spiders use silk for building, they make many different kinds of webs.

2. Build homes, snares, tightropes, tunnels, and bridges.

3. Spiders use their special fingerlike spinnerets for spinning God made this tiny, amazing creature.

4. Spiders can make sticky silk lines for trapping insects or dry ones to walk on.

> Challenge Exercise >

Answer these questions about the verb **be.**

1. Which form of **be** is used only with the subject **I**?

2. Which form of **be** must be used with the helping verb **have, has,** or **had**?

3. Which form of **be** needs another form of **be** as a helping verb?

4. Which form of **be** is used in a command?

33. Helping Verbs and Verb Phrases

A group of words working together as one verb is called a **verb phrase.** A verb phrase is made of a **main verb** and one or more **helping verbs.** In this sentence, the verb phrase is in bold print and the main verb is underlined.

They **had been <u>studying</u>** quietly.

The main verb in a verb phrase may show action or being.

Action: had been **studying**
Being: may have **been**

In a verb phrase, the last word is always the main verb. Every word before the main verb is a helping verb.

Be sure you know these helping verbs by memory.

Forms of *be*: am, is, are, was, were, be, been, being
H **triplets:**   have, has, had
D **triplets:**   do, does, did
M **triplets:**   may, might, must
Three sets of twins:
                can—could, shall—should, will—would

Some words that act as helping verbs can also stand alone as main verbs. Forms of **be, have,** and **do** can be used both ways. Other helping verbs cannot be used as main verbs. Forms of **may, can, shall,** and **will** can be helping verbs but not main verbs.

Sometimes a verb phrase is divided by a word such as **not** or **never.** These words are not verbs. They are not part of the verb phrase.

Male <u>ants</u> | <u>do</u> **not** <u>work</u>.
<u>We</u> | <u>may</u> **never** <u>see</u> the lost book again.

Remember: A group of words working together as one verb is a verb phrase. The last word in a verb phrase is the main verb, and all the others are helping verbs. A main verb can be an action verb or a form of **be.**

 Oral Drill

A. Give the definition of a verb.

B. Say the forms of **be** from memory.

C. Say the other helping verbs by memory.

D. Read the verb phrase in each sentence, and tell which word is the main verb. Tell whether the main verb shows **action** or **being.**
1. A barn swallow is sitting on the telephone wire.
2. Many birds are migrating south this time of year.
3. The sky was filled with birds.
4. The geese were flying.
5. The birds have been flying south all week.
6. The children have never been there.
7. Jeffrey does do good work.
8. The geese may be in the South soon.
9. Jean might not have been on time.
10. You must work harder on your penmanship.
11. Every little letter does make a difference.
12. Your effort will be rewarded.

> **Written Practice** >

A. Write the definition of a verb.

B. Write in order all the verbs that can be used as helping verbs.

C. Copy all the verbs and verb phrases. Underline the main verb in each verb phrase.
1. I am watching an ant nest.
2. One worker ant is carrying a large load.
3. He will take it to his nest.
4. Some workers are moving cocoons to another room.
5. Queen ants lay the eggs.
6. One ant was repairing the nest with a leaf.
7. You could never build a nest as perfect as an ant's nest.
8. You might not agree, but just try it sometime.

9. Ants work together by instinct.
10. Some ants may not be friendly to other ants.
11. God did make the ants and all other creatures.
12. We should learn lessons from the ants.

Go to the ant, thou sluggard; consider her ways, and be wise.

Proverbs 6:6

> Review and Practice

A. Make a noun from each word by adding the suffix **-ness,
-ment, -ity,** or **-ion.** Use the dictionary if you need help.
1. ignite
2. mature
3. lengthy
4. judge
5. opportune
6. faithful
7. measure
8. estimate

B. Find each word that should begin with a capital letter, and
write it correctly.
1. When we visited florida in april, daniel martin took us to
see the gulf of mexico on wednesday afternoon.
2. At the fulton christian school, brother joseph told his pupils
to read the book of proverbs in the old testament before
thanksgiving day.
3. On a trip to british columbia with floyd burkholder and
his family, we visited the glacier national park.

34. Learning to Outline

Did you ever see a house before the siding and roofing were put on? If you did, you saw the frame of the house. You could see what size and shape the house would be. The frame is the part to which the other materials are fastened.

An outline is to a composition what a frame is to a house. It is the plan upon which a composition is built. It provides an orderly pattern for the composition to follow.

Making an outline helps us when we study what others have written. An outline gives a summary of a composition. It shows what the main thoughts are and how they are organized.

Study the following pattern for outlining.

    I. First main topic
      A. Subtopic
      B. Subtopic
   II. Second main topic
      A. Subtopic
      B. Subtopic
  III. Third main topic

Notice that Roman numerals are used with main topics, and capital letters are used with subtopics. A period is placed after the number or letter that comes before each point. Every main topic and subtopic begins with a capital letter. Also notice that all the Roman numerals are lined up vertically and that all the capital letters are lined up vertically.

Remember that every paragraph has a topic sentence. The topic sentence gives the main idea of the paragraph. This is shown as the main topic on the outline. The rest of the sentences in the paragraph develop the topic sentence. These are shown as subtopics on the outline.

Study the following paragraphs, in which the topic sentences are underlined. Then look at the outline below them. Notice that the boldface words in the paragraphs are the same as the words

on the outline. Also notice that the outline and the paragraphs have the same title.

How Stars Are Different From Planets

<u>Stars are **much larger than planets**</u>. They only seem to be about the same size because stars **are much farther away than planets.** Stars **produce their own light** in the same way that the sun does. They **seem to twinkle** as they shine.

<u>Planets **are fairly small bodies** in comparison with stars.</u> They **travel around the sun as the earth does.** They **do not produce light, but simply reflect sunlight.** Planets **shine with a steady light** in the night sky.

How Stars Are Different From Planets

I. Stars
   A. Are much larger than planets
   B. Are much farther away than planets
   C. Produce their own light
   D. Seem to twinkle
II. Planets
   A. Are fairly small bodies
   B. Travel around the sun as the earth does
   C. Do not produce light, but simply reflect sunlight
   D. Shine with a steady light

Remember: An outline is the frame or plan of a composition. It shows how the ideas in a composition are organized.

> Oral Drill >

Tell how to outline the following paragraphs. Tell which points are main topics and which ones are subtopics.

African and Asiatic Elephants

African elephants live in central Africa. They are huge, fierce animals, and they have large ears that cover their shoulders. They have a dip in their backs. African elephants have two knobs of flesh at the tip of their trunks, which they use for picking up small things.

Asiatic elephants live in southeastern Asia. They are smaller and easier to train than African elephants. They have smaller ears that do not cover their shoulders, and they have a hump on their backs. Asiatic elephants have only one knob of flesh at the tip of their trunks.

> Written Practice

A. Read the following paragraphs. Copy and complete the outline, which shows how the paragraphs are organized.

The Inside Parts of a Flower

The male part of a flower is the stamen. It has a threadlike part called a filament and an enlarged tip called an anther. The male part bears pollen, which is needed for producing seeds.

The female part of a flower is the pistil. It has a stemlike part called a style and a sticky tip called a stigma. The female part produces seeds in the ovary, which is at its base.

The Inside Parts of a Flower

I. Male part
   A. Is the _____
   B. Has a _____
   C. Has an _____
   D. Bears _____
II. Female part
   A. Is the _____
   B. Has a _____
   C. Has a _____
   D. Produces _____

B. Read the parable of the sower in Luke 8:5–15. Then copy and complete the following outline.

Four Kinds of Soil

   I. Soil by the wayside
     A. Seed was _____
       down.
     B. Seed was _____ by birds.
     C. This is like people who _____.
  II. Thin soil over a rock
     A. Seed grew but _____.
     B. Seed lacked _____.
     C. This is like people who _____.
 III. Soil with thorns
     A. Thorns _____ with the seed.
     B. Thorns _____ the seed.
     C. This is like people who _____.
 IV. Good, deep soil
     A. Seed _____.
     B. Seed bore _____.
     C. This is like people who _____.

Review and Practice

Diagram the skeleton of each sentence. An expression like **wolf spider** is a noun phrase.

1. Did you see that spider?
2. Harry, count its eyes.
3. Wolf spiders and lynx spiders chase and catch insects.

© Corel

4. A raft spider builds a raft and floats downstream.
5. From the raft, it grabs swimming insects and small fish.
6. Spiders have many legs, but they are not insects.
7. There is a spider web in the window.
8. Brother John teaches science in an interesting way, but we must work hard too.

35. Agreement of Subjects and Verbs

The subject and the verb must work together in a sentence. If the subject is singular, the verb must be singular. If the subject is plural, the verb must be plural.

Wrong: <u>Ralph</u> <u>write</u> his memory verses.
Right: <u>Ralph</u> <u>writes</u> his memory verses.

Remember that a **singular** noun names only one, and a **plural** noun names more than one. A verb that goes with a singular subject is a **singular verb.** A singular verb usually ends with **-s.** A verb that goes with a plural subject is a **plural verb.**

You may remember from earlier grades that the singular form of the verb may be called the **-s form** of the verb. The **-s** form is used only in the present tense. Past tense verbs do not need **-s.**

Singular verbs usually end with **-s.** This is different from nouns. With nouns, the plural form usually ends with **-s.** So in the present tense, either the subject or the verb usually ends with **-s.**

> The **trees grow** taller and taller.
> **Judy paints** beautiful pictures.

When the subject of a sentence is singular, be sure to use the singular form of the verb.

> The <u>mailman</u> <u>drops</u> the mail into this box.
> <u>Grandfather</u> <u>passes</u> our house on his way to work.

When the subject of a sentence is plural or compound, be sure to use the plural form of the verb.

> The <u>girls</u> <u>paint</u> beautiful pictures.
> <u>Grandfather</u> and <u>Grandmother</u> <u>pass</u> our house each day.

Be sure verbs agree with pronoun subjects. Use a plural verb with the subjects **I** and **you.**

> <u>I</u> <u>eat</u> cheese with apples.
> <u>You</u> <u>eat</u> peanut butter with apples.
> <u>She</u> <u>eats</u> mustard on eggs!
> <u>They</u> <u>eat</u> lunch at twelve o'clock.

> **Remember:** A singular verb must be used with all singular subjects except **I** and **you**. A plural verb must be used with a plural subject. A singular verb usually ends with **-s.**

⟩ Oral Drill ⟩

A. Tell whether **see** or **sees** would fit in each blank.
1. The baby —— the bird.
2. The children —— new birds every day.
3. John and Joe —— where the tracks go.
4. I —— the top of the mountain.
5. You ——, we will soon be there.
6. He —— the end of the trail.

B. Tell which verb is correct.
1. Harold (write, writes) a letter to his grandmother every month.
2. You (write, writes) faithfully to your aunt.
3. My cat (catch, catches) mice.
4. All our cats (catch, catches) mice.
5. Charles and Paul (find, finds) arrowheads in this field.
6. We (leave, leaves) today.
7. He (leave, leaves) tomorrow.
8. John and Betty (leave, leaves) at nine o'clock.

⟩ Written Practice ⟩

Write the correct verbs.
1. I (read, reads) my Bible every day.
2. They (read, reads) a chapter every morning.
3. We (sing, sings) a new song every week.
4. Karl (wait, waits) at the bridge every morning.
5. Carla and Joyce (jump, jumps) rope together.

6. The trap-door spider (live, lives) in a silk-lined tunnel.
7. Harvester ants (dig, digs) burrows in the ground.
8. Some wasps (build, builds) paper nests.
9. The mud dauber (build, builds) a nest of mud.

Review and Practice

A. Write the definition of a noun. Then write the definition of a verb.

B. Rewrite the following sentences. Change all the nouns to plural nouns.
   1. The family visited a church in this state.
   2. The leaf drops off the bush.
   3. My brother saw a deer under that tree.
   4. The echo rings through the valley.
   5. The book on this shelf is a dictionary.
   6. A slug is a snail without a shell.

C. Write **A** or **D** to tell whether each sentence has an appositive or a noun of direct address. Then copy each word that should have a comma after it, and add the missing comma.
   1. My grandfather received this beautiful drawing from Laura Johnson an artist.
   2. Sarah do you like to draw?
   3. Joyce Hannigan my grandmother has a small garden in her back yard.
   4. May we see your garden Grandma?

> Challenge Exercise >

In the following lists are some pronouns that you may not recognize as pronouns. When you use them as subjects, you must use the correct verb form with them.

Singular pronouns:

each, one, everybody, nobody, someone, something

Plural pronouns:

both, few, several, many

Examples:

Everybody <u>was</u> on time. (not **were**)

<u>Each</u> of the children <u>is</u> drawing a picture.

(The subject is never in a prepositional phrase.

The verb agrees with **each,** not **children.**)

<u>Few</u> of the people <u>are</u> still outside.

Write the correct verb for each sentence.

1. Each of the students (is, are) writing a report.
2. Both of the dogs (is, are) mine.
3. Somebody (have, has) broken the window.
4. Both of the girls (is, are) ready to help.
5. Many of the students (was, were) ready for the test.
6. One of the doughnuts (is, are) missing.
7. Nobody (have, has) eaten it.
8. Someone (have, has) taken it.
9. (Do, Does) one of the boys have it in his lunch?
10. Everybody (work, works) hard on this job.

36. Using Forms of *Be* and *Do*

Forms of the verbs **be** and **do** are often used incorrectly. This lesson will show you some of these common mistakes and the ways to correct them.

1. When you use forms of **be** and **do,** make sure the subjects and verbs agree. Use a singular verb with a singular subject except **I** and **you.** Use a plural verb with a plural or a compound subject.

   > The <u>women</u> <u>do</u> sewing for poor people. (not **does**)
   > <u>Alice</u> and <u>Mary</u> <u>are</u> in school. (not **is**)
   > <u>Howard</u> and <u>Kevin</u> <u>do</u> the chores. (not **does**)

2. Use the forms of **be** correctly with pronoun subjects. Be especially careful with **we, you,** and **they.** These always take a plural verb.

   > **Wrong:** We was looking at pictures yesterday.
   > **Right:** <u>We</u> <u>were</u> looking at pictures yesterday.

   > **Wrong:** They was taken many years ago.
   > **Right:** <u>They</u> <u>were</u> taken many years ago.

   > **Wrong:** In one picture you was just a baby.
   > **Right:** In one picture <u>you</u> <u>were</u> just a baby.

3. When you use forms of **be** in contractions, be sure the verb agrees with the subject. Do not use the contraction **ain't.** Use **am not, isn't,** or **aren't.**

   > <u>Mother</u> <u>isn</u>'t back yet.
   > The <u>boys</u> <u>aren</u>'t in their room.
   > <u>James</u> and <u>Mark</u> <u>aren</u>'t here.
   > I **am not** ready yet. (not **ain't**)

4. Use the contractions **don't** and **doesn't** correctly. Remember to use **doesn't** with a singular subject. Use **don't** with plural subjects, compound subjects, and the pronouns **I** and **you.**

> **Wrong:**
>> He don't come very early.
>
> **Right:**
>> He <u>does</u>n't come very early.
>> The <u>men</u> <u>don</u>'t plow on Sunday.
>> <u>Ruth</u> and <u>Katie</u> <u>don</u>'t plan to go.
>> <u>I</u> <u>don</u>'t know who wrote the Book of Job.

If you are not sure whether to use **don't** or **doesn't,** try **do not** or **does not** first.

> **Wrong:**
>> He do not come often.
>> He don't come often.
>
> **Right:**
>> He <u>does</u> not come often.
>> He <u>does</u>n't come often.

5. Make sure the verb agrees with the subject in a sentence that begins with **here** or **there.**

> Here <u>are</u> a <u>box</u> and a <u>bag</u> for you.
> There <u>is</u> my <u>shoe</u>.

Remember: Use the forms of **be** and **do** correctly. Use the contractions **don't** and **doesn't** correctly. Do not use **ain't.**

> **Oral Drill** >

Choose the correct words in parentheses. Practice reading each sentence correctly.

1. I (am, is) in the fifth grade.
2. They (was, were) the tallest boys in the class.
3. We (wasn't, weren't) looking for a change of weather.
4. Genesis and Exodus (isn't, aren't) the names of men.
5. I (ain't, isn't, am not) planning to go along.
6. They (ain't, isn't, aren't) going either.
7. We (don't, doesn't) know how long Job had boils.
8. Father (don't, doesn't) know either.
9. Sue and Bill (don't, doesn't) eat eggs for breakfast.
10. He (don't, doesn't) try as hard as he should.
11. Sharon (don't, doesn't) waste time in school.
12. There (is, are) some visitors at the door.
13. Here (is, are) my papers.
14. There (was, were) bigger fish in this area long ago.

> **Written Practice** >

A. Choose and write the correct words in parentheses.

1. Margaret (do, does) the cleaning each Saturday.
2. We (is, are) in the fifth grade.
3. (Wasn't, Weren't) you on time today?
4. Joshua and Caleb (was, were) spies.
5. Revelation (is, are) the last book in the Bible.
6. It (don't, doesn't) matter where you put the box.
7. You (don't, doesn't) catch fish when you are noisy.
8. This jar (don't, doesn't) have a lid.
9. I (ain't, aren't, am not) forgetting my lessons.
10. These colors (isn't, aren't) bright.
11. The children (isn't, aren't) playing in the sandbox.
12. He (don't, doesn't) go fishing very often.

13. She (don't, doesn't) like to do her lessons over.
14. They (was, were) building snowmen.
15. There (is, are) several high mountains in Palestine.
16. There (is, are) three deer.
17. There (is, are) more hope for a fool than for a man who is hasty in his words.
18. Here (is, are) a small trout.

B. Write four sentences of your own, using **do, does, don't,** and **doesn't** correctly.

> Review and Practice

A. Write whether each sentence is a **statement, question,** or **command.** Also write the correct end punctuation.
   1. Are you holding a box turtle
   2. Box turtles like to eat vegetables, earthworms, and insects
   3. Give him raw hamburger, a special treat
   4. Watch out for that snapping turtle

B. Which sentence in Part A would probably be said with strong feeling? Write it as an exclamation, using the correct end punctuation.

C. Write the possessive form of each noun.
   1. turtle
   2. foxes
   3. sheep
   4. children

37. Verb Tense

Tense means "time." Verbs show tense. They can have present tense, past tense, and future tense.

Verbs in the **present tense** tell about things that happen now, in the present time. They tell about things that are happening right now.

> He **tries** very hard.
> We **study** the Bible.
> Amy **makes** the cookies.

Verbs in the **past tense** tell about things that have already happened. The past tense of regular verbs is formed by adding **-ed.** The past tense of irregular verbs is formed in various ways.

Regular verbs:
> The children **play** outside. (present)
> The children **played** outside. (past)
>
> Mother **waits** for us. (present)
> Mother **waited** for us. (past)

Irregular verbs:
> The birds **sing** cheerily. (present)
> The birds **sang** cheerily. (past)
>
> Father **drives** carefully. (present)
> Father **drove** carefully. (past)

Verbs in the **future tense** tell about things that will happen sometime, in the future. The words **shall** and **will** are used as helping verbs to show future tense.

> I **write** a letter today. (present)
> I **shall write** a letter tomorrow. (future)
>
> Mother **helps** us. (present)
> **Will** Mother **help** us? (future)

The following chart shows the present, past, and future tenses of two regular verbs and two irregular verbs.

Present	Past	Future
care	cared	will care
talk	talked	will talk
buy	bought	will buy
get	got	will get

Remember: Tense means "time." A verb can show present tense, past tense, and future tense.

> Oral Drill

A. Give all three tenses for each verb. The first one is done for you.

Present	Past	Future
1. try	tried	will try
2. know	——	—— ——
3. ——	washed	—— ——
4. ——	——	will see
5. are	——	—— ——
6. ——	carried	—— ——

B. Say each verb or verb phrase, and tell what tense it is.
   1. I shall visit my elderly neighbor.
   2. Barry learned his lesson.
   3. I have a pretty scrapbook from my friends.
   4. The teacher will explain the lesson.
   5. Father waited patiently.
   6. Fools despise wisdom and understanding.
   7. Will the girls help?

> Written Practice >

A. Write all three tenses for each verb. The first one is done for you.

Present	Past	Future
1. touch	touched	will touch
2. find	——	—— ——
3. ——	——	will travel
4. repair	——	—— ——
5. ——	brought	—— ——
6. ——	——	will do
7. study	——	—— ——
8. am	——	—— ——

B. Copy each verb or verb phrase. After it write **present, past,** or **future** to tell what tense it is.
1. Envy and anger shorten a man's life.
2. Enoch walked with God in daily fellowship.
3. Two men went to the temple to pray.
4. We shall read the story.
5. The Pharisee stands to pray.
6. In his prayer he boasted about himself.
7. Will the publican pray?
8. You will learn the lesson.

C. Write three sentences of your own. Use each of the three tenses.

> **Review and Practice**

A. Write the following things.
   1. the definition of a verb
   2. the forms of the verb **be**
   3. the other helping verbs by groups

B. Correct each sentence by writing it properly as a compound sentence, or by dividing it into two sentences. Correct the fragments by adding the missing parts.
   1. All insects have six legs most insects have wings.
   2. Have two feelers on their heads.
   3. Grasshoppers and beetles.
   4. Spiders are not insects, they have eight legs.
   5. Webs of sticky silk.

C. Combine each pair of choppy sentences, using as few words as possible.
   1. Land turtles breathe with lungs. Water turtles breathe with lungs.
   2. Most turtles can pull their heads into their shells. They can pull their legs and tails into their shells.
   3. Sara fed her turtle some cantaloupe. It was a box turtle. The cantaloupe was fresh.
   4. The turtle's neck swayed back and forth. It was long and thin.

38. More About Outlining

You have learned that an outline is like the framework of a building. It is an orderly arrangement of main ideas and less important ideas. An outline shows how the ideas in a composition are organized. This makes it easy to see how the ideas are related to each other.

To make an outline, write in order the main topic of each paragraph. Place a Roman numeral before each main topic. Place a capital letter before each subtopic under a main topic.

Sometimes an outline shows ideas that are even less important than subtopics. These ideas may be called details, and they are marked with Arabic numerals (1, 2, and so on). Study the following form of an outline. Notice how subtopics come under main topics, and details come under subtopics.

  I. First main topic
     A. Subtopic
     B. Subtopic
        1. Detail
        2. Detail
 II. Second main topic
     A. Subtopic
        1. Detail
        2. Detail
     B. Subtopic
III. Third main topic

Remember: An outline shows how the ideas in a composition are organized. Main topics are marked with Roman numerals, subtopics are marked with capital letters, and details are marked with Arabic numerals.

Oral Drill

Read these paragraphs. The outline that follows them shows how they are organized. Work together as a class to complete it on the chalkboard.

The Three Largest of the Great Lakes

Lake Superior is the largest and the farthest west of the five Great Lakes. This is the largest freshwater lake in the world. Its area is 31,700 square miles, or a little greater than the area of South Carolina. Lake Superior is also the highest and deepest of the Great Lakes. Its surface is 600 feet above sea level, and its depth is 1,333 feet.

Lake Huron is the second largest of the Great Lakes. This lake has the same elevation as Lake Michigan. The surface of both lakes is 579 feet above sea level. But Lake Huron is only 750 feet deep, while Lake Michigan is 923 feet deep. Lake Huron was named for the Huron Indians who lived on its shores.

Lake Michigan is the third largest of the Great Lakes. This is the only one of the Great Lakes entirely within the United States. It is the largest freshwater lake in the United States. Its area is 22,300 square miles, or about half as great as the area of Pennsylvania. Lake Michigan received its name from the Indian name *Michi-guma,* which means "big water."

The Three Largest of the Great Lakes

I. Lake Superior

    A. Is the _____ and the _____

    B. Is the largest_____

       1. Area is_____

       2. Area is_____

    C. Is the _____ and _____

       1. Surface is _____

       2. Depth is_____

II. Lake Huron
   A. Is the _____
   B. Has the same _____
      1. Surface of_____
      2. Lake Huron _____,
         while Lake Michigan_____
   C. Was named for_____
III. Lake Michigan
   A. Is the _____
   B. Is the only _____
   C. Is the largest_____
      1. Area is _____
      2. Area is _____
   D. Received its name _____

Written Practice

Read the following paragraphs. Copy and complete the outline, which shows how the paragraphs are organized.

Corn and Its Uses

The corn plant has a tall central stalk. It has underground roots that supply water and minerals to the plant, and prop roots that support the plant. The stalk has a soft, spongy center. At the top it has tassels that bear pollen. The leaves have a long, swordlike shape, and they grow from each joint of the stalk. The ears have a round, firm cob in the center. They have many kernels, which are the seeds of corn. The ears have a leafy covering of husks.

Corn has many uses. It is used as food for hogs, cattle, sheep, and poultry. It is a good food for people too. Corn is cooked and eaten as a vegetable. It may be made into cereals, cornmeal, cornstarch, corn oil, and other things. It is also eaten indirectly as meat from animals raised on corn. Many things other than food are made from corn. Cornstalks are used in wallboard and paper, and corncobs are burned as fuel or used to make fertilizer. Corn syrup is used to make alcohol, which is used in plastics, brake fluid, and many other products.

Corn and Its Uses

I. The corn plant
   A. Stalk
      1. Has underground _____
      2. Has prop _____
      3. Has _____ center
      4. Has _____
   B. Leaves
      1. Have _____
      2. Grow from _____
   C. Ears
      1. Have _____
      2. Have many _____
      3. Have leafy _____
II. Uses for corn
   A. Food for _____
   B. Food for _____
      1. Is cooked _____
      2. Is made into _____
      3. Is eaten indirectly _____
   C. Other uses
      1. Cornstalks used in _____
      2. Corncobs _____ or _____
      3. Corn syrup used to make _____, which
         is used in _____

> Review and Practice

Write **true** or **false.**
1. When you write about a personal experience, you need to include interesting details.
2. **Worthwhile** is a more exact word than **good.**
3. A paragraph is a group of sentences that develop several topics.
4. The sentences in a paragraph should be written in an order that is easy to understand.
5. When all the sentences in a paragraph tell about the same topic, the paragraph has unity.
6. The sentences in a paragraph should be of equal lengths.
7. In a description that uses steps, something is described in a certain order, such as from top to bottom or from left to right.
8. An outline shows how the ideas of a composition are organized.

> Challenge Exercise

Write an outline of a sermon that you hear in church.

39. The Principal Parts of Verbs

Verbs have three main forms. They are the present form, the past form, and the past participle. These are the three **principal parts** of verbs.

The first principal part is the **present** form. This is the main form of the verb, and it is used for the present tense.

The twins **like** chocolate ice cream.
The pupils **study** the countries of Africa.
We **enjoy** watching the birds.
The girls **rub** soap over the clothes.

The second principal part is the **past** form. It may also be called the **simple past form.** This form is used for the past tense.

Be sure to spell past forms correctly. Study the following rules for spelling the past forms of regular verbs.

a. For most regular verbs, simply add **-ed** to the present form.

> **Present:** We **help** Mother with the dishes.
> **Past:**   We **helped** Mother with the dishes.

b. If a verb ends with **e,** drop the **e** before adding **-ed.**

> **Present:** The twins **like** chocolate ice cream.
> **Past:**   The twins **liked** chocolate ice cream.

c. If a verb ends with **y** after a consonant, change the **y** to **i** and add **-ed.**

> **Present:** The pupils **study** the countries of Africa.
> **Past:**   They **studied** the countries of Asia last year.

d. If a verb ends with **y** after a vowel, simply add **-ed.**

> **Present:** We **enjoy** watching the birds.
> **Past:**   We **enjoyed** watching the birds.

e. If a one-syllable verb ends with a single consonant after a short vowel, double the final consonant before adding **-ed.**

> **Present:** The girls **rub** soap over the clothes.
> **Past:**   The girls **rubbed** soap over the clothes.

Notice how verb **tenses** are different from verb **forms.** Different verb tenses are the different **times** that verbs tell about (present, past, and future). Different verb forms are the different **spellings** that are used to show different tenses.

The third principal part of verbs is the **past participle.** It may also be called the **helper form.** This form often tells about something that has already happened and is finished.

In regular verbs, the past participle is spelled the same as the past form. Both forms are made by adding **-ed** to the present form. The helping verb **have, has,** or **had** must be used with the past participle.

> I **have signed** my name.
> Karen **has cleaned** her room.
> Charles **had answered** correctly.

Remember: The three principal parts of verbs are the present form, the past form, and the past participle.

> **Oral Drill**

A. Give the missing verbs for this chart, and tell how to spell them. The first one is done for you.

Present	Past	Past Participle
1. clean	cleaned	(have) cleaned
2. sign	———	(has) signed
3. answer	———	(had) answered
4. listen	———	——— ———
5. ———	stayed	——— ———
6. ———	stopped	(had) stopped
7. hurry	———	——— ———
8. ask	———	——— ———

B. Say each verb or verb phrase. Tell whether it is the **present** form, the **past** form, or the **past participle.**

1. The children listen well.
2. Bartimaeus sat by the highway.
3. He begged for alms.
4. Have mercy on me.
5. Many people have heard him.
6. The Master stood still.
7. They have called the blind man.
8. Jesus healed him immediately.

> **Written Practice** >

A. Copy the chart, and add the missing words. The first one is done for you.

Present	Past	Past Participle
1. pack	packed	(have) packed
2. fill	———	——— ———
3. climb	———	(had) climbed
4. ———	carried	——— ———
5. study	———	——— ———
6. ———	brushed	——— ———
7. hike	———	——— ———
8. tag	———	——— ———
9. destroy	———	——— ———

B. Copy each verb or verb phrase. After each one, write **present, past,** or **past participle** to tell which form it is.

1. The Philistines gathered against Israel.
2. David spoke to King Saul.
3. I have slain a lion and a bear.
4. Five smooth stones go into his shepherd's bag.
5. David has killed Goliath.
6. Good shepherds carefully watch their sheep.
7. Our parents care for us.

8. The fifth graders have learned a new song.
9. The people have recited Psalm 19.
10. The students repeated their verses every day.

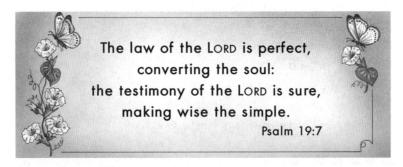

The law of the LORD is perfect,
converting the soul:
the testimony of the LORD is sure,
making wise the simple.

Psalm 19:7

> **Review and Practice**

A. Diagram the skeletons of these sentences.
   1. The men were hunting for sponges.
   2. Real sponges are animals.
   3. Large crews went out and hunted for sponges.
   4. There was danger in that business.
   5. The cook and his helper worked together on the sponge boat.
   6. Would you like the smell of drying sponges?
   7. Natural sponges were in great demand a few years ago.
   8. Artificial sponges are used today.

B. Choose and write the correct words in parentheses.
   1. I (like, likes) to make bouquets.
   2. We (was, were) finding many kinds of wildflowers.
   3. James and Mary (bring, brings) wild violets to Mother.
   4. The yellow violets (ain't, aren't) blooming yet.
   5. Here (is, are) some purple flowers.
   6. He (don't, doesn't) know what kind they are.

Principal Parts of Common Verbs

(Some verbs on this chart have alternate forms.)

First	Second	Third	First	Second	Third
(Present)	*(Past)*	*(Past Participle)*	*(Present)*	*(Past)*	*(Past Participle)*
be (is)	was	(have) been	*lie	lay	(have) lain
begin	began	(have) begun	pay	paid	(have) paid
blow	blew	(have) blown	put	put	(have) put
break	broke	(have) broken	*raise	raised	(have) raised
bring	brought	(have) brought	read	read	(have) read
*burst	burst	(have) burst	ride	rode	(have) ridden
buy	bought	(have) bought	ring	rang	(have) rung
catch	caught	(have) caught	*rise	rose	(have) risen
choose	chose	(have) chosen	run	ran	(have) run
*come	came	(have) come	*see	saw	(have) seen
cost	cost	(have) cost	send	sent	(have) sent
cut	cut	(have) cut	*set	set	(have) set
dig	dug	(have) dug	shine	shone	(have) shone
*do	did	(have) done	shoot	shot	(have) shot
*drag	dragged	(have) dragged	shut	shut	(have) shut
draw	drew	(have) drawn	sing	sang	(have) sung
drink	drank	(have) drunk	sink	sank	(have) sunk
*drown	drowned	(have) drowned	*sit	sat	(have) sat
eat	ate	(have) eaten	sleep	slept	(have) slept
fight	fought	(have) fought	speak	spoke	(have) spoken
find	found	(have) found	steal	stole	(have) stolen
fly	flew	(have) flown	swim	swam	(have) swum
forget	forgot	(have) forgotten	*swing	swung	(have) swung
freeze	froze	(have) frozen	*tag	tagged	(have) tagged
give	gave	(have) given	take	took	(have) taken
*go	went	(have) gone	teach	taught	(have) taught
hold	held	(have) held	tear	tore	(have) torn
hurt	hurt	(have) hurt	tell	told	(have) told
keep	kept	(have) kept	think	thought	(have) thought
know	knew	(have) known	wear	wore	(have) worn
*lay	laid	(have) laid	weep	wept	(have) wept
*leave	left	(have) left	win	won	(have) won
*let	let	(have) let	write	wrote	(have) written

*These troublesome verbs are often used incorrectly.

40. Principal Parts of Irregular Verbs

Verbs have three main forms, which are called their three principal parts. In the last lesson you studied the principal parts of regular verbs. The past form and the past participle of regular verbs are made by adding **-ed** to the present form.

In this lesson you will study the principal parts of irregular verbs. The past form and the past participle of these verbs are not formed by adding **-ed** to the present form. Instead, they are formed in a number of different ways. Their principal parts have irregular spellings.

Some irregular verbs have the same spelling for the past form and the past participle.

Present	Past	Past Participle
feel	felt	(have) felt
lay	laid	(has) laid
leave	left	(had) left

Other irregular verbs have three different forms: one for the present form, another for the past form, and still another for the past participle.

Present	Past	Past Participle
eat	ate	(have) eaten
do	did	(has) done
go	went	(had) gone

A few irregular verbs have the same spelling for all three principal parts.

Present	Past	Past Participle
burst	burst	(have) burst
cost	cost	(has) cost
set	set	(had) set

The chart before this lesson shows the principal parts of many other irregular verbs. Use the chart or a dictionary whenever you do not know the correct forms of a verb. If no principal parts are shown, the past and the past participle are formed in the regular way, by adding **-ed.** If only one principal part is shown, the past and the past participle are the same.

Remember to always use the helping verb **have, has,** or **had** with the past participle. Many past forms that need helpers end with an **n** or **un** sound.

have see**n**	had go**ne**
has **run**	have s**ung**

Remember: The past forms of irregular verbs are not made by adding **-ed** to the present form. The past participle must always be used with the helping verb **have, has,** or **had.**

> **Oral Drill**

A. Say and spell the correct past form of each word in parentheses.
1. Susan has (write) a note to the teacher.
2. Reuben (ring) the doorbell.
3. The children (sing) for Grandmother.
4. Father (pay) the bill promptly.
5. Mary has (set) the table.
6. She (find) the napkins in the drawer.
7. Little Samuel has (wear) his new coat.
8. Gideon had (break) his pitcher.
9. Not one person (drown) after the ship was broken.
10. Have you ever (draw) water from a well?
11. The stars (shine) brightly last night.
12. Jesus asked where they had (lay) Lazarus.
13. He (weep) at the grave of Lazarus.

14. Lazarus had (lie) in the grave four days.

15. He (rise) when Jesus called him.

B. Say and spell the words that belong in the blanks on this chart. You may use the chart on the page before this lesson if you are not sure.

Present	Past	Past Participle
1. ——	held	—— ——
2. think	——	—— ——
3. fly	——	(had) flown
4. ——	swam	—— ——
5. know	——	(has) known
6. bring	——	—— ——
7. ——	wrote	—— ——
8. ——	tore	(has) torn
9. go	——	(had) gone
10. dig	——	—— ——
11. ——	shot	—— ——
12. teach	——	—— ——
13. ——	——	(have) sunk
14. ——	chose	—— ——
15. shut	——	—— ——

C. Use a dictionary, and see how it shows the principal parts of the following verbs. Say the parts.

1. throw

2. climb

3. fall

> Written Practice >

A. Write the correct past form of each word in parentheses.

1. Have you (study) Genesis 40?

2. Who (write) the story of Joseph?

3. Potiphar (buy) Joseph from the Ishmaelites.

4. Joseph (keep) all the prisoners that were in prison.
5. Pharaoh (send) the butler and the baker to prison.
6. They have (know) Pharaoh's anger.
7. Joseph (know) they were sad.
8. They had (tell) their dreams to Joseph.
9. In my dream I (see) a grapevine with ripe grapes.
10. The birds have (fly) to the basket on his head.
11. The servants have (go) to Pharaoh's birthday feast.
12. The butler (bring) the cup to Pharaoh.
13. He has (forget) Joseph.
14. Joseph has (wait) two years.
15. He has (ride) in a chariot throughout Egypt.

B. Copy the chart, and fill in the blanks.

Present	Past	Past Participle
1. ——	blew	—— ——
2. drink	——	—— ——
3. ——	ran	—— ——
4. ——	——	(have) swung
5. sleep	——	(has) slept
6. speak	——	—— ——
7. ——	read	(have) read
8. ——	sat	—— ——
9. come	——	—— ——
10. cut	——	(have) cut
11. ——	dragged	—— ——
12. raise	——	—— ——
13. put	——	(have) put
14. ——	began	—— ——
15. cost	——	—— ——

C. Write sentences as directed.
1. Three sentences using the three forms of **take** correctly.
2. Three sentences using the three forms of **see** correctly.

> Review and Practice >

Write **A** or **D** to tell whether each sentence has an appositive or a noun of direct address. Then copy each word that should have a comma after it, and add the missing comma.

1. Mary come and see this strange animal!
2. It looks like a stick that is walking Susan.
3. Girls it is a walking stick.
4. This animal an unusual insect has no wings.
5. Its shape Mary protects it from enemies.
6. The common walking stick a brown or green creature is two or three inches long.

41. Using Verb Forms Correctly

You have learned that verbs have three principal parts: the **present,** the **past,** and the **past participle.** Be sure to use these forms correctly when you speak and write.

Forms of the verbs **come** and **see** are often used incorrectly. Study this chart and the sentences that follow it.

Present	Past	Past Participle
come	came	(have) come
see	saw	(have) seen

Wrong	**Right**
He come here today.	He **came** here today.
	He **has come** here today.
He had came before.	He **came** before.
	He **had come** before.
I seen a bluebird.	I **saw** a bluebird.
	I **have seen** a bluebird.
I had saw it before.	I **saw** it before.
	I **had seen** it before.

The verbs **tag** and **drag** are also used incorrectly sometimes. These are regular verbs whose past forms are made by adding **-ed** to the present form. Do not give irregular spellings to regular verbs. Study this chart and the sentences below it.

Present	**Past**	**Past Participle**
tag	tagged	(have) tagged
drag	dragged	(have) dragged

Wrong	**Right**
I tug you.	I **tagged** you.
I had tug you.	I **had tagged** you.
Spot drug the shoes out.	Spot **dragged** the shoes out.
He has drug them out before.	He **has dragged** them out before.

There are other irregular verbs whose past forms are used incorrectly. Study the chart before Lesson 40 again. Remember to use a dictionary when you are not sure about a verb form.

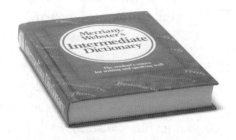

> Oral Drill >

A. Read each sentence, using all three principal parts.

Example: Doctor Brown sees many patients every day.
Answer: Doctor Brown **sees** many patients every day.
          Doctor Brown **saw** many patients every day.
          Doctor Brown **has seen** many patients every day.

1. The girls come early.
2. I see a balloon floating in the sky.
3. She weeps over the loss.
4. The bird flies swiftly.
5. The ducks swim across the creek.
6. The truck sinks in the mud.
7. I keep all my papers.
8. George rides in the back.
9. The frozen pipe bursts.
10. David buys paper and pencils.
11. The tomato plants freeze overnight.
12. I see you.
13. Julie comes home.
14. The pipe breaks.
15. The boys catch muskrats.
16. Father wears a hat.
17. Alfredo speaks Italian.
18. The teacher shuts the door.
19. Elmer drags the board.
20. We forget the answer.

B. Read each sentence correctly.
1. The wind blowed fiercely.
2. The disciples seen Jesus walking on the sea.
3. Peter has chose to walk to Jesus.
4. Peter come down out of the ship to go to Jesus.
5. Peter was afraid and sunk in the water.
6. Jesus stretched out His hand and catched him.

7. The vase has broke.

8. William's dog has came to school with him.

9. The cover has teared.

10. We have not boughten much this time.

11. The dog brung home a skunk.

12. He keeped his bat in the car.

13. The hunter had saw a deer in the woods.

14. The hunter shot the deer and tug it.

15. Someone has stole my toolbox.

16. The pond has froze all the way across.

> Written Practice >

A. Write the correct past form of the incorrect verb in each sentence. Write the helping verb **have, has,** or **had** each time you use the past participle.

Examples: a. Have you ever rode in an airplane?

　　　　　　b. Roger thrown the junk away.

Answers:　a. Have ridden

　　　　　　b. threw

1. Jesus seen great multitudes.

2. Jesus knowed their hearts.

3. Jesus give them a parable.

4. A sower gone forth to sow his seed.

5. The fowls had saw the seeds on the path.

6. The birds have ate the seeds.

7. Some people had soon forgot the Word of God.

8. Some seeds have fell on stony places.

9. The plants have growed rapidly.

10. I have saw thin, withered plants.

11. The thorns have came up.

12. Other seeds have took root in the good ground.

13. We seen a sparkling lake on the mountaintop.

14. Who blowed up the balloon?

15. Robert has shook the rugs for you.
16. She tored my book.
17. The ice has froze hard.
18. Have you got the mail yet?
19. Harold come in late last night.
20. She has wore that dress before.
21. Who has stole the chickens?
22. God has spoke, and His Word will not change.
23. My brother has broke out with chicken pox.
24. Most birds have flew many miles.
25. He has not drove very long.

B. Write sentences using **see, saw,** and **had seen** correctly.

C. Write sentences using **come, came,** and **had come** correctly.

> Review and Practice

A. Choose and write the correct words in parentheses.
   1. They (was, were) raising hamsters.
   2. I (ain't, aren't, am not) fond of hamsters.
   3. She (don't, doesn't) know what to feed the hamster.
   4. There (is, are) several library books about pets.
   5. There (is, are) a book on hamsters.

B. Write the plural form of each noun.
   1. canary   5. wolf   8. chief
   2. salmon   6. alto   9. glass
   3. fox   7. goose   10. tomato
   4. child

C. Write the **singular possessive** and **plural possessive** forms
   for numbers 1–8 in Part B.

42. Giving Directions Orally

Sometimes a friend asks you how to do something. Or you may simply be asked to choose something and tell how to do it. In either case, you need to know how to give directions orally.

First of all, be sure you know how to do the thing yourself. If you are not sure of all the details, look up the information or ask someone who knows. Do not just guess how to do it. Write brief notes on the information, and be sure they are accurate. One wrong measurement or direction can completely spoil the end result.

Second, put your ideas in the order of time. This means that the points must be written in the order each step should be done. Number the first step **1,** the second step **2,** and so on. Start a new line for each point. You do not need to use complete sentences for your notes.

Write a good beginning and ending for your directions. For the beginning, write an interest-catching title. Make your directions so interesting and helpful that others will want to try them. For a good ending, give suggestions on how to use the information you have just given. Your reasons should sound convincing.

Here is a sample set of notes for giving directions orally.

Flatboat Sandwiches—a Quick, Simple Meal

1. Preheat oven to 350 degrees.
2. Place five or six slices of bread on cookie sheet.
3. Put slice of luncheon meat on each slice of bread.
4. Spread layer of baked beans evenly on top.
5. Heat in oven 20–30 minutes or until hot.
6. Top with slice of cheese.
7. Return to oven 5–10 minutes or until cheese melts.
8. If you serve it to your friends, make it educational. Show picture of flatboat. Tell interesting things about flatboats on the Mississippi River.

Whenever you can, show your listeners how to do the thing you are describing. For giving directions on making flatboat sandwiches, you could bring a cookie sheet and pieces of paper cut to the size of slices of bread. Then you could show how to arrange the bread on the sheet. You could bring an actual can of baked beans. One with a colorful label picturing the beans would be ideal. Hold up the can while you tell about using the beans. Write the oven temperature on the chalkboard to help your listeners remember it.

The best way to give directions is to use the actual materials and show the whole process. Perhaps you are telling how to dust a room. Bring a dustcloth and a can of dusting spray, and show your listeners the correct way to spray and dust. You could show some incorrect ways too. Draw diagrams and pictures on the chalkboard, or make colorful posters with diagrams and illustrations on them. Use your imagination to make your directions as interesting as you can.

Practice giving your directions orally. Practice so much that you hardly need to look at your notes. Keep them handy, though, just in case you need them. Use good expression. Show that you are really interested in what you are saying and that you think your classmates should be interested too.

Remember the rules for speaking well. Stand with your weight on both feet, your back straight, and your hands in front of you. Look at your listeners, and use complete sentences. Speak slowly, clearly, and loudly enough so that everyone can hear. Avoid awkward posture. If you use gestures, be sure they are meaningful; do not make unnecessary motions.

Remember, you may be a little nervous. But your nervousness can actually give you energy to do a good job!

Remember: When giving oral directions, choose something that is interesting to you. Make sure your directions are accurate. Speak clearly enough to be understood easily.

Oral Drill

With your classmates, discuss things you have made and enjoy making. As you share, you may give someone else a good idea, and someone may give an idea to you.

Written Practice

A. Choose a topic to tell about. The following ideas may help you. Choose something that is interesting and enjoyable to you.
 1. Tell how to play a game you enjoy, such as hopscotch or a jump rope game.
 2. Show and tell how to draw an animal step by step.
 3. Show and tell how to draw a house in perspective.
 4. Tell how to make something good to eat, using a simple recipe.
    Examples: a. Mint candy   c. Oven doughnuts
    　　　　　　 b. No-bake cookies   d. Wacky cake
 5. Tell how to plan a simple meal.
 6. Tell how to make a simple toy out of wood.
 7. Tell how to sew something such as a simple pocketbook or doll quilt.
 8. Show and tell how to make something of folded paper, such as a boat.
 9. Give an interesting scientific demonstration, such as floating a needle on water. Explain why it works.

B. Organize a set of notes, and write them neatly. Make sure you have written your information accurately. Practice giving your directions aloud to someone at home.

C. Give your oral directions on the day assigned to you. Your teacher will grade your notes as well as your oral directions.

> Review and Practice >

A. Make a noun from each word by adding the suffix **-ness, -ment, -ity,** or **-ion.** Use the dictionary if you need help.

1. tolerate
2. bewilder
3. great
4. reject

5. human
6. good
7. hostile
8. state

B. Copy all the nouns in the following sentences, including the possessive forms. Use apostrophes and capital letters where they are needed.

1. The deers tails are white.
2. The geeses pen should be cleaned.
3. The king of israel met with the king of judah.
4. The courage of joshua is an example for all men.
5. The class was encouraged by marys cheerfulness.
6. The five students diligence was rewarded when they took the test.

43. Chapter 4 Review

> Oral Drill

A. Do the following things.
  1. Give the definition of a verb.
  2. Give the forms of **be.**
  3. Read the sentences, and fill in the blanks.
    a. A group of verbs working together is a —— ——.
    b. The last word in a verb phrase is the —— ——.
  4. Give all the helping verbs in their groups.

B. Give the verbs in these sentences. Tell whether the main verbs show **action** or **being.**
  1. We have been through the Mont Cenis (mōn· sə· nē′) tunnel.
  2. This eight-mile tunnel connects France and Italy.
  3. The tunnel does go through the Alps.
  4. It was the world's first major tunnel through solid rock.
  5. The tunnel was finished in 1871.
  6. It has been very useful in transportation.

C. Give the verbs in these sentences. Tell whether they are in the **present, past,** or **future** tense.
  1. The men drill holes in the rock.
  2. They filled the holes with dynamite.
  3. Then they blast the rock away.
  4. They will use the road for many years.
  5. It took more than ten years.
  6. Soon workers will invent better methods.

> Written Practice

A. Write the definition of a verb.

B. Write all the helping verbs in their groups.

C. Write the missing verb forms. When a helping verb is needed, use **have.**

Present	Past	Past Participle
1. raise	———	(have) raised
2. lay	laid	——— ———
3. leave	———	(have) left
4. think	———	——— ———
5. fly	———	——— ———
6. bring	brought	——— ———

D. Write the correct verbs.
1. We (was, were) on this path before.
2. Arnold (come, comes) this way too.
3. Bradley and Louis (collect, collects) rock samples.
4. I (ain't, am not, is not) good at sorting rocks.
5. He (don't, doesn't) know if this is limestone or sandstone.
6. It (don't, doesn't) look like quartz.
7. Mary and Judy (don't, doesn't) know what it is either.
8. Father (don't, doesn't) have a book about rocks.
9. The books (ain't, aren't) at school either.

E. Write the correct past form of each verb in parentheses. When there is the helping verb **have, has,** or **had,** write it with the main verb.
1. Samuel and Eli have (go) to bed.
2. Eli (know) that the Lord had called the child.
3. Samuel (answer) the call.
4. The wind has finally (stop).
5. The students have (study) the states and capitals.
6. The Martins (fly) on Monday.
7. They had never (fly) before.
8. I have never (sing) that song before.

F. Read the following paragraphs. Copy and complete the outline, which shows how the paragraphs are organized.

Kinds of Turtles

There are many kinds of freshwater and land turtles. The largest group of freshwater turtles is the pond and marsh turtles. Many of these turtles are brightly colored. Most of them are less than a foot long. There are about fifty species of side-necked turtles. They bend their necks sideways to get them inside their shells. They live mainly in areas south of the equator.

Sea turtles live in warm seas throughout the world. They are among the largest of all turtles. The leatherback may weigh fifteen hundred pounds. Sea turtles lay their eggs on land, the same as all other turtles.

Kinds of Turtles

I. Freshwater and land turtles
   A. Pond and marsh turtles
      1. Are brightly _____
      2. Are less than _____
   B. Side-necked turtles
      1. Are about _____
      2. Bend _____
      3. Live _____
II. Sea turtles
   A. Live _____
   B. Are among _____
   C. May weigh _____
   D. Lay _____

G. Write answers to the following questions.
   1. What must you know before you can give directions well?
   2. In what order should you say things when you give directions?
   3. What is better than just **telling** how to do something?

Verbs are followed by . . .

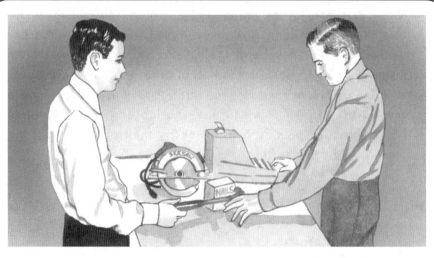

Direct Objects:
Father is buying a hammer, a saw, and some nails.

Predicate Nouns:
Brother Mark is a good friend and a kind teacher.

Chapter 5

More About Verbs

Predicate Adjectives:
A baby is sweet and lovable.

44. Sentences With Direct Objects

Some sentences have direct objects. A **direct object** is a noun or pronoun that receives the action of a verb. A direct object is a sentence part. It may be a noun or a pronoun.

> Jesus <u>blessed</u> the **children.**
>> The noun **children** receives the action of **blessed.**
> Jesus <u>loves</u> **us** too.
>> The pronoun **us** receives the action of **loves.**

Not all verbs pass action to a receiver. Forms of **be** express being, not action. So they can never pass action to a direct object.

Remember that the last verb in a verb phrase is the main verb. So if a verb phrase ends with a form of **be,** there can be no direct object.

> Sister Jane <u>has been</u> my teacher. (no direct object)

Many action verbs pass action to a receiver. But not every action verb has a direct object. To find a direct object, use the following steps.

a. First, find the main verb in the simple predicate. If it is a form of **be,** your work is finished. There cannot be a direct object.

> David <u>**is**</u> my cousin. (no direct object)
> David <u>will **be**</u> the song leader. (no direct object)

b. If the main verb is an action verb, find the simple subject. Remember that the simple subject and the simple predicate together are the skeleton.

c. Say the sentence skeleton, and ask **whom** or **what** after it. If there is a noun or a pronoun that answers the question, it is the direct object.

Father has driven the bus.
> The main verb is **driven.** It is an action verb.
> The sentence skeleton is **Father has driven.**
> Father has driven **what**? Bus.
> **Bus** is the direct object.

Father drove carefully.
> The main verb is **drove.** It is an action verb.
> Father drove **what**? There is no noun or pronoun to answer the question. (**Carefully** tells **how,** not **what.**)
> This sentence has no direct object.

Peter had a new knife.
> Peter | had **what**? Knife.
> **Knife** is the direct object.

A direct object is never found in a prepositional phrase.

We ate in the morning.
> We | ate **what**? We did not eat **morning. Morning** comes after the preposition **in.**
> There is no direct object in this sentence.

On a sentence diagram, the direct object is written on the base line after the skeleton. A vertical line separates the direct object from the verb. This line does not go through the base line, but rests on it. Study the following examples.

Father	has driven	bus

Peter	had	knife

> **Remember:** A direct object is a noun or pronoun that receives the action of a verb.

> Oral Drill >

Tell which sentences have direct objects. On the chalkboard, diagram each sentence skeleton and direct object.

1. He is diligent.
2. Everyone sang hymns.
3. We ate under the tree.
4. Erma and I are visiting Nancy.
5. The Lord is good to all.
6. Jesus fed a multitude of people.
7. Paul preached mightily.
8. He had been in a shipwreck.
9. The righteous man prayed fervently.
10. David wrote many psalms.
11. God's loyal followers trust Him.
12. The teacher read a poem to us.

> Written Practice >

A. Diagram each sentence skeleton and direct object.

1. The boys stopped at the corner.
2. The boys stopped the horse.
3. The children were being very helpful.
4. Brother Avery is running this machine.
5. Harlan and Larry caught six fish.
6. Mary and Joseph went to Bethlehem.
7. Jacob and Esau were brothers.
8. David killed Goliath.
9. Samson was a very strong man.

10. He carried the gates of the city.

11. Judas had the bag of money.

12. The children obeyed their parents.

13. Joseph's angry, jealous brothers sold him.

14. The twelve disciples followed Jesus.

B. Write a direct object for each blank. Diagram each sentence skeleton with the direct object you added.

1. The fifth grade teacher gives interesting ———.

2. Four purposeful young students wrote ——— yesterday.

3. My father bought a helpful ——— yesterday.

> Review and Practice

Write whether each sentence is a **statement, question, command,** or **exclamation.** (There are only two exclamations.) Also write the correct end punctuation.

1. Did you know that a hamster is a rodent

2. Common hamsters grow to be about a foot long

3. Feed them grain, fruit, seeds, and insects

4. What an interesting pet a hamster is

5. Golden hamsters are about seven inches long

6. A hamster crams food into his cheek pouches and stores it in his home

7. What a little hoarder he is

8. Tell me how long a hamster lives

9. A hamster lives about three years

45. Sentences With Compound Direct Objects

If two sentences have the same skeleton but different direct objects, they can be combined into one sentence that has a **compound direct object.** In such a sentence, more than one noun or pronoun receives the action of a verb. See how the two sentences below are combined into one sentence that has a compound direct object.

Jesus blessed the loaves.

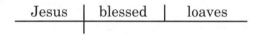

He blessed the fishes.

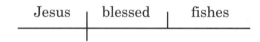

Jesus blessed the loaves and the fishes.

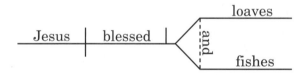

Do not forget the vertical line between the skeleton and the direct object. If there is a compound direct object, a fork comes **after** the vertical line.

Remember the steps you learned in the last lesson for finding a direct object. If a sentence has a compound direct object, there will be more than one word to answer the question **whom** or **what.**

Ziba brought bread and raisins to David.

The sentence skeleton is **Ziba brought.**

Ziba brought **what**? Bread and raisins.

The two nouns **bread** and **raisins** make up the compound direct object.

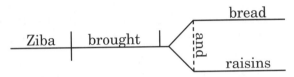

Sometimes a sentence has three direct objects. Then it is diagramed as shown here.

Grandmother is making the bread, cakes, and pies.

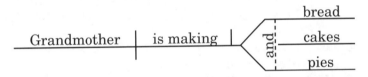

Remember: A sentence may have a compound direct object.

> **Oral Drill**

A. Tell how to combine the following sentences.
1. Ezra taught statutes.
   Ezra taught judgments.
2. David killed a lion.
   David killed a bear.
3. The boys enjoyed the forests.
   They enjoyed the mountains.
4. Barbara sent Uncle Amos a card.
   Barbara sent Uncle Amos a letter.

B. On the chalkboard, diagram the sentence skeletons and the direct objects.
   1. My sister fried eggs and bacon.
   2. The carpenters have built a shed and a barn.
   3. Father is buying a hammer, a saw, and some nails.

C. Decide whether each sentence has a direct object. If it does, diagram the skeleton and the direct object on the chalkboard.
   1. These little flowers are pansies and violets.
   2. Aunt Sarah gave these apples and pears.
   3. The child's pets were a little brown dog, two orange cats, and a parakeet.
   4. God has given faithful teachers and parents.
   5. We were hiking in the morning.
   6. We heard warblers and orioles in the trees.

Written Practice

A. Combine each pair of sentences.
   1. Verna visited Uncle John.
      Verna visited Aunt Anna.
   2. We saw a fat chickadee.
      We saw a saucy blue jay.

B. Decide whether each sentence has a direct object. If it does, diagram the skeleton and the direct object.
   1. God made the beautiful sunrises and sunsets.
   2. Miriam's brothers were Aaron and he.
   3. Aaron wore a coat and a robe.
   4. Mother bakes delicious cookies, cakes, and pies.
   5. The students wrote stories and poems.
   6. We will be cleaning on Friday and Saturday.
   7. Our mailman comes in the morning.
   8. Elmer got a hammer and some nails.

9. A large tree fell to the ground.
10. You should not play in the rain.
11. Alfredo can speak Spanish and Italian.
12. Mr. Benson has been a carpenter and a mason.

C. Write two sentences of your own. Put a compound direct object in each one.

> Review and Practice >

Write **C, F, RO,** or **CS** to tell whether each sentence is correct, is a sentence fragment, is a run-on sentence, or has a comma splice.

1. I heard an eerie sound it woke me up.
2. It was a strange, trembly sound, it seemed to run down the musical scale.
3. Then a dark, silent shadow.
4. Floated from one tree to another.
5. What could this mysterious creature be?
6. Soon the sound came again, and now it was in the tree just outside my window!
7. I shone my flashlight into the tree, I saw a pretty screech owl!
8. God made the screech owl with an eerie call and silent wings the owl is a better hunter that way.

46. Principal Parts of Common Irregular Verbs

You have learned three principal parts of verbs: the present, the past, and the past participle. The past participle is used with the helping verb **have, has,** or **had.**

For **regular verbs,** the past and the past participle are formed by adding **-ed** to the present form. For **irregular verbs,** the past and the past participle are formed in other ways. There are no special rules for the forms of irregular verbs. You must practice using the right ones until you memorize them.

The past participle of many irregular verbs ends with an **n** or **un** sound. Remember that the past participle must be used with the helping verb **have, has,** or **had.**

Present	Past	Past Participle
see	saw	(have) seen
know	knew	(have) known
fall	fell	(have) fallen
ring	rang	(have) rung
sink	sank	(have) sunk

See the chart on page 167 if you are not sure which verb form to use. A dictionary also gives the spellings of irregular verb forms.

Remember: Use the helping verb **have, has,** or **had** with the past participle of a verb.

 Oral Drill

A. For each of the following verbs, fill in these blanks with the correct form.

> Today I ———.
> Yesterday I ———.
> I have ———.

1. give		6. write	
2. see		7. find	
3. buy		8. catch	
4. keep		9. weep	
5. dig		10. break	

B. Say the principal parts of the following verbs. Use the chart before Lesson 40 if you need help.

    1. begin   2. sink   3. ride

C. Choose the correct words in parentheses. Say the helping verb **have, has,** or **had** with the past participle.

    1. Sheila (wore, wored, worn) a coat yesterday.

    2. Mattie has (wore, worn) her coat for a month already.

    3. Jennie (drew, drawed) a picture of a cat.

    4. She has (drew, drawn) pictures of different animals.

    5. Her mother (teached, taught) her to draw well.

D. Give the correct past form of each verb in parentheses.

    1. The little salmon (swim) downstream yesterday.

    2. We have often (put) up nets to catch the fish coming upstream.

    3. How much had the nets (cost)?

    4. Has the store (cut) the price lately?

    5. The fishermen (drag) the nets to the shore.

E. Tell how to correct the following sentences.

    1. The water in this bucket has froze solid.

    2. The men drug the logs out of the woods.

    3. The sun shined brightly this morning.

    4. My brother seen six deer running across the field.

    5. A fox had stole some of our chickens.

> Written Practice >

A. Write the correct verb forms. Include the helping verb **have,**
   has, or **had** whenever it is part of the verb.
   1. Jesus (saw, seen) a great company of people.
   2. They have (brung, brought) the children along.
   3. They could not have (bought, boughten) enough bread.
   4. The lad (give, gave) his lunch to Jesus.
   5. They (began, begun) by sitting down on the grass.
   6. Jesus (broke, broken) the loaves.
   7. He has (gave, given) the pieces to the disciples.
   8. They (saw, seen) the miracle that Jesus did.
   9. They gathered up the fragments that had been (broke,
      broken).
   10. Wear gloves so that your hands don't (freeze, froze).
   11. Yesterday the creek (freezed, froze) over.
   12. The lake had (froze, frozen) already last week.

B. Write the correct past form of each verb in parentheses. Also
   write the helping verb **have, has,** or **had** if it is used in the
   sentence.
   1. Aunt Ellen (buy) a lemon pie at the market.
   2. We have (keep) it as a surprise for Mother.
   3. Anna scrubbed the mirrors till they (shine).
   4. The ice cream (freeze) in less than half an hour.
   5. The water has (freeze) in the pipes.
   6. It has (cost) much money to repair the damage.

C. Rewrite the following sentences correctly.
   1. God had gave them instructions.
   2. Achan has stole silver and gold.
   3. God seen him do it.
   4. Achan digged a hole under his tent.
   5. The people throwed stones at Achan.

D. Use the following forms correctly in sentences of your own.
1. the past form of **bring**
2. the past participle of **sing**
3. the past participle of **begin**
4. the past form of **climb**

> Challenge Exercise >

A. Verbs actually have five different forms: the present, the past, the past participle, the **-s** form, and the present participle (**-ing** form). Copy and complete the following chart, spelling all the forms correctly. A dictionary may help you.

Present	Past	Past Participle	-S form	Present Participle
1. eat	ate	(have) eaten	eats	eating
2. get	——	——	——	——
3. bring	——	——	——	——
4. choose	——	——	——	——
5. buy	——	——	——	——
6. come	——	——	——	——
7. ride	——	——	——	——
8. steal	——	——	——	——
9. write	——	——	——	——

B. Use all five forms of **bring** and **come** in sentences of your own.

47. Observing, Listening and Taking Notes

What are the most precious gifts God has given you? You could name many things, and high on the list would likely be your five senses—sight, hearing, touch, taste, and smell. Think what it would be like not to have these five senses. You would be living in a dark, silent world—never a glowing sunset, never a snow-capped mountain, no rippling creek music or happy voices of loved ones. Suppose you could never taste a bit of food again, or smell the spicy fragrance of leaves in an autumn woods, or feel the soft touch of a baby's hand. What price would you take for your five senses? Surely none, for they are priceless.

One important use of our five senses is observation. Observing things is a needful preparation for writing. Think of your senses as gateways for observing the wonderful works of our great Creator.

Another important use of our five senses is careful listening. We should listen to the beautiful sounds God has put in nature for us to enjoy. We should also listen in order to learn valuable and interesting things from others. The Bible says, "Be swift to hear, slow to speak" (James 1:19). Older people can tell us many things that we could never learn by ourselves. We need to listen carefully when they speak to us.

One more way to use our five senses is by reading. Do you expect that you will ever fly to Tibet? Likely not, but through reading you can be well acquainted with the people, animals, and customs of that country. Reading is a wonderful form of observation that takes us to strange lands and faraway places. You can sit down with a book and travel anywhere in the world without leaving your chair.

Through reading we can discover things that happened many centuries ago and even in eternity past, before the earth was created. The Bible tells us that Jesus was in heaven with God before the world began. Through reading we can learn some things that will happen in eternity future, after this earth has passed away. The Bible reveals these wonderful things to us.

How can we remember accurately all the things we observe and read? One excellent way is to take notes. When we do this, we do not forget as much. We do not get the facts confused with our own ideas.

What is a good way to take notes? Write down only main ideas and key words. Do not copy whole sentences. Notes are usually short phrases that are written quickly. Some notes may be short sentences, but they do not need to be punctuated as sentences.

Suppose you are taking notes about people who live in highlands. In reference books, you might find the following paragraphs. How would you take notes on this information?

First reference book:

The Swiss Alps are some of the highest mountains in Europe. Many people of the Alps live in houses high up on mountain slopes. In summer the children help to care for cattle, goats, and sheep that graze in lofty mountain pastures. In winter the children may ski down to a village school. They can come down a mountain in just a few minutes, but it may take an hour or more to climb back to their homes.

Second reference book:

The country of Tibet in south central Asia is so high that it is called the Roof of the World. Mount Everest, the highest mountain in the world, lies on its border. Many people of Tibet live in two-story houses with goats, yaks, and cows on the ground floor. The Tibetan town of Ka-erh is over fifteen thousand feet above sea level. It is thought to be the highest town in the world.

Third reference book:

People of the Puna region in the Andes Mountains have learned how to live in a harsh land more than fifteen thousand feet above the sea. Constant winds tear at the treeless wastes about them. Temperatures often drop below freezing at night, and the peaks of surrounding volcanoes are always covered with snow. The people build sturdy houses of stone and thatch in the shelter of rocky clefts. Their houses are the highest permanent dwelling places of man on earth.

These paragraphs tell about highland people of three different places. You can take notes on the main ideas about people in each place.

People of the Highlands

Swiss Alps
    houses high on mountain slopes
    summer—children care for cattle, goats, sheep
    winter—children ski to village school
Tibet
    town of Ka-erh is over 15,000 feet above sea level
    Ka-erh is thought to be highest town in world
Puna region in Andes Mountains
    more than 15,000 feet above the sea
    houses of stone and thatch in shelter of rocky clefts
    highest permanent dwelling places of man on earth

To write a paragraph about highland people, you would use your notes to write sentences in your own words.

People of the Highlands

Various people around the world live at high altitudes. In the Swiss Alps, people live in houses high on mountain slopes. Children help to care for cattle, goats, and sheep during the summer, and in the winter they ski down the mountain to a village school. In Tibet is the town of Ka-erh, which is fifteen thousand feet above sea level. This is thought to be the highest town in the world. The Puna region in the Andes Mountains is more than fifteen thousand feet above the sea. People there build houses of stone and thatch in the shelter of rocky clefts. These are the highest permanent dwelling places of man on earth.

Notice how the paragraph above is written. The writer first took notes on paragraphs in three reference books. Then he used the notes to write a paragraph in his own words. The paragraph has ideas from all three reference books, but it is not copied from any of them.

Remember: To be a good writer, you must observe and listen carefully, and you must take accurate notes. You should write by using your notes, not by copying someone else's writing.

> Oral Drill

A. How well have you observed and listened today?
1. Without looking, tell your teacher what is on the bulletin board in your room.
2. Give the main points that your teacher had in devotions this morning.
3. Describe the outside of your school building.

B. Work together with your classmates to take notes on the following paragraphs. Your notes should be about customs in Tibet.

Many customs of people in Tibet are different from those of American people. Some Tibetans are nomads who live in tents of yak hair. Others live in houses, usually of two stories. Animals are kept on the ground floor, and the living quarters are on the second floor.

Most Tibetans eat two meals a day. The main crop is barley, and the main foods are made from barley flour. A favorite drink is Chinese tea flavored with salt, soda, and yak butter. Tibetans also drink the milk of goats or yaks.

Many people wear shoes made of yak leather, and some ride in boats made of yak skin. Tibetans in general are hard-working people who make good use of the things they have.

> Written Practice >

A. Use the paragraphs below to write a set of notes about two animals of highland people. Arrange your notes in an orderly way.

First reference book:

The yak is an important animal of Tibet. It is a kind of ox that looks like a hairy buffalo. Yaks have long silky hair, which the people use to make cloth, mats, and tent coverings. They use the hide for shoes, whips, and boats. Tibetans even use the yak's bushy tail as a fly chaser and an ornament. Yaks also provide the Tibetans with food. Wealthy people drink the rich milk of the yak, or they make cheese and butter from it. The meat is eaten dried or roasted. Life would be much harder for the people in Tibet if they did not have yaks.

Second reference book:

> Llamas haul loads of tin ore, bags of grain, and blocks of salt for their Indian masters in the Andes Mountains. They can carry burdens weighing up to one hundred pounds. But if a llama is overloaded, it promptly lies down and refuses to move. The Indians spin yarn and make cloth from llama wool. They drink the llama's milk and eat its meat. The llama is valuable even after it dies, for its bones can be made into weaving tools and its hide into sandals.

B. Use your notes from Part A to write a paragraph about two important animals of highland people. Be sure to write in your own words. Give your paragraph the title "Two Valuable Animals of Highland People."

> **Challenge Exercise**

Ask a returned missionary to tell you something about the foreign country he was in. Ask polite questions. Listen carefully, and take notes. Then organize your notes, and write a paragraph from them. Be ready to read your paragraph to the class.

48. Using *Raise* and *Rise*

Some verbs are very much alike, yet they have different meanings. Learn to use them correctly.

The verb **raise** means "to cause something to go up or grow up." **Raise** needs a direct object. There must be a noun or a pronoun to tell who or what was raised.

> We <u>raise</u> calves on our farm.
> We raise **what**? Calves.
> **Calves** is the direct object.

Notice the direct object in each sentence below.

The teacher <u>will raise</u> the **windows.**

The teacher <u>raised</u> the **windows** yesterday.

The teacher <u>has raised</u> **them** often this week.

Our neighbor <u>raises</u> **pumpkins.**

My cousin <u>raised</u> **cantaloupes** last year.

The verb **raise** is a regular verb. Its principal parts are as follows: **raise, raised, (have) raised.**

The verb **rise** means "to get up or go up." **Rise** never takes a direct object.

The workers <u>rise</u> early every morning.

The sun <u>rises</u> in the east.

Jesus said, "I <u>will rise</u> on the third day."

The verb **rise** is an irregular verb. Its past form and past participle are not spelled with **-ed.** Its principal parts are as follows: **rise, rose, (have) risen.**

The sun <u>rose</u> while you were sleeping.

I <u>have risen</u> early every day this week.

Risen always needs the helping verb **have, has,** or **had.** Never use a helping verb with **rose.**

Wrong:

The temperature has rose quickly this morning.

Right:

The temperature **has risen** quickly this morning.

Remember: The verb **raise** means "to cause something to go up or grow up." **Raise** needs a direct object. Its principal parts are as follows: **raise, raised, (have) raised.**

The verb **rise** means "to get up or go up." **Rise** never takes a direct object. Its principal parts are as follows: **rise, rose, (have) risen.**

> Oral Drill >

A. Read each sentence, changing the verb to the past form and then to the past participle.

Example: The sun rises through the mist.
Answer: The sun rose through the mist.
             The sun has risen through the mist.

1. Brother Mark raises wheat in that field.
2. The bread dough rises to twice its former size.
3. The smoke rises into the blue sky.
4. Father raises the window.

B. Tell which verb is correct. If you use a form of **raise,** also give the direct object. Read each sentence correctly several times.

1. Paul has not (raised, risen) from his bed for a whole week.
2. The minister (raised, rose) an important question.
3. The mother sheep (raised, rose) two lambs.
4. The bread will not (raise, rise) if it is too cold.
5. A cloud of dust (raised, rose) over the road.
6. We (raise, rise) our hands when we need help.
7. The old man has (raised, risen) from his chair to greet us.
8. We rejoice because Jesus has (raised, risen).

C. Give the correct form of **raise** or **rise** for each blank. Give the direct object when you use a form of **raise.**
1. The people ——— to their feet for the benediction.
2. If you can come and help, please ——— your hand.
3. Peter ——— Dorcas and presented her alive to the people.
4. The full moon ——— after the sun sets.
5. Jesus had ——— Lazarus from the dead.
6. Lazarus ——— and walked out of the tomb when Jesus called him.

> Written Practice >

A. Rewrite each sentence, changing the verb to the past form and then to the past participle.
1. Calvin raises rabbits to sell.
2. The rocket rises above our heads.
3. The pupils raise their hands.
4. Several geese rise from the pond.

B. Copy the correct verbs. When you choose a form of **raise,** write the direct object after it.
1. John (raised, rose, risen) the window.
2. Mr. Brown (raised, rose) turkeys last year.
3. Has the temperature (raised, risen) this morning?
4. The moon had not (raised, rose, risen) yet.
5. The kites (raise, rise) swiftly in this strong wind.
6. The leader (raised, rose) to speak.
7. The children (raise, rise) little chicks as a hobby.
8. During the recent rain, the streams have (raised, risen) to the flood stage.
9. The Lord has (raised, risen) indeed.
10. Joshua (raised, rose) early in the morning.
11. The disciples had (raised, risen) a hard question.

12. Before John finished speaking, Mr. Smith had (raised, risen) to his feet.

13. I will (raise, rise) and give thanks.

C. Write the correct form of **raise** or **rise** for each blank. When you choose a form of **raise,** also write the direct object.

1. Please ——— the bed a little.
2. Last year the children ——— a few baby chicks.
3. The store has ——— the price of beef.
4. Grandmother had ——— the window shade.
5. We ——— at six o'clock.
6. Gladys and Marjorie will ——— watermelons.
7. The sun ——— high during summer days.
8. It had ——— early.
9. The government officials ——— the taxes.
10. Bread ——— because it contains yeast.
11. Our bread dough has ———.

Check your work in Parts B and C. Did you write a direct object each time you chose a form of **raise**?

D. Write sentences using these forms of **raise** and **rise.**

1. the present form of **raise**
2. the past form of **rise**
3. the past participle of **raise**
4. the past participle of **rise**

■◆■◆■◆■◆■◆

49. Using *Set* and *Sit*

Do bicycles **set** or **sit** in the driveway? Do students **set** or **sit** in their seats? Do they **set** or **sit** their books on their desks? Learn to use **set** and **sit** correctly.

Set means "to put or place something." **Set** must have a direct object. There must be a noun or a pronoun after the verb to tell what was **set.**

> You may <u>set</u> the vase on this desk.
>> You may set **what**? Vase.
>> **Vase** is the direct object.
>
> God <u>set</u> the **stars** in the firmament.
> You <u>may set</u> **it** on the table.

Set is an irregular verb. Its present and past forms are the same. Its principal parts are as follows: **set, set, (have) set.**

Sit means "to rest or be seated." **Sit** never takes a direct object.

> The bicycle <u>sits</u> in the driveway.
> You <u>will sit</u> in this chair.
> You <u>sat</u> in that chair this morning.
> We <u>have sat</u> here a long time.

Sit is an irregular verb. Its principal parts are as follows: **sit, sat, (have) sat.**

Remember: The verb **set** means "to put or place something." **Set** needs a direct object. Its principal parts are as follows: **set, set, (have) set.**

The verb **sit** means "to rest or be seated." **Sit** never takes a direct object. Its principal parts are as follows: **sit, sat, (have) sat.**

▷ Oral Drill ▷

A. Read each sentence, changing the verb to the past form and then to the past participle.

1. The boys will set the packages on the table.

2. The children sit outside in the sun.

3. The old cabin sits there year after year.

4. We shall set a date and time for the meeting.

B. Tell which verb is correct. Give the direct object when you choose a form of **set.** Read each sentence correctly several times.

1. Please (set, sit) this bowl on the table.

2. The children (set, sat) on the grass.

3. Mark (set, sat) a good example.

4. Carol has (set, sat) too near the fire.

5. The shed has (set, sat) there for too many years.

6. He always (sets, sits) in the same chair.

7. We (set, sat) a date for the next meeting.

8. Someone has (set, sat) a barrel on our porch.

9. Mary (set, sat) at Jesus' feet.

10. We must (set, sit) the clock in a suitable place.

C. Tell how to correct each of the following sentences that is incorrect. Read each sentence correctly.

1. The king sets on his throne.

2. Do not sit up late.

3. Two blind men set by the roadside that day.

4. Jesus sits at the right hand of God.

5. Janet sat the dishes on the table.

6. Abraham set near his tent door.

7. You may sit the box on the floor.

8. God will set His saints on high.

> **Written Practice** >

A. Write the correct verbs. Write the direct object if you choose a form of **set.**

1. The Great Dane has (set, sat) on Mother's geraniums.

2. Paul (set, sat) at the feet of Gamaliel to learn from him.

3. The Israelites (set, sat) the ark of God on a new cart.
4. The ark did not (set, sit) very firmly.
5. Do not (set, sit) down in the most honorable seat.
6. Jesus commanded the people to (set, sit) down by companies on the grass.
7. The people (set, sat) down in ranks.
8. The disciples (set, sat) the food before them.
9. God has (set, sit) up a kingdom that shall never be destroyed.
10. King Nebuchadnezzar (set, sat) on the throne.

B. Write the correct form of **set** or **sit** for each blank. Write the direct object if you choose a form of **set.**
   1. Jesus has —— down at the right hand of God.
   2. I have —— before thee an open door.
   3. The judges have —— at the gate.
   4. God will —— His glory among the heathen.
   5. Why do we —— here until we die?
   6. Ye shall also —— upon twelve thrones.
   7. I will —— no wicked thing before my eyes.
   8. Believers —— together in heavenly places in Christ.
   9. The Lord had —— a mark upon Cain.
   10. Go and —— down to eat.

   Check your work in Parts A and B. Did you write a direct object each time you chose a form of **set**?

> Review and Practice >

A. Write the correct verbs. When you choose a form of **raise,** write the direct object after it.
   1. We (raise, rise) tomatoes every year.
   2. Have you ever (raised, rose, risen) produce to sell?
   3. The balloon (raised, rose, risen) into the air and soon disappeared.
   4. Do not (raise, rise) your voice so much.

5. The sun (raises, rises) early on summer mornings.
6. The temperature in the car (raised, rose, risen) quickly because all the windows were closed.
7. Gasoline prices have (raised, rose, risen) this month.
8. The station has also (raised, rose, risen) the price of kerosene.
9. The new skyscraper was (raising, rising) quickly.
10. Eunice (raised, rose) Timothy to serve the Lord.

B. Copy all the nouns in these sentences. Capitalize the proper nouns, and underline the plural nouns.
1. The home of peter was in the village of bethsaida.
2. A teacher named gamaliel taught paul in jerusalem.
3. A captain called naaman came from syria to see elisha in israel.
4. The prophet told him to wash in the jordan river.
5. "Are not abana and pharpar, rivers of damascus, better than all the waters of israel?" asked naaman.
6. But he dipped in the jordan river as the man of god had said, and he was healed.
7. From the land of moab, ruth and orpah began to follow naomi back to israel.
8. The donkeys owned by kish were lost, and saul went to look for them.
9. Many proverbs spoken by king solomon are written in the bible.

50. Using *Lay* and *Lie*

Which is correct? Jerry **has laid** the paper on the table, or Jerry **has lain** the paper on the table? Betty **has lain** in bed all day, or Betty **has laid** in bed all day? He **lay** on the sofa, or he **laid** on the sofa? Learn to use all the forms of **lay** and **lie** correctly.

Lay means "to put or place something." **Lay** needs a direct object. A noun or a pronoun must follow the verb to tell what was put or placed.

> The men <u>lay</u> blocks.
>> The men lay **what**? Blocks.
>> **Blocks** is the direct object.

> We <u>laid</u> the **baby** in the crib.
> The hen <u>has laid</u> an **egg.**
> Take these papers, and <u>lay</u> **them** on my desk.

Lay is an irregular verb. Its principal parts are as follows: **lay, laid, (have) laid.**

Lie means "to rest or recline." **Lie** never takes a direct object.

> <u>Lie</u> down, Rover.
> He <u>lay</u> on the grass.
> He <u>has lain</u> down to rest.

Lie is an irregular verb. Its principal parts are as follows: **lie, lay, (have) lain.**

Remember: The verb **lay** means "to put or place something." **Lay** needs a direct object. Its principal parts are as follows: **lay, laid, (have) laid.**

The verb **lie** means "to rest or recline." **Lie** never takes a direct object. Its principal parts are as follows: **lie, lay, (have) lain.**

> Oral Drill >

A. Read each sentence, changing the verb to the past form and then to the past participle.

1. The men will lay bricks.
2. The cat lies on the porch.
3. I shall lie down to rest.
4. He will lay the book on the table.

B. Tell how to correct each sentence that has a mistake. Practice reading the sentences correctly.

1. After the sun went down, Jacob lay down to sleep.
2. I have lain the foundation.
3. They laid Jesus in a new sepulcher.
4. Lazarus had laid in the grave four days.
5. Three flocks of sheep laid by the well.
6. The manna lay on the ground.
7. The baby lay the flowers on the floor.
8. Baby Jesus laid in a manger.
9. Peter's wife's mother lay sick with a fever.
10. We laid paper on the shelves.
11. Who lay my books on the chair?
12. Paul is lying bricks for the porch floor.
13. Ruth has lain the baby in the bed.

14. Robert lay his aching head on the desk.
15. The man with palsy lay on a bed.
16. Snow lays on the mountain peak all year.

> **Written Practice**

A. Rewrite each sentence, changing the verb to the past form and then to the past participle.
   1. He lays his plans carefully.
   2. The apples lie on the ground.
   3. The cat lies on the old rug.
   4. We lay our papers on the desk.

B. Write the correct verbs. If you choose a form of **lay,** also write the direct object.
   1. Frank (laid, lay) his coat on the shelf.
   2. The dog (laid, lay) on the floor near the stove.
   3. That village (lays, lies) near the mountain.
   4. The wood has (laid, lain) on the ground all winter.
   5. They had (laid, lain) the injured boy on the bed.
   6. A cloud of smoke (laid, lay) over the ruined house.
   7. The chicken (laid, lay) brown eggs.
   8. This field has (laid, lain) idle for too many years.
   9. Mary brought the clothes inside and (laid, lay) them on the table.
   10. Darrel is (laying, lying) on the sofa because he is sick.

C. Follow these directions.
   1. Write two original sentences using the present form of **lay** and **lie.**
   2. Write two original sentences using the past form of **lay** and **lie.**
   3. Write two original sentences using the past participle of **lay** and **lie.**

> **Review and Practice** >

A. Write the correct verb for each sentence.
  1. (Raise, Rise) your Bibles high.
  2. The moon (raised, rose, risen) early on that clear night.
  3. Joseph had (raised, rose, risen) to a high position.
  4. Betty, (set, sit) this vase on the shelf.
  5. The car has (set, sat) in the lane for two days.
  6. You may (set, sit) your books and papers here.
  7. Andrew (laid, lay) on the sofa until morning.
  8. Thomas can (lay, lie) blocks and bricks.
  9. The baby has (laid, lain) in the crib all night.

B. Diagram the skeletons and direct objects of the sentences in Part A. Remember that forms of **raise, set,** and **lay** are followed by direct objects.

---

51. Using *Let* and *Leave*

Should you say "Please **let** me go" or "Please **leave** me go"? When you forget something, do you **let** it somewhere or **leave** it somewhere? Learn the correct usage of **let** and **leave.**

Let means "to allow or permit." All three of its principal parts are the same: **let, let, (have) let.**

Let is always followed by another verb form. The other verb may be written or understood.

> <u>Let</u> me **stay.**
> He <u>let</u> me **go** yesterday.
> He had never <u>let</u> me (**go**) before.
> Father <u>lets</u> me **walk** to school.
> He <u>let</u> me (**walk**) every day last week.

Leave means "to go away from or depart." Its principal parts are as follows: **leave, left, (have) left.**

> We <u>leave</u> early.
>
> He <u>leaves</u> his snowy boots at the door.
>
> The Browns <u>left</u> yesterday.
>
> They <u>have left</u> their dog at home.

Leave is sometimes followed by a direct object and sometimes not. Can you tell which sentences above have direct objects?

The forms of **leave** are never followed by another verb, either written or understood.

> **Wrong:** Father left me climb the ladder.
>
> **Right:**   Father <u>let</u> me **climb** the ladder.

> **Wrong:** We wanted to cook, so Mother left us (cook).
>
> **Right:**   We wanted to cook, so Mother <u>let</u> us (**cook**).

> **Remember:** The verb **let** means "to allow or permit." **Let** is always followed by another verb form. Its principal parts are as follows: **let, let, (have) let.**
>
> The verb **leave** means "to go away from or depart." **Leave** may be used with or without a direct object. Its principal parts are as follows: **leave, left, (have) left.**

 Oral Drill

A. Read each sentence, changing the verb to the past form and then to the past participle.

1. I shall let Shirley mix the lemonade.
2. Brother Paul will leave for Paraguay.
3. The children will let the cats eat the fish.
4. We shall leave a note in the door.

B. Tell how to correct the sentences that use **let** or **leave** incorrectly. When **let** is used, give the other verb form that follows it. Practice reading each sentence correctly.

1. Do you know why God does not leave us have everything we want?
2. Some people need to leave their father and mother for Jesus' sake.
3. Leave me go.
4. Who let his toothbrush in the kitchen?
5. Boaz said, "Let her glean even among the sheaves."
6. Daniel left me see the clock he had made.
7. Leave me know when this job is finished.
8. Jesus said, "I will not leave you comfortless."
9. May I let my books on the table?
10. Mother leaves me read when my work is finished.
11. The woman let her waterpot behind and went into the city.
12. The soldiers quickly left Paul when they learned that he was a Roman citizen.

C. These sentences review the verbs you have been studying. Find the mistake in each one, and read the sentence correctly several times.

1. The sun has not yet raised this morning.
2. Melinda is laying on the sofa.
3. Please lie the book down.
4. The bird was setting in the tree.

5. Please leave me stay here.
6. Shall we go home and let the dog here?
7. Gail sets quietly in her seat.
8. Rise your hand if you want to help.
9. My bicycle is setting in the garage.
10. Yesterday he laid in bed all day.
11. The workers lay new carpet in my bedroom yesterday.
12. Brother John has risen the windows.

> **Written Practice** >

A. Write the correct verb for each sentence. When you write **let,** also write the other verb form that follows it.
   1. The boys have (let, left) their coats on the porch.
   2. Mother (let, left) me use the telephone.
   3. Do not (let, leave) the cats come into the house.
   4. You must not (let, leave) anything on the steps.
   5. Someone has (let, left) a book on the table.
   6. Will you (let, leave) me use your crayons?
   7. (Let, Leave) sleeping dogs lie.
   8. The boys will never (let, leave) us forget it.
   9. He dropped the towel and (let, left) it there.
   10. It is time now to (let, leave) this matter.

B. Rewrite each sentence, changing the verb to the form named in parentheses.
   1. James leaves the easy parts for me. (past)
   2. He lets me work slowly. (past participle)
   3. We leave the house early. (past)
   4. The children let the chickens get out. (past participle)

C. Follow these directions.
   1. Write two original sentences, one with **let** and one with **leave.**
   2. Write an original sentence using **left.**

> Review and Practice >

A. Write the correct verb for each sentence.
1. A sandy beach (lays, lies) along the ocean here.
2. The ocean tides (raise, rise) two times each day.
3. The gravity of the moon (raises, rises) the water.
4. Have you ever (set, sat) and watched the waves rolling in?
5. Father does not (let, leave) us play in the water alone.
6. He is (setting, sitting) on the deck right now.
7. Last night a lovely full moon (raised, rose) over the ocean.
8. I could see the moon as I (laid, lay) in my bed.
9. You may (set, sit) this large shell on the table.
10. We have (laid, lain) other shells there already.
11. We will (let, leave) them here until we go home.
12. Sometimes I have (let, left) things here that I wanted to take along.

B. Write the correct words for these sentences.
1. (There's, There are) sea animals that look like stars.
2. (There is, There are) harmless insects that look like stinging insects.
3. A bird usually (don't, doesn't) capture an insect that looks dangerous.
4. (There is, There are) two crocodiles in the water.
5. A beaver and a mink (was, were) inspecting the beaver dam.

52. Making an Outline for a Report

In Lessons 34 and 38 you learned about outlines. In Lesson 47 you learned about taking notes. Now you are ready to take notes and make an outline from them. An outline is a great help in writing a good report.

First, choose a topic that is interesting to you. Your teacher may help you choose a topic that is suitable.

Then find information on the topic you have chosen. Use textbooks, encyclopedias, and other books from your library at school or at home.

Take notes from at least two different books. Use the questions **who, what, when, where, why,** and **how** to help you find details. If you find something that is especially interesting, be sure to include it in your notes.

Remember to write down only main ideas and key words. Do not copy whole sentences. Notes are usually phrases and short sentences that are written quickly. Do not worry about writing complete sentences when you take notes.

Suppose you are taking notes for a report on the Milky Way. Here is what your list might look like.

The Milky Way

a galaxy
diameter about 100,000 light-years
diameter about ten times greater than thickness
people long ago thought it looked like a stream of milk
   across the sky
made of billions of stars
home of solar system
name became widely used
official scientific name today
top view—like a huge pinwheel
side view—like a cookie with filling heaped in middle

After you have enough notes, organize them into an outline.

Do this by deciding which notes should be grouped together. Decide what the main topic is in each group, and write the main topics on another paper. Put the main topics in a sensible order, and number them with Roman numerals.

Next, find the notes that fit under each main topic. (These are the subtopics that you studied in Lesson 34.) Put them in order under the main topics where they fit, and write capital letters before them. If there are any details, put them where they belong, and write Arabic numerals before them. Do not copy any note unless it fits under one of the topics on the outline. You may need to drop some notes in order to keep your report brief.

Here is an example of what your outline might look like.

The Milky Way

I. How it got its name
    A. People long ago thought it looked like a stream of milk across the sky.
    B. The name became widely used.
    C. It is the official scientific name today.

II. What it is
    A. A galaxy
    B. Made of billions of stars
    C. Home of solar system

III. What it looks like
    A. Top view—like a huge pinwheel
    B. Side view—like a cookie with filling heaped in middle

IV. How big it is
    A. Diameter about 100,000 light-years
    B. Diameter about ten times greater than thickness

Organizing your notes into an outline is important for writing an orderly, meaningful report. Later you will learn how to write an actual report by using an outline.

Oral Drill

Using this list of notes, work together as a class to write an outline on the chalkboard.

Kangaroos

a furry marsupial (mammal with a pouch to carry its young)

native to Australia

five main kinds: antelope kangaroo, eastern gray kangaroo, western gray kangaroo, red kangaroo, wallaroo

may stand 6 feet tall and weigh 100 pounds or more

powerful back legs for hopping

can hop 40 miles per hour

can leap over obstacles 6 feet high

large tail for balancing

Australian names: males—boomers, females—flying does, young ones—joeys

first seen by white men in 1770

discovered by Captain James Cook and his men

> **Written Practice** >

A. Make an outline from the list of notes below. Use the title and main topics shown. You do not need to write **Mercury** or **Venus** in each subtopic. (Save your outline for Lesson 56.)

Title: **The Two Planets Closest to the Sun**

Main topics: I. Mercury is closest to sun
                  II. Venus is second closest to sun

Mercury orbits sun in 88 earth days
Mercury's diameter is about 3,000 miles
Venus orbits sun in 225 earth days (about 7½ months)
Venus's diameter is about 7,500 miles
Venus is 67 million miles from sun
Mercury is 36 million miles from sun
Mercury's temperature is -315° to 650° F
Venus's temperature is about 850° F
Romans named it Venus because of its brightness and beauty
Romans named it Mercury ("swift messenger") because of its
   fast movement

B. Copy and complete this outline by using the notes below. Put two subtopics in a sensible order under each main topic where they fit. (Save your outline for Lesson 56.)

The Pony Express
    I. Where and when it was operated
   II. Who operated it
  III. How fast it was
   IV. When and why it ended

carried mail between St. Joseph, Missouri, and Sacramento,
   California

daring young men rode horses at top speed from one station to
   another

trips usually took 8 or 9 days

began on April 3, 1860, and lasted about 19 months
first trip took 10 days
ended on October 24, 1861
station keepers provided fresh horses
telegraph ended need for Pony Express

> Review and Practice >

Answer the following questions in complete sentences. You may look back in the composition lessons if you need help.

1. What is a paragraph?
2. When does a paragraph have unity?
3. What is one good way to develop a paragraph?
4. What is a good way to take notes?
5. What does an outline show?

53. Linking Verbs

Some verbs are used as **linking verbs.** A linking verb links the subject to a word in the predicate that renames or describes the subject.

Robert is my **brother.**
> The noun **brother** renames the subject **Robert.** The verb **is** links the two words.

Babies are **lovable.**
> The adjective **lovable** describes the subject **babies.** The verb **are** links the two words.

Most linking verbs are forms of **be.** Review the eight forms of **be.**

am, is, are, was, were, be, been, being

Linking verbs may be in verb phrases. Review the list of helping verbs.

Forms of *be:* am, is, are, was, were, be, been, being
H **triplets:**   have, has, had
D **triplets:**   do, does, did
M **triplets:**   may, might, must
Three sets of twins:
          can—could, shall—should, will—would

If a verb phrase ends with a form of **be,** it is often a linking verb phrase.

should have **been**   will **be**   is **being**

Jonathan will be the **teacher.**
> The linking verb phrase **will be** links the subject **Jonathan** to the noun **teacher,** which renames the subject.

The little child is being **obedient.**
> The linking verb phrase **is being** links the subject **child** to the adjective **obedient,** which describes the subject.

There are some other linking verbs besides the forms of **be.** They may be called the "**sometimes linking verbs.**" Memorize the ones in this list.

taste, feel, smell, sound, look, appear

These verbs are called "sometimes linking verbs" because they can also be action verbs. To tell when they are action verbs, see if the subject is performing any action.

I **tasted** the pie.
> The subject **I** performs the action. The verb **tasted** is an action verb.

The pie **tasted** good.

> Pies do not have tongues. They cannot taste. **Tasted** links **pie** to **good.**

I **felt** the ice.

> The subject **I** performs the action. The verb **felt** is an action verb.

The ice **felt** cold.

> Ice does not have skin. It cannot feel. The verb **felt** links **ice** to **cold.**

We **looked** at the pictures.

> The subject **we** performs the action. The verb **looked** is an action verb.

The pictures **looked** lovely.

> Pictures cannot look. The verb **looked** links **pictures** to **lovely.**

To tell when **taste, feel, smell, sound, look,** or **appear** is a linking verb, see if it can be replaced by a form of **be.** If the sentence still makes sense, the verb is a linking verb. If the sentence does not make sense, the verb is an action verb.

The cake **smells** delicious.

> **Try saying:** The cake **is** delicious. (sensible; linking)

Donna **smelled** the roses.

> **Try saying:** Donna **was** the roses. (not sensible; action)

Kay **felt** the cloth.

> **Try saying:** Kay **was** the cloth. (not sensible; action)

Kay **felt** sick yesterday.

> **Try saying:** Kay **was** sick yesterday. (sensible; linking)

A linking verb can never have a direct object. It does not show action, so it cannot pass action to a receiver.

> **Remember:** A linking verb is a word that links the subject to some other word in the sentence. Forms of **be** and the "sometimes linking verbs" can be used as linking verbs.

> **Oral Drill**

A. Say the forms of **be** and the "sometimes linking verbs" from memory.

B. Tell whether each boldface verb or verb phrase is a **linking verb** or an **action verb.**
   1. The Lord **is** King.
   2. The disciples **ate** the Passover with Jesus.
   3. The women **had** some sweet spices.
   4. The disobedient people **were being** very careless.
   5. The Israelites' situation **was** very serious then.
   6. The Good Samaritan **was helping** the wounded man.
   7. Sally **appears** very bashful.
   8. Strawberry ice cream **tastes** delicious.

C. Tell whether each verb is a **linking verb** or an **action verb.** If it is a linking verb, also give the form of **be** that can be used to replace it.
   1. The echoes in the valley **sounded** loud.
   2. This pudding **tastes** good.
   3. Will you **taste** this bread?
   4. The baby's hands **feel** cold.
   5. I **felt** how cold they were.
   6. **Look** at the beautiful sunset!
   7. Mother **looks** tired.
   8. These potatoes **smell** burnt.
   9. Can't you **smell** them?
   10. **Look** in the kettle on the stove.

> Written Practice >

A. Write **linking** or **action** for each boldface verb or verb phrase.
1. The Lord **is** great.
2. The twelve disciples gladly **followed** Jesus.
3. My brother **is** a plumber.
4. My brother **called** the plumber.
5. Brother Benjamin **will visit** our neighbor.
6. Brother Benjamin **will be** our neighbor.
7. This dog **was** the thief.
8. This dog **was chasing** the thief.

B. If the boldface verb can be replaced by a form of **be,** write that form of **be.** If it cannot be replaced with a form of **be,** write **A** for action verb.
1. The children **tasted** the fresh cookies.
2. The cookies **tasted** spicy and sweet.
3. The roses in the garden **smell** fragrant.
4. I could **smell** them through my window.
5. The priests **sounded** the trumpets.
6. The trumpet **sounds** very loud.

C. For each boldface verb, write **L** for linking or **A** for action. If the action verb has a direct object, write the direct object.
1. Susan **tasted** the tea.
2. The tea **tasted** too sweet.
3. Samuel **looks** mischievous.
4. **Look** up here.
5. The new idea **sounded** good.
6. Father **smelled** the smoke from the fire.
7. The smoke **smelled** terrible.
8. The fire **felt** extremely hot.
9. The firemen **sounded** the alarm.

> Review and Practice >

Write **A** or **D** to tell whether each sentence has an appositive or a noun of direct address. Then copy each word that should have a comma after it, and add the missing comma.

1. Janet how much of the earth's surface is covered with water?
2. It is over 70 percent Sister Maria.
3. The highest spot in Europe Mount Elbrus is found in Russia.
4. How high James is the highest mountain in the world?
5. Mount Everest the highest mountain in the world is 29,028 feet high.

◆━◆━◆━◆━◆━◆━◆━◆

54. Linking Verbs With Predicate Nouns

When a linking verb is followed by a noun, the noun renames the subject. In such a sentence, the linking verb is like an equal sign in an arithmetic problem. Remember, "7 x 9 is 63" means the same as "7 x 9 = 63."

<u>Jesus is</u> our **Helper.**
   Jesus = Helper

<u>Columbus was</u> an **Italian.**
   Columbus = Italian

A noun that follows a linking verb and renames the subject is a **predicate noun.** It is called a predicate noun because it is in the predicate, but it names the same person, place, or thing as the subject. If a sentence does not have a linking verb, it cannot have a predicate noun.

My <u>brother</u> <u>is</u> my **teacher.**

> **Brother** and **teacher** name the same person. The verb **is** links the two nouns.

In a sentence with a predicate noun, the subject and the predicate noun can be exchanged, and the sentence still means the same. A subject and a direct object cannot be exchanged in this way.

> My brother is my teacher.
> **Try saying:** My teacher is my brother.
> (same meaning)

The ravens fed Elijah.
> **Try saying:** Elijah fed the ravens.
> (different meaning)

A predicate noun is diagramed on the base line after the sentence skeleton. A slanted line is placed before the predicate noun. This line slants toward the subject to show that the predicate noun renames the subject.

Jesus is the King.

In diagraming sentences with predicate nouns, first find the verb. Then ask **who** or **what** with the verb to find the subject. Next, find the noun in the predicate that renames the subject. Then say the skeleton and the predicate noun together to see if they make sense.

God is the Creator of heaven and earth.

The verb is **is.**

Who is? God.

Which noun renames the subject? **Creator.**

God is Creator makes sense.

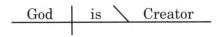

Predicate nouns cannot follow action verbs. Nouns in the predicate that receive action are direct objects. Notice which of the following sentences has a direct object and which one has a predicate noun. Direct objects follow action verbs (labeled **A**). Predicate nouns follow linking verbs (labeled **L**).

The children ate the mangoes.

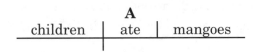

This yellow fruit is a mango.

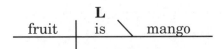

A sentence may have a compound predicate noun. When such a sentence is diagramed, the fork comes **after** the slanted line.

My father is a carpenter and teacher.

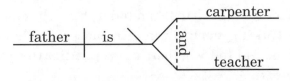

> **Remember:** A predicate noun is a noun that follows a linking verb and renames the subject.

Oral Drill

A. Say all the verbs you have learned that can be used as linking verbs.

B. Choose the correct words.
1. A linking verb may be followed by a (direct object, predicate noun).
2. An action verb may be followed by a (direct object, predicate noun).
3. A (direct object, predicate noun) renames the subject.
4. A (direct object, predicate noun) receives action.

C. Say the sentence skeleton and the predicate noun in each sentence.
1. These green fruits are avocados.
2. James Buchanan was the president before Abraham Lincoln.
3. Menno Simons had been a Catholic priest.
4. Later he was an Anabaptist.
5. That man on the platform is the president.
6. A young kangaroo is a joey.
7. Jason is a good friend and helper.
8. Are you a teacher?

D. Give each sentence skeleton, and tell if the verb is an **action verb** or a **linking verb.** Then give each noun that follows the skeleton, and tell whether it is a **predicate noun** or a **direct object.**
1. Those men are farmers.
2. They have been raising corn and wheat.

3. In the cornfield, Robert saw a deer.

4. This building is a school and a meetinghouse.

5. Our teacher sang the new song.

6. My younger brother is an active child.

7. He rode my new bicycle awhile.

8. Those birds are not pheasants.

E. On the chalkboard, diagram the skeletons, predicate nouns, and direct objects of numbers 1–4 in Part D. Above each main verb, write **L** for linking or **A** for action.

> **Written Practice**

A. Diagram the sentence skeletons and predicate nouns.
1. His name is Rover.
2. He is my dog.
3. Benjamin Franklin was a famous inventor.
4. David and Solomon were kings of Israel.

B. Diagram the sentence skeletons, predicate nouns, and direct objects. Above each main verb, write **L** for linking or **A** for action.
1. This young man is a skillful carpenter.
2. Our neighbor has been a farmer all his life.
3. These purple flowers are asters.
4. Mother has planted some pink asters too.
5. The asters are growing well.
6. Grandmother sees the flowers from her window.
7. Betsy is my sister.
8. Betsy made some biscuits.
9. Abner tasted the biscuits.
10. Brother Joel will be our teacher tomorrow.

C. Follow these directions.
1. Write the definition of a linking verb.
2. Write all the verbs you have learned that can be used as linking verbs.
3. Write the definition of a predicate noun.
4. Write a sentence of your own, using a predicate noun.

> **Review and Practice** >

Write the correct verb for each sentence.
1. Please (raise, rise) your hand before you speak.
2. I (raise, rise) at six o'clock in the morning.
3. (Lay, Lie) the book on the table.
4. (Lay, Lie) down and rest a few minutes.
5. Will you (let, leave) me go tomorrow?
6. Be sure you (let, leave) my books here.
7. We have (set, sat) the dishes on the table.
8. We (set, sat) down to eat.

55. Linking Verbs With Predicate Adjectives

You have learned that a linking verb is followed by a word that renames or describes the subject. If the word renames the subject, it is a predicate noun. But if the word describes the subject, it is a **predicate adjective.**

God is **great.**

Great is an adjective that describes **God.** The verb **is** links the two words.

The <u>sky</u> <u>was</u> **blue.**

> **Blue** is an adjective that describes **sky.** The verb **was** links the two words.

Only linking verbs are followed by predicate adjectives. If a sentence has an action verb, it cannot have a predicate adjective.

Review the linking verbs. They are the forms of **be** and the "sometimes linking verbs."

> **am, is, are, was, were, be, been, being**
> **taste, feel, smell, sound, look, appear**

In the following two sentences, adjectives in bold print come after the skeletons. But they are not predicate adjectives. Can you tell why?

> Texas is a **large** state.
> Paul's nephew was a **courageous** boy.

The adjective **large** does not modify the subject **Texas.** It describes the predicate noun **state.** The adjective **courageous** does not modify the subject **nephew.** It describes the predicate noun **boy. Large** and **courageous** are in the predicate, but they are not predicate adjectives. A predicate adjective must describe, or modify, the subject.

But the sentences above can be changed so that **large** and **courageous** are predicate adjectives. The following sentences show how.

> Texas is large.
> Paul's nephew was courageous.

Texas

Predicate adjectives are diagramed in the same way as predicate nouns. First find the sentence skeleton. If there is a linking verb, look for an adjective in the predicate that describes the subject.

These boards feel very smooth.

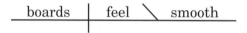

The sentence skeleton is **boards feel.** Which word after the skeleton is an adjective that describes the subject? Try putting the words before the subject. **Very boards** does not make sense. **Smooth boards** does, so **smooth** is the predicate adjective.

This tree is huge.
   Think: huge tree.
   Huge is a predicate adjective.

The tree looks extremely old.
   Think: not **extremely tree,** but **old tree.**
   Old is a predicate adjective.

A sentence may have a compound predicate adjective. When such a sentence is diagramed, the fork comes **after** the slanted line.

The <u>rolls</u> <u>smell</u> **sweet** and **spicy.**

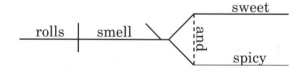

In a question, the predicate adjective does not come directly after the linking verb. Changing the question to a statement makes it easier to find the predicate adjective.

Is the bed soft?
(the bed Is soft)

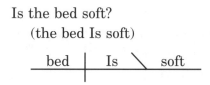

Remember: A predicate adjective is an adjective that follows a linking verb and describes the subject.

> **Oral Drill** >

A. On the chalkboard, diagram each sentence skeleton and predicate adjective.
   1. The doughnuts smelled delicious.
   2. The autumn leaves were crisp and colorful.
   3. The sky looked dark and stormy.
   4. Was the peach ripe?
   5. Our gracious God is most merciful.
   6. Were the people diligent or careless?

B. Change these sentences so that the adjectives in the predicate become predicate adjectives.
   1. John is a careful boy.
   2. May is a cheerful girl.
   3. This baby is a sweet and happy child.
   4. That book is a valuable one.

> **Written Practice** >

A. Diagram the sentence skeletons and predicate adjectives.
   1. The morning was bright.
   2. The lemonade tastes delicious.
   3. The wind felt raw and unpleasant.

4. Was the sky cloudy?

5. The weather was very warm and humid.

6. The steers sounded nervous and fearful.

7. Were the wicked people sorry?

8. God's commandments are righteous.

9. Our heavenly Father is just.

10. Job was perfect and upright.

B. Rewrite each sentence so that the adjective in the predicate becomes a predicate adjective.

1. Solomon was a wise king.

2. Are you a friendly person?

3. Those children are diligent workers.

> **Review and Practice** >

Combine each pair of choppy sentences, using as few words as possible.

1. The American black bear may act playful. The American black bear may do amusing things.

2. But black bears are strong. Black bears are fierce.

3. A black bear might suddenly hit the person who tries to feed him. He might suddenly bite the person who tries to feed him.

4. Black bears are not really tame. They are not really friendly.

5. Mother bears are interesting to watch from a distance. Their cubs are interesting to watch from a distance.

56. Writing a Report

You have learned how to take notes for writing a report and how to organize your notes into an outline. The next step is to actually write the report. Your outline shows the main topics, subtopics, and details that will be in your report. It also shows the order in which things will be said. The most important thing now is to put those things in paragraphs and to write in a clear, interesting way.

Write in complete sentences, and write one paragraph for each main idea on your outline. Skip every other line so that you can make changes later. This is your first draft.

Think of ways to improve your report. Did you write sentences of different patterns? Are your sentences of different lengths? Do they begin in different ways? Write notes on the first draft to show the improvements you want to make.

Then check for mistakes in spelling, punctuation, and grammar. Also correct these mistakes on the first draft.

Finally, write the second draft of your report. Write as neatly as you can, and make the corrections you have marked.

> Oral Drill >

Tell how to write a report from the outline on the Milky Way that is given in Lesson 52. With the help of your teacher and classmates, write at least the first paragraph on the chalkboard.

> Written Practice >

A. Write a report from your outline in Lesson 52, Part A ("The Two Planets Closest to the Sun"). Write one paragraph for each main topic. Skip lines on the first draft, make improvements, and rewrite the report.

B. Write a report from your outline in Lesson 52, Part B ("The Pony Express"). You may add more details from an encyclopedia if you wish. Put each added detail under the main topic where it fits.

---

57. More Troublesome Verbs

What is the difference between asking "**Can** I read this book?" and "**May** I read this book?" What is the difference between **teaching** a song and **learning** a song? Learn the meanings and correct usages of the following verbs.

Can means "to be able."

> My little brother **can** ride a bicycle.
> We **can** understand the Bible.
> **Can** you speak German?
> **Can** we see God's wonderful works?

May means "to be permitted."

> You **may** not go outside now.
> We **may** sing for Grandmother soon.
> **May** I borrow your pen?
> **May** we read a book?

Teach means "to give knowledge or instruction."

> Lord, **teach** us to pray.
> Jesus **taught** His disciples to pray.
> My father **teaches** me many things.
> He **is teaching** me to be honest.

Learn means "to gain knowledge."

> **Learn** to obey.
> Betty **is learning** to sew.
> She **had** already **learned** to cook.
> Robert **learns** easily.
> He **has learned** the alphabet.

Do you know what is wrong with the following sentence?

> I would of helped you if I could of.

Of is not a verb. It is not correct to use **could of, should of,** and **would of.** These phrases come from carelessly saying **could have, should have,** and **would have.**

> **Wrong:** Jeroboam should of obeyed the Lord.
> **Right:** Jeroboam **should have** obeyed the Lord.

Remember: Can means "to be able." **May** means "to be permitted." **Teach** means "to give knowledge or instruction." **Learn** means "to gain knowledge." Do not use **could of, should of,** and **would of** for **could have, should have,** and **would have.**

Oral Drill

Some of the following sentences have mistakes. Practice reading each one correctly.

1. The teacher said we can choose a poem.
2. I can learn this poem.
3. The younger boys can climb this rope.
4. Can I have a drink, please?
5. Can I go downstairs to study?
6. Can we play tag at recess?
7. The Lord will learn the meek His ways.

8. Have you learned to be content in any situation?
9. The prophet learned the people every day.
10. Jesus began to teach by the seaside.
11. We should first learn to be kind at home.
12. Learn the young women to be sober.
13. I should of known better.
14. I could of done much more.
15. I wish I would of been more careful.

Written Practice

A. Write the correct words.
1. (Can, May) I please see your book?
2. Father will (teach, learn) me how to make a birdhouse.
3. I (should have, should of) done my lessons sooner.
4. I (could have, could of) finished by now.
5. My sister (taught, learned) me this new song.
6. (Can, May) I come to your house?
7. (Can, May) you jump that high?
8. Everyone should (teach, learn) to be patient.
9. My mother (taught, learned) me how to sew.
10. Will you (teach, learn) me too?

B. Write sentences of your own, using **can, may, teach, learn, should have,** and **would have.**

Review and Practice

A. Diagram the sentence skeletons and the direct objects, predicate nouns, or predicate adjectives.
1. Righteous Naboth had a vineyard near the palace.
2. The grapes tasted delicious.
3. Ahab was Israel's king.
4. King Ahab wanted Naboth's vineyard.
5. His face looked sullen.

6. He did not taste any bread.
7. The queen was wicked and cruel.
8. That wicked woman must have been Jezebel.
9. That plan sounded very easy.
10. The letters will be short and clear.
11. Two men will be false witnesses.
12. Carry him out of the city.

B. Make a noun from each word by adding the suffix **-ness, -ment, -ity,** or **-ion.** Use the dictionary if you need help.
1. ship
2. rare
3. gentle
4. imitate
5. exaggerate

58. Chapter 5 Review

Oral Drill

A. Give the answers.
1. What is a verb?
2. What is a direct object?
3. What are the three principal parts of verbs?
4. What must be used with the past participle?
5. Give the meaning and the three principal parts of each verb. For letters a–f, tell whether the verb needs a direct object.
   a. raise
   b. rise
   c. set
   d. sit
   e. lay
   f. lie
   g. let
   h. leave
   i. teach
   j. learn

6. Give the meanings of **can** and **may.**
7. What is a linking verb?
8. Name the linking verbs you learned.
9. What is a predicate noun?
10. What is a predicate adjective?

B. On the chalkboard, diagram each sentence skeleton and direct object, predicate noun, or predicate adjective. Above each main verb, write **A** for action or **L** for linking. Write **DO** above each direct object, **PN** above each predicate noun, and **PA** above each predicate adjective. (**Mountain lion** is a noun phrase.)

1. The cougar is a mountain lion.
2. Cougars hunt small game.
3. They attack deer and other animals.
4. Its scream sounds strange.
5. Robert tasted the cookie.
6. The crackers tasted stale.
7. The teacher feels happy.
8. The principal sounded the alarm.
9. The smoke looked real.
10. It was only a drill.

C. Give the missing forms of the following verbs.

Present	Past	Past Participle
1. dig	——	—— ——
2. fight	——	—— ——
3. find	——	—— ——
4. shine	——	—— ——
5. catch	——	—— ——
6. teach	——	—— ——
7. write	——	—— ——

D. Give the correct past form of each verb in parentheses.
1. Mother said the book (cost) too much.
2. Jane had (bring) a book about snowflakes.
3. Yesterday I (see) the lovely pictures in it.
4. I have never (see) such a book before.
5. Janice (draw) a picture of a snowman.
6. I had never (draw) a horse before.
7. Yesterday I (do) try drawing a rabbit.
8. I had not (do) it before.
9. We (steal) quietly through the baby's room.
10. The lost puppy had not been (steal).

E. Tell how to correct the following sentences.
1. Sister Mary, can I get a drink?
2. My mother learned me how to knit.
3. I could of learned it before.
4. You should of seen the balloon that landed in our field yesterday.
5. Mother, can I go home with John?
6. My teacher learned me to keep a neat desk.
7. My brother left me use his bat.
8. The stewardess told us to let the suitcase with her.
9. Leave me help you carry those boxes.
10. Do not leave the cat come into the house.

F. Answer these questions.
1. What are some things you should do in order to become a good writer?
2. What should you do when you take notes?
3. What should you not do when you take notes?

G. Tell whether each statement is **true** or **false.** If it is false,
   tell how to correct it.
   1. When you write a report, you should choose a topic that is
      interesting to you.
   2. You may take notes by copying sentences and paragraphs
      from a reference book.
   3. Most notes are phrases and short sentences that are written
      quickly.
   4. When you first write your report, you should try to do it so
      well that you will not need to rewrite it.

> Written Practice >

A. Write all the correct words for each sentence. Some sentences
   have more than one answer.
   1. An action verb can have a (direct object, predicate noun,
      predicate adjective) after it.
   2. A linking verb can have a (direct object, predicate noun,
      predicate adjective) after it.
   3. A (direct object, predicate noun, predicate adjective)
      renames the subject.
   4. A (direct object, predicate noun, predicate adjective) receives
      action.
   5. A (direct object, predicate noun, predicate adjective)
      describes the subject.
   6. A predicate adjective follows (an action, a linking) verb.
   7. On a sentence diagram, a slanted line is placed before a
      (direct object, predicate noun, predicate adjective).

B. Diagram each sentence skeleton and each direct object, predicate noun, or predicate adjective.
   1. It is raining, and the swollen creek is rising.
   2. The water is brown and muddy.
   3. Set the bottles and boxes down here.

4. A panther was lying on a low branch of the tree.
5. Do not leave the lambs in that meadow.
6. They are helpless animals.
7. The ewe and her lambs lay in the sun yesterday.
8. We will lay the tools here.
9. A screwdriver is a handy tool.
10. Their fence is white.
11. Grandmother's bread tastes delicious.
12. It looks fluffy and white.
13. Raise your hands.
14. John left the box here.
15. My father is a farmer.

C. Write the missing verb forms.

Present	**Past**	**Past Participle**
1. bring	——	—— ——
2. drag	——	—— ——
3. break	——	—— ——
4. wear	——	—— ——
5. freeze	——	—— ——
6. swim	——	—— ——
7. buy	——	—— ——

D. Write the correct words in parentheses. Also write the direct object if there is one.
1. Please (raise, rise) the windows for more air.
2. "(Raise, Rise) and say your poem together," said the teacher.
3. "Whose bicycle is (setting, sitting) in the driveway?" asked Father.
4. Jerry is sick and must (lay, lie) in bed all day.
5. Those workmen (lay, lie) new carpets every day.
6. They (laid, lay) the carpet in our living room yesterday.
7. Harold has often (laid, lain) in that hammock for a nap.
8. Jesus has (raised, risen) from the dead.

9. Jesus (raised, rose) from the dead on the first day of the week.
10. Jesus (raised, rose) the little girl from the dead.
11. The masons have (laid, lain) a new wall of red bricks for us.
12. Judy (set, sat) her little brother in the wagon and gave him a ride.

E. Take three notes on the following paragraph for a report on controlling mosquitoes. One note should be about something that does not work, and two should be about things that do work.

Mosquitoes are especially bothersome in damp, low-lying areas. Spraying clouds of poison into the air does not bring much relief. This is because mosquitoes develop from eggs that hatch in pools of stagnant water. Public health workers have learned that the best way to fight these pests is to drain the pools or to cover them with a film of oil. These methods greatly reduce the torment of mosquitoes.

F. Copy and complete the following outline by using the notes below. (You will not use all of them.) Put three subtopics under each main topic where they fit. Read Deuteronomy 3:3, 11 and 1 Samuel 17:4, 51 if you need help.

Two Giants in the Bible
  I. Og
  II. Goliath

was king of Bashan
was from Gath
had an iron bedstead nine cubits long
wore a crown that weighed one talent
had a height of six cubits and a span
was killed by David
had hands with six fingers and feet with six toes
was killed by Israelites in Moses' time

●━●━●━●━●━●━●━●

Personal Pronouns

Nominative Pronouns

	Singular	*Plural*
*First person:	I	we
Second person:	you	you
Third person:	he, she, it	they

Objective Pronouns

	Singular	*Plural*
First person:	me	us
Second person:	you	you
Third person:	him, her, it	them

Possessive Pronouns

	Singular	*Plural*
First person:	my, mine	our, ours
Second person:	your, yours	your, yours
Third person:	his, her, hers, its	their, theirs

First person pronouns refer to the speaker himself.
Second person pronouns refer to the person spoken to.
Third person pronouns refer to the person spoken about.

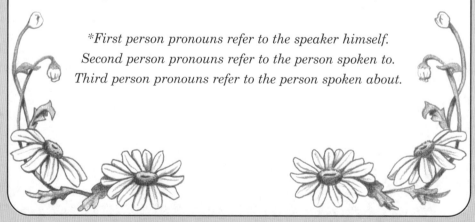

Chapter 6
Pronouns

This

These

That

Those

59. Pronouns Stand for Nouns

A pronoun is another of the eight parts of speech. A pronoun is a word that takes the place of a noun.

God created the heaven and the earth.
He made everything good.

Adam and Eve were the first people.
They lived in the Garden of Eden.

The pronoun **He** takes the place of the noun **God.** The pronoun **they** takes the place of the nouns **Adam** and **Eve.**

An **antecedent** is a word for which a pronoun stands. In the sentences above, **God** is the antecedent of the pronoun **He. Adam** and **Eve** are the antecedents of the pronoun **they.** In the following sentence, **Eve** is the antecedent of **her.**

God made Eve and brought **her** to Adam.

There are different classes of pronouns. The first class you will study is the **personal pronouns,** which refer mainly to persons. Pronouns like **you, she, him, it,** and **them** are personal pronouns. They are the most common pronouns we use.

Personal pronouns have three **cases:** the **nominative** case, the **objective** case, and the **possessive** case. (See the chart at the beginning of the chapter.) You will learn more about these cases in later lessons.

Pronouns can be singular or plural. Singular pronouns name only one. **I, he, she,** and **it** are some singular pronouns. Plural pronouns name more than one. **We** and **they** are two plural pronouns. **You** can be either singular or plural.

A plural pronoun can stand for a plural noun, or it can stand for more than one noun. In the sentence **They lived in the Garden of Eden, they** stands for the nouns **Adam** and **Eve.** Also look at these examples.

The **disciples** followed Jesus.
Peter and **John** followed Jesus.
They followed Jesus.

In the last sentence, **they** can mean **the disciples,** or it can mean **Peter and John.**

Remember: A pronoun is a word that takes the place of a noun. An antecedent is a word for which a pronoun stands.

> Oral Drill

A. Replace the words in bold print with suitable pronouns.

One Sunday the apostle Paul preached to the people at Troas. Paul had so many things to say that (1) **Paul** continued speaking to (2) **the people** until midnight.

A certain young man named Eutychus was sitting in a window. Because it was so late, (3) **Eutychus** went to sleep and fell down from the third story. (4) **Eutychus** was taken up dead.

Paul went down to Eutychus and embraced (5) **Eutychus.** Paul said to the people, "Do not trouble yourselves, for (6) **Eutychus's** life is in (7) **Eutychus.**" (8) **The people** were greatly comforted because (9) **Eutychus** was alive.

B. Give plural pronouns to take the place of the words in bold print.
1. **Jason and I** made furrows in the garden.
2. **Ruth and Rebecca** planted bean seeds in **the furrows.**
3. Did **you and the girls** plant all the seeds?
4. The twins helped **Jason and me** to cover the seeds.
5. Mother watched **you and the girls,** and she said the work was well done.

C. Give each pronoun and its antecedent.
1. Jesus said to His disciples, "I am the vine, and you are the branches."
2. "Janet said that she is coming to my house on Sunday," said Julie.
3. The cub followed its mother to their den in the woods.
4. The children love Aunt Mary. She tells them stories.
5. Michael forgot to study, and he will soon be sorry.
6. Martin, this paper is for you and Jerry. Please show it to him.

D. Tell which pronouns in Part C are plural pronouns.

> Written Practice >

A. Write suitable pronouns to replace the words in bold print.

King Herod arrested Peter and put (1) **Peter** into prison. (2) **King Herod** delivered (3) **Peter** to sixteen soldiers. One night the angel of the Lord came and awoke Peter, saying, "Rise up quickly." The chains fell off (4) **Peter's** hands. (5) **Peter** followed (6) **the angel** and went out, but (7) **Peter** thought (8) **Peter** was seeing a vision. They came to the iron gate that led to the city. (9) **The gate** opened to (10) **Peter and the angel** of its own accord. Then the angel departed from Peter. (11) **Peter** went to the house of Mary, where the people were praying for (12) **Peter.**

Peter stood outside knocking. A girl named Rhoda came to the door, but (13) **Rhoda** was so happy to hear (14) **Peter's** voice that (15) **Rhoda** forgot to open (16) **the door.** Peter kept on knocking, and finally (17) **the people** let (18) **Peter** in. How happy (19) **the people** were that God had answered (20) **the people's** prayers!

B. Write each pronoun and its antecedent.
1. This present is for Anna. She does not know about it.
2. The baby has closed his eyes.
3. The girls have done their work well.
4. Ray can read. He could read last year.
5. Children should obey their parents.

C. Write plural pronouns to take the place of the words in bold print.
1. **My parents** are coming to visit school today.
2. **Martha and I** set up the chairs.
3. Will you help **Mary and me**?
4. **Joseph and you** may wash the windows.
5. The teacher will help **June and you.**
6. Who will help **the boys** carry the tables?

D. Write the definition of **pronoun** and of **antecedent.**

> Review and Practice >

Write the correct past form of each verb in parentheses.
1. David (come) to the Israelite camp.
2. He (hear) Goliath challenging Israel's army.
3. Goliath had (defy) the Israelites for forty days.
4. The Israelites (think) no one could defeat Goliath.
5. David had (keep) his father's sheep.
6. He (know) that God could help him.
7. David (tell) Saul that he would fight Goliath.
8. He (go) out and (fight) the giant.
9. The stone (hit) Goliath in the forehead, and he (fall) to the ground.
10. David had (win) a great victory.

60. Nominative Case Pronouns

A pronoun may be used as the subject of a sentence.

He drew a picture. **She** admired it.
They drew other pictures.

When a pronoun is used as the subject of a sentence, it must be in the **nominative case.** Learn the nominative case pronouns.

I, you, he, she, it, we, they

Usually when a pronoun is a subject, you use the right form without thinking about it. But if the subject is compound, you may use the wrong form. Choosing the correct form is simple if you use the pronoun alone in the sentence.

Robert and (**I** or **me**?) studied the lesson.
> **You do not say:**   Me studied the lesson.
> **So do not say:**   Robert and me studied the lesson.
> **You say:**   I studied the lesson.
> **So you must say:** Robert and **I** studied the lesson.

Sometimes a pronoun subject is followed by an appositive (a noun that makes the pronoun clearer). The boldface nouns in these sentences are appositives.

We **girls** have finished the cleaning.
Have you **boys** finished your work?

Now look at this sentence. Do you know which pronoun is the correct one to use?

(**We** or **Us**?) boys saw the fox's den.

Boys is not the subject of this sentence. It is an appositive, and the subject is a pronoun. So the pronoun must be in the nominative case.

We boys saw the fox's den.

Saying the subject without the appositive is one good help in choosing the right form.

(**We** or **Us**?) children walked home.

> **You do not say:**   Us walked home.
> **So do not say:**   Us children walked home.
> **You say:**   **We** walked home.
> **So you must say: We** children walked home.

Pronouns can also be used as **predicate nominatives.** So far, you have known these as **predicate nouns** and **predicate pronouns.** Predicate nominatives are nouns or pronouns in the predicate that rename the subject. They follow linking verbs.

> My father is the **man** in the dark suit.
>   (noun used as a predicate nominative)
> My father is **he.**
>   (pronoun used as a predicate nominative)

Pronouns used as predicate nominatives must be in the nominative case. This is so because a subject and a predicate nominative can be exchanged, and the sentence means the same.

> **He** is my **father.** My **father** is **he.**
> **They** were his **helpers.** His **helpers** were **they.**

Remember that a predicate nominative is diagramed on the base line after the verb. A slanted line is placed before the predicate nominative to show that it refers to the subject.

The teachers are they.

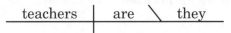

teachers	are \ they

A sentence may have a compound predicate nominative.

My cousins are he and she.

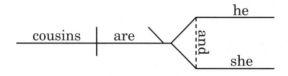

The twins are Joan and she.

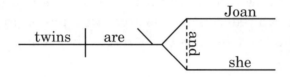

In the Bible, the archaic pronouns **thou** and **ye** are used for **you** in the nominative case.

> "**Thou** shalt not be afraid for the terror by night; nor for the arrow that flieth by day" (Psalm 91:5).
>
> "**Ye** shall find the babe wrapped in swaddling clothes" (Luke 2:12).

Remember: The nominative case pronouns are **I, you, he, she, it, we,** and **they.** A pronoun used as a subject or a predicate nominative must be in the nominative case.

> Oral Drill

A. Replace the words in bold print with suitable pronouns.
1. **Shirley** and **George** are waiting.
2. **The boys** have found a turtle. **The turtle** was hiding.
3. The visitors are **those people.**

4. **The boy** knows the answer, and **the girl** does too.
5. The carpenter is **that man.**

B. On the chalkboard, diagram the skeletons and the predicate nominatives of the sentences in numbers 1 and 5 of Part A.

C. Choose the correct pronouns in parentheses. Tell whether the pronoun you choose is a **subject** or a **predicate nominative.** Read each sentence correctly several times.
1. James and (I, me) will help.
2. The first ones were Alice and (she, her).
3. Wasn't it (they, them)?
4. (We, Us) boys saw it.
5. Surely it was (he, him).
6. You and (I, me) have seen God's wonders.
7. (Thou, Thee) art our Father.
8. Daniel said to Nebuchadnezzar, "It is (thou, thee), O king, that art grown and become strong."

> Written Practice >

A. Write the nominative case pronouns, and memorize them. Also write the nominative case pronouns that are the archaic forms of **you.**

B. Write pronouns to take the place of the words in bold print.
1. **The fishermen** were Peter and **John.**
2. The woman was **her mother.**
3. It was **John the Baptist** who baptized Jesus.
4. Philip and **Nathanael** followed Jesus.
5. Mary and **Martha** were Jesus' friends.

C. Choose the correct pronouns in parentheses. After each pronoun, write **S** for subject or **PN** for predicate nominative.
1. My sister and (I, me) sing songs together.
2. (She, Her) and I also enjoy Old Testament Bible stories.

3. (We, Us) girls have read the Old Testament together.
4. The twins are Jacob and (he, him).
5. My brother and (I, me) were sick on Sunday.
6. My parents and (we, us) children were happy.
7. My parents, my brother, and (I, me) listened eagerly.
8. The two sisters were Leah and (she, her).
9. Are James and (he, him) brothers?
10. The youngest brothers are Joseph and (I, me).
11. Did Paul and (he, him) write New Testament books?
12. The children were she and (they, them).

D. Diagram the skeletons and predicate nominatives of sentences 8–10 in Part C. Use the correct pronouns.

> Review and Practice >

Correct numbers 1–3 by writing them as compound sentences, using a different conjunction each time. Correct numbers 4–6 by joining the sentences, using as few words as possible.

1. Most animal mothers bring food to their babies the mother bear takes her babies to the food.
2. A bear cub learns to fish, soon he can throw a swimming fish right out of the water!
3. Keep away from a mother bear and her cubs, the mother may attack you.
4. Never hand food to a bear. Never hand other things to a bear.
5. Bears are very fast. Bears are very strong.
6. A bear is an animal. A bear is wild. He is not a pet.

61. Objective Case Pronouns

When a pronoun is used as an object, it must be in the objective case. Learn the objective case pronouns.

me, you, him, her, it, us, them

The pronouns **you** and **it** are the same in the nominative case and the objective case.

A pronoun used as a direct object must be in the objective case. Study the following sentence.

My little brother follows **me.** (not **I**)

Be careful when a direct object is compound. It is helpful to use the pronoun alone to decide which is the correct form.

Mother heard Mary and (**she** or **her**?).
You do not say: Mother heard she.
So do not say: Mother heard Mary and she.
You say: Mother heard **her.**
So you must say: Mother heard Mary and **her.**

Also try using the pronoun alone when a direct object pronoun is followed by an appositive.

Mother thanked (**we** or **us**?) girls.
Think: Mother thanked **us.**
Say: Mother thanked **us** girls.

In the Bible, the archaic pronoun **thee** and the pronoun **you** are used for **you** in the objective case.

"Whosoever shall compel **thee** to go a mile, go with him twain" (Matthew 5:41).

"I brought **you** up from the land of Egypt" (Amos 2:10).

Remember: The objective case pronouns are **me, you, him, her, it, us,** and **them.** A pronoun used as a direct object must be in the objective case.

Oral Drill

A. Replace the words in bold print with suitable pronouns.
1. The teacher called **Anna** and **Marvin.**
2. We surprised **Uncle James** on his birthday.
3. The children told **their parents** about the bird.
4. Karen saw **Mother and Charlotte.**
5. The bus left **Ernest** and **Ellen** behind.

B. Tell which pronoun is correct and why. Then read each sentence aloud, using the correct pronoun.
1. Father told John and (I, me).
2. The dog followed James and (she, her).
3. Herbert and (we, us) boys went into the cabin.
4. (We, Us) children saw the smoke from the fire.
5. Irene and (we, us) will look at the old coins.
6. We needed Mildred and (she, her) for the project.
7. The teacher helped (we, us) pupils with the work.
8. Mother called (I, me), and (I, me) went inside.
9. Return, (we, us) beseech (Thou, Thee), O God of hosts: look down from heaven.
10. (Thou, Thee) art my God, and I will praise (Thou, Thee).

C. Change each sentence by switching the subject and the direct object.
Example: I saw them.
Answer: They saw me.
1. We heard her.
2. They followed him.

3. She told me.
4. You paid him.
5. Thou hast told us.

D. This part reviews the usage of nominative and objective pronouns. Tell how to correct each sentence and why it needs correction. Then read it correctly several times.

1. Robert and me worked hard.
2. The visitors are them.
3. The helpers were her and him.
4. Jerry invited Daniel and I.
5. The twins are Martha and her.
6. Her and me sat beside Mother.
7. We watched Nancy and she.
8. Mervin and them helped Jonathan.
9. Mae knows Marcia and she.
10. Our family visited Grandmother and he.

> **Written Practice** >

A. Write the objective case pronouns, and memorize them. Also write the objective case pronoun that is an archaic form of **you**.

B. Replace the words in bold print with suitable pronouns.
1. God sent Moses and **Aaron** to Pharaoh.
2. **Moses and Aaron** approached **Pharaoh** with God's message.
3. **Pharaoh** would not release **the Israelites.**
4. God plagued **the Egyptians** until Pharaoh let the Israelites go.
5. Soon **the Egyptians** pursued the Israelites.
6. God divided **the Red Sea** until the Israelites had crossed.
7. The Red Sea covered **the chariots and horsemen of Pharaoh.**
8. **Miriam** sang a song of praise.

> Review and Practice

A. Choose the correct pronouns. After each answer, write **S** for subject or **DO** for direct object.
1. God called Paul and (he, him) into special service.
2. Jesus visited Mary and (she, her).
3. Did He rebuke Martha or (she, her)?
4. Robert and (they, them) gave the book to us.
5. Mother called you and (I, me).
6. (Thou, Thee) preparest a table before me.
7. Take Arlene and (they, them) with you.
8. He told (we, us) girls about it.
9. (We, Us) children received a package yesterday.
10. We thanked Grandfather and (she, her).

B. Write the correct words.
1. Please (set, sit) here beside me.
2. You may (set, sit) the box right there.
3. Please (raise, rise) the window.
4. Someday we shall (raise, rise) to meet the Lord in the air.
5. Please (lay, lie) your coats on this table.
6. Do not (let, leave) the dog (lay, lie) on the sofa.

7. (Can, May) I borrow this book?
8. (Can, May) you read it in two days?
9. (Teach, Learn) me how to knit, please.
10. You will (teach, learn) fast.
11. I (could of, could have) learned it at school.
12. I (should of, should have) practiced more.

62. The Form of a Friendly Letter

God says in the Book of Hebrews, "To do good and to communicate forget not: for with such sacrifices God is well pleased"
(Hebrews 13:16). Writing friendly letters is one important way
of communicating with others.

Do you like to get letters? How long is it since you have
written to a friend or relative? Read the following letter and
rules, and think how they compare with the letters you write
and receive.

Heading {
Route 1, Box 15
Greensburg, KY 42743
April 22, 20--

Greeting   Dear Joseph,

Body {
    Greetings in Jesus' Name. "The joy of the Lord is your strength" (Nehemiah 8:10). We learned this verse in school last week, and I like it very much.

    How is your broken leg by now? I hope it is healing fast. Maybe the crossword puzzles I am sending will help to pass the time.

    Guess what is new on our farm, Joseph. Do you remember our pony, Ginger? She has a frisky little colt named Spice. Come and visit us this summer, and then you can see it.

Closing
        Your friend,

Signature
        Wayne

The five parts of a friendly letter are shown beside the sample letter. The first part is the heading, which shows the address of the writer and the date of writing. The other four parts are the greeting, body, closing, and signature.

Use correct capitalization when you write a friendly letter. The first word in the greeting of a letter and the first word in the closing must be capitalized. Capital letters are used for all proper nouns, such as the names of streets, cities, states, and months. The abbreviations **Mr.** and **Mrs.** are always capitalized. Titles of respect, such as **doctor** and **uncle,** are capitalized when they are used with names: **Doctor Early, Dr. Early, Uncle Will.**

Use correct punctuation in a friendly letter. In the heading, place a comma between the route number and the box number, between the name of the city and the state or province, and between the number of the day and the year. Do not place a comma between the house number and the street name, between the state name and the Zip Code, or between the province name and the postal code. Put a comma after the greeting and after the closing.

Wrong: 1124, Applebutter Road
Bethlehem, PA, 18015
Oct. 6 20—

Right: 1124 Applebutter Road
Bethlehem, PA 18015
Oct. 6, 20—

Notice where the heading, closing, and signature are written. The heading is close to the right margin. The left edge of the heading, closing, and signature are in line with each other.

For state names, the postal service has developed a list of two-letter abbreviations to be used with Zip Codes. These are completely capitalized and have no end punctuation.

PA 17519   MD 21641   NY 11223

> Oral Drill >

A. Do the following things with the letter in the lesson.
   1. Point out and name the five parts.
   2. Tell how it follows the rules of capitalization.
   3. Tell how it follows the rules of punctuation.
   4. Tell what makes this letter interesting to Joseph.

B. Tell which part of a friendly letter each of the following belongs to. Tell which words should be capitalized. Tell where punctuation marks are needed.

   1. 271 grant street
      brinkhaven oh 43006
      march 12 20—
   2. how is your sister ann
   3. dear cousin Julia
   4. dennis martin

   5. dear uncle ben
   6. route 1 box 200
      emerald wi 54012
      october 4 20—
   7. with deep affection
   8. marilyn

> Written Practice >

A. Write each letter part correctly.

   1. route 3 box 3114
      lowville ny 13367
      aug 23 20—
   2. 518 olga place
      fort hill pa 15540
      jan 12 20—

   3. sincerely yours
   4. bernice
   5. my dear friend
   6. dear frank
   7. your sister
   8. mary

B. Choose one of the topics below, and write a short friendly letter. Include all the five parts. If you write to a real person, you may want to send the letter after your teacher has checked it.
   1. Write a letter thanking your grandmother (or someone else) for a birthday gift.
   2. Write a letter inviting a friend to your house.

3. Write a letter to encourage your friend who is ill.
4. Write a letter to tell your cousin about something exciting that happened to you.

> **Review and Practice** >

Write the correct words in parentheses.
1. A (topic, descriptive) sentence gives the main idea of a paragraph.
2. A paragraph is a group of sentences that develop (a single topic, several topics).
3. A paragraph has (unity, sentence variety) when all the sentences tell about the same topic.
4. Two words more exact than **slow** are (sluggish, creeping, silent).
5. Two words more exact than **bad** are (faulty, rapid, destructive).
6. (A topic sentence, An outline) shows how the ideas of a composition are organized.
7. A good way to take notes is to (copy sentences, write main ideas).
8. A paragraph has (unity, order) when ideas are given step by step.

63. Possessive Case Pronouns

Possessive case pronouns show ownership or relationship. The following words are possessive pronouns.

my, mine, your, yours, his, her, hers, its, our, ours, their, theirs

Some possessive pronouns are used as adjectives: **my, your, his, her, its, our, their.** Other possessive pronouns are used as pronouns: **mine, yours, his, hers, its, ours, theirs.** Notice that **his** and **its** may be used either way.

When a possessive pronoun modifies a noun, it is used as an adjective. When it stands alone, it is used as a pronoun.

My book is blue. (adjective)	**Mine** is blue. (pronoun)
His shoes are new. (adjective)	**His** are new. (pronoun)
Her pen is lost. (adjective)	**Hers** is lost. (pronoun)
Our house is old. (adjective)	**Ours** is old. (pronoun)

You know that an apostrophe is used to make the possessive form of a noun. But an apostrophe is never used to form a possessive pronoun.

This book is **Carol's.**	This book is **hers.** (not **her's**)
Bob's bat is broken.	**His** bat is broken. (not **his'**)
Which is the **Ebys'** car?	Which is **theirs**? (not **their's**)

Do not confuse contractions and possessive pronouns. The only time an apostrophe is used with a personal pronoun is to form a contraction.

It's means "it is."
It's time to give the calf **its** milk.

You're means "you are."
You're not doing **your** own work.

They're means "they are."
They're riding **their** bicycles.

In the Bible, the archaic pronoun **thy** is used for **your,** and **thine** is used for **yours. Thine** is also used for **your** before words that begin with a vowel sound.

"**Thy** will be done" (Matthew 6:10).
    Thy means "your."

"**Thine** is the kingdom" (Matthew 6:13).
  Thine means "yours."

"Incline **thine** ear unto me" (Psalm 17:6).
  Thine means "your."

Remember: The possessive case pronouns are **my, mine, your, yours, his, her, hers, its, our, ours, their,** and **theirs.** The apostrophe is used in possessive nouns but never in possessive pronouns.

> **Oral Drill** >

A. Tell which words are pronouns. Tell whether each pronoun is in the **nominative, objective,** or **possessive** case.
  1. Jesus said, "Fear not; I am the first and the last."
  2. He had in His right hand seven stars, and out of His mouth went a sharp two-edged sword.
  3. Follow Me, and I will make you fishers of men.
  4. She poured the ointment on His feet and wiped them with the hairs of her head.
  5. She said, "They have no wine."
  6. He turned the water into wine. It tasted better than their wine.
  7. Be thou diligent to know the state of thy flocks, and look well to thy herds.
  8. If thine enemy hunger, feed him.

B. Tell which is the correct word in parentheses.
  1. (Their, They're) house is the red brick one.
  2. (Its, It's) never too late to do good.
  3. Look at that bright star. We know (its, it's) not a planet, because (its, it's) light twinkles.
  4. (Its, It's) the star called Rigel.
  5. (Your, You're) eyes are better than mine.

6. (Your, You're) seeing stars I cannot see.

7. (Your, You're) hearing must be good too.

> **Written Practice**

A. Copy the pronouns in these sentences. After each one, write **N** for nominative, **O** for objective, or **P** for possessive.

1. He lifted his rod over the sea.
2. The waters parted, and they crossed over.
3. They took their children and all their cattle with them.
4. She lifted her voice in thankful praise.
5. The Lord has done great things for us.
6. I will praise His Name forever.
7. He will bless you too.
8. We will sing with you and them.
9. Be Thou exalted, Lord, in Thine own strength: so will we sing and praise Thy power.
10. Unto Thee will I pray. My voice shalt Thou hear in the morning, O Lord.

B. Write the correct words.

1. (Their, They're) coming to see (your, you're) new house.
2. (Their, They're) house is a hundred years old.
3. (Its, It's) walls are made of heavy logs.
4. (Its, It's) interesting to see old houses.
5. (Your, You're) standing in the room where the slaves hid.
6. (Your, You're) head almost touches the ceiling.

> **Review and Practice**

A. Answer these questions from the "Remember" boxes in this chapter.

1. What are two ways that nominative case pronouns can be used?
2. What is one way that objective case pronouns can be used?

B. Copy the correct pronouns. Be ready to tell in class why you chose the pronoun you did.

1. Judy and (I, me) have finished sweeping the porches.
2. Was it (they, them) at the door?
3. Did Jerry see (they, them)?
4. The song leader was (he, him).
5. Judy welcomed the visitors and (she, her).
6. (We, Us) fifth graders will study adjectives next.
7. The sisters are Janet and (she, her).
8. The ministers will be Brother Stephen and (he, him).
9. The other students and (I, me) learned a new song last week.
10. Brother John taught the fourth graders and (we, us) about electricity.

C. Diagram each skeleton and each direct object, predicate nominative, or predicate adjective.

1. The unselfish lad shared his lunch.
2. The fish were small.
3. Jesus blessed the fish and bread.
4. Soon He had fed five thousand people.
5. Everyone was satisfied.
6. God's Word is bread for our souls today.

64. Nominative, Objective, and Possessive Pronouns

Pronouns have three cases: the **nominative case,** the **objective case,** and the **possessive case.** How can you be sure to use pronouns correctly in each case? Review the following points.

The nominative case pronouns are **I, you, he, she, it, we, they,** and the archaic pronoun **thou.** A nominative case pronoun may be used as a **subject** or a **predicate nominative** in a sentence.

> **Subject: They** walk to school.
> **Predicate nominative:** I am **he.**

Be sure to use the correct form when a subject is compound or when it is followed by an appositive. Use the pronoun alone in the sentence to help you choose the correct one.

> The teacher and (**they** or **them**?) cleaned the rooms.
> **Think: They** cleaned the rooms.
> **Say:**   The teacher and **they** cleaned the rooms.

> (**We** or **Us**?) girls washed the windows.
> **Think: We** washed the windows.
> **Say:**   **We** girls washed the windows.

A predicate nominative is a noun or pronoun that follows a linking verb and renames the subject. Pronouns used as predicate nominatives must be in the nominative case. Be especially careful with compound predicate nominatives.

> My sisters are **they.** (not **them**)
> The twins are **he** and **she.** (not **him** and **her**)

The objective case pronouns are **me, you, him, her, it, us, them,** and the archaic pronoun **thee.** An objective case pronoun may be used as a **direct object.** Remember that a direct object is a noun or pronoun in the predicate that receives action.

> **Direct object:** Mother brought **me.**

Be careful when a direct object is compound or is followed by an appositive. It is helpful to use the pronoun alone to decide which is the correct form.

Mother brought James and (**I** or **me**?).
>**Think:** Mother brought **me**.
>**Say:**   Mother brought James and **me**.

Sister Julia helped (**we** or **us**?) girls.
>**Think:** Sister Julia helped **us**.
>**Say:**   Sister Julia helped **us** girls.

The possessive case pronouns are listed below.

**my, mine, your, yours, his, her, hers, its,
our, ours, their, theirs**
(archaic forms) **thy, thine**

An apostrophe is used to form a possessive noun, but never to form a possessive pronoun.

>**Right:** Mary's doll   Ben's gloves
>**Wrong:** her' doll   his' gloves

Do not confuse contractions and possessive pronouns. The only time an apostrophe is used with a personal pronoun is to form a contraction.

>**It's** means "it is."   **It's** lying on **its** side.
>**You're** means "you are."   **You're** losing **your** keys.
>**They're** means "they are." **They're** picking **their** peas.

Study the following diagrams to review what you have learned.

>**Pronoun used in a compound subject:**
>Melinda and she came early.

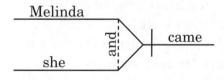

Pronoun used in a compound direct object:
Father helped Daniel and me.

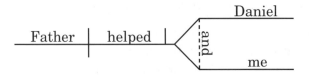

Pronoun used in a compound predicate nominative:
The workers were they and she.

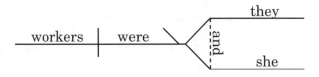

> Oral Drill

A. Read each sentence correctly. If it has a mistake, tell why it is wrong. If it has no mistake, say **correct.**
1. Their flying in the morning.
2. It's time to go for them.
3. Your plane was quite late.
4. You're dog is at the neighbor's house.
5. Margaret and her took care of the baby.
6. We called Joshua and he, but no one answered.
7. It was him that called us.
8. Grandmother thanked we girls for the work we did.
9. Us boys threw some hay down for the cows.
10. Thee hast proved my heart and tried me.
11. Alan and him did their work well.
12. You should thank Grandmother and she for it.
13. Gerald's guests are Herbert and him.
14. The visitors were Grace and she.
15. It was they and she.
16. Thou visitest the earth and waterest it, O Lord.

B. Choose the correct pronouns in parentheses. Diagram the skeletons, direct objects, and predicate nominatives on the chalkboard. Write **A** above each action verb and **L** above each linking verb. Write **DO** above each direct object and **PN** above each predicate nominative.

1. Philip and (he, him) followed Jesus.
2. Lillian and (she, her) called Linda and (we, us).
3. Your helpers will be Dale and (he, him).
4. It was (they, them).
5. Harlan will lead (they, them) and (we, us) through the city.
6. (I, Me) will guide (thou, thee) with Mine eye.

> Written Practice >

A. Write the correct pronouns. After each one, write **S** for subject, **DO** for direct object, or **PN** for predicate nominative.

1. Melody and (she, her) sing well.
2. The bricklayers are Richard and (he, him).
3. You should tell Nancy and (she, her).
4. (Thou, Thee) shalt love thy neighbor as thyself.
5. Noah and (he, him) brought the strawberry plants.
6. We could hear (he, him) from outside.
7. The caller was (he, him).
8. The Lord will help (thou, thee).
9. (We, Us) boys sang while we worked.
10. Nelson knew (we, us) boys.
11. (Thou, Thee) hast delivered me.
12. I thank (Thou, Thee).

B. Write the correct words.

1. (Its, It's) nearly time to leave.
2. (Its, It's) nest has green and blue threads in it.
3. (Your, You're) pens are in (your, you're) pocket.
4. (Your, You're) welcome to come again.

5. (Their, They're) coming to paint the porch.

6. (Their, They're) children have gone to school.

C. Write the correct pronouns. Then diagram the sentence skeletons, direct objects, and predicate nominatives.

1. Irma and (I, me) found a bird's nest.

2. The teachers are Sister Joyce and (she, her).

3. You should call (she, her).

4. We will help Mark and (he, him).

5. Esther and (they, them) picked the apples.

6. Rebecca and (she, her) are the waitresses.

7. The peddler was (he, him).

8. Father will pay Edwin and (he, him).

> Review and Practice >

Write **S, Q, C,** or **E** to tell whether each sentence is a statement, question, command, or exclamation. (There are only two exclamations.) Also write the correct end punctuation.

1. Who gave supplies to Moses for the tabernacle

2. God said the people should give supplies

3. Give offerings willingly

4. What a great amount of gold and silver they brought

5. Where did the children of Israel get all the gold

6. The Egyptians gave the Israelites gold and other precious things before they left Egypt

7. How beautiful the tabernacle must have been

8. God wanted to dwell among His people

65. Demonstrative Pronouns

A **demonstrative** pronoun is used to point out something. The four demonstrative pronouns are **this, that, these,** and **those.**

> **This** is my book; **that** is yours.
> **These** are my papers; **those** are yours.

Use **this** and **these** to refer to things nearby. Use **that** and **those** to refer to things farther away. When pointing out a single person, place, or thing, say **this** or **that.** They are singular pronouns. When pointing out more than one person, place, or thing, say **these** or **those.** They are plural pronouns.

This, that, these, and **those** are often used as adjectives that tell **which.** When they modify nouns, they are used as adjectives. Otherwise, they are used as pronouns.

> **This** book is mine. (adjective that tells which book)
>
> **That** pen is yours. (adjective that tells which pen)
> **This** is my book. (pronoun that means **this book**)
> **That** is your pen. (pronoun that means **that pen**)

Do not say **this here** or **that there.** Using **here** and **there** with demonstrative pronouns is unnecessary because these pronouns already point out things.

> **Wrong:** This here is a rare bird.
> **Right:** **This** is a rare bird.

> **Wrong:** Have you read that there book?
> **Right:** Have you read **that** book?

Never use the word **them** as a demonstrative pronoun.

> **Wrong:** Them are high mountains.
> **Right:** **Those** are high mountains.

> **Remember:** The demonstrative pronouns are **this, that, these,** and **those.** They are used to point out things. Do not use **here** or **there** with demonstrative pronouns. Do not use **them** as a demonstrative pronoun.

Oral Drill

A. Correct the following sentences. Read each sentence correctly several times.
1. These are ripe, but them are still green.
2. I will take those there.
3. These here apples are better than them.
4. Whose paper is this here?
5. This here dog belongs to my brother and me.
6. That stool under my feet is higher than this one in the far corner.
7. Them are my boots.

B. Tell whether each boldface word is an **adjective** or a **pronoun.**
1. **These** birds are rare.
2. **That** is another rare bird.
3. The bird in **this** picture is extinct.
4. What kind of birds are **these**?
5. **Those** are sea gulls.
6. **That** bird is an albatross.
7. **This** is a penguin from Antarctica.
8. **Those** birds live in Australia.

Written Practice

A. Write these sentences correctly.
1. Them scissors are dull.
2. Those there clouds look like rain clouds.

Photodisc by Getty Images

3. These mountains in the distance are very high.
4. This here is my favorite season.
5. Them trousers have worn well.
6. These here are sweeter than them.
7. Please give me those there books.
8. That there is the tallest building in the world.

B. Write **adj.** or **pron.** to tell whether each boldface word is an adjective or a pronoun.
1. **This** has been a rainy year.
2. **That** year was dry.
3. **These** are weather records.
4. **This** instrument is a barometer.
5. What do **these** numbers mean?
6. **That** is a cumulus cloud.
7. What kind of clouds are **those**?
8. **Those** cirrus clouds are several miles high.

C. Use all the demonstrative pronouns in sentences of your own. Use them as pronouns and not as adjectives. Tell about things you saw on your last school trip or on a family trip.

> **Review and Practice** >

Copy the chart, and fill in the missing words.

Singular	Singular Possessive	Plural	Plural Possessive
1. cat	———	———	———
2. mouse	———	———	———
3. ox	———	———	———
4. sheep	———	———	———
5. tree	———	———	———
6. child	———	———	———
7. boy	———	———	———
8. man	———	———	———
9. brother	———	———	———
10. woman	———	———	———

> **Challenge Exercise** >

Find and write inspiring verses from the Bible that use **thou, ye, thee, thy,** and **thine.** Find two examples for each archaic pronoun.

66. Writing an Interesting Friendly Letter

Friendly letters are written for various reasons. The most common reason is simply to share news and information. We may write to tell about a special happening. Or we may just tell about everyday happenings, such as the weather, things at school, and things at home.

When you write a letter, think of things your friend enjoys. If he likes to watch birds, describe the unusual birds you have seen lately. If he enjoys traveling, write about a trip you have taken. Be sure to answer any questions the other person asked when he last wrote to you.

Write simply and sincerely, just as if you were speaking to the other person. Do not try to copy another person's way of writing. Express yourself in a way that is natural for you, remembering to use good grammar.

Sometimes a friendly letter has a special purpose. Perhaps we want to invite a friend to come for a visit. We may be answering an invitation we have received. We may write to get advice, help, or information. Or we may write to apologize for a wrong we did or a mistake we made. Some letters are written for more than one purpose.

When we have stayed in another family's home overnight, we may write a thank-you letter for their hospitality. (A letter thanking someone for meals and lodging is sometimes called a bread-and-butter note.) Writing a thank-you letter is especially proper when we have received a gift or special favor from someone.

Be specific when you write for a special purpose. If you are thanking someone for a gift, name the gift and tell why it pleases you or how you will use it. If you are apologizing for a wrong, be sure to say clearly what you did and why you see that it was wrong. If you are asking for information, be careful to state exactly what you want.

Write courteously by making your letter neat, correct, and easy to read. Always write kindly and considerately. Use clear sentences, and choose exact words. Proofread your letter for correct grammar, punctuation, and spelling, and for neat penmanship. Always be sure the letter you send is the kind of letter you would like to receive.

A. Read the following letter, and answer the questions below.

> 234 Angel Lane
> Beaver, AR 72613
> September 22, 20—
>
> Dear Uncle George,
>
> I was really surprised when Father gave me the present you sent with him! I have wanted a handbook on birds ever since I began to learn about birds in school. We have many kinds of birds around our place, and I would really like to identify them better. The fine book you gave is a great help in doing that. I have already discovered that we have two kinds of wrens right near the house. Thank you for such a suitable gift and for your thoughtfulness in giving it.
>
> Your loving nephew,
> Wilbur

1. What special purpose does this letter have?
2. What did Wilbur write to show that the gift was something he truly appreciated?
3. For what two things did Wilbur thank his uncle?
4. What writing skills did Wilbur use to make the letter clear and courteous?

B. Tell what kind of letter should be written for each occasion listed below. Choose from these: **sharing, invitation, answer to an invitation, thank-you letter, special request, apology.**

1. You want to ask James to go to the zoo with your family.
2. Keith has been sick for a long time and feels discouraged.
3. Margaret made a scrapbook for you while you were sick.
4. Uncle Mark has invited you to go along to Ohio.
5. You had promised to write to Grandmother soon, but forgot it for a month.
6. You want Marie's recipe for gingerbread.

> **Written Practice**

A. Write a letter for one of the occasions in Oral Drill, Part B.

B. Write a thank-you letter to your grandmother for the enjoyable week-long visit you had recently. Mention some specific things that you especially appreciated. Use correct letter form, neat handwriting, and proper spelling, grammar, and punctuation.

67. Indefinite Pronouns

Some pronouns do not refer to definite persons, places, things, or ideas. They are **indefinite pronouns.** Here is a list of indefinite pronouns.

one	**no one**	**each**
anyone	**anybody**	**both**
everyone	**everybody**	**few**
someone	**somebody**	**several**
	nobody	**many**

The indefinite pronouns in the following list are singular. They must be used with a singular verb.

one	**no one**	**each**
anyone	**anybody**	
everyone	**everybody**	
someone	**somebody**	
	nobody	

One is always singular, and **body** is too. So an indefinite pronoun with **one** or **body** in it is singular. It takes a singular verb.

> **Everyone** <u>is</u> in his seat.
>
> **Nobody** <u>wants</u> to lose his place.
>
> **Everybody** <u>has brought</u> a note.
>
> **Anybody** <u>is</u> welcome.

The following indefinite pronouns are plural and must be used with plural verbs.

> **both**   **few**   **several**   **many**
>
> **Both** <u>write</u> to Grandmother regularly.
>
> **Many** <u>have</u> never <u>seen</u> a comet.

In some sentences, an indefinite pronoun is followed by a **prepositional phrase.** A prepositional phrase begins with a **preposition** and ends with a noun or a pronoun (the **object** of the preposition). Some prepositional phrases are **in the tree, for you, of the men,** and **with them.**

The prepositional phrase after an indefinite pronoun usually begins with **of.** Here are four examples. Do you know which verb form to use?

> One **of the girls** (**is** or **are**?) here.
> Each **of the children** (**bring** or **brings**?) a lunch.
> Several **of the pupils** (**walk** or **walks**?) to school.
> Many **of them** (**come** or **comes**?) early.

The verb in a sentence must agree with the subject, not with some other word. The subject of a sentence is never in a prepositional phrase. The verbs in the sentences above must agree with the subjects, not with the objects of the prepositions.

> <u>One</u> of the girls <u>is</u> here.
> (One is here.)

> <u>Each</u> of the children <u>brings</u> a lunch.
> (Each brings a lunch.)

> <u>Several</u> of the pupils <u>walk</u> to school.
> (Several walk to school.)

> <u>Many</u> of them <u>come</u> early.
> (Many come early.)

Remember: Indefinite pronouns do not refer to definite persons, places, things, or ideas. Indefinite pronouns like **someone, anybody,** and **each** must be used with a singular verb. The indefinite pronouns **both, few, several,** and **many** must be used with a plural verb.

◇ Oral Drill ◇

Tell which words are indefinite pronouns, and whether each pronoun is singular or plural. Then choose the correct verb in parentheses. Read each sentence correctly several times.

1. Everybody (have, has) studied the lesson.
2. No one (was, were) disappointed with the new books.
3. Somebody (have, has) left those books here.
4. (Was, Were) both of the windows broken?
5. Both (was, were) cracked.
6. One of the doors (was, were) open.
7. Several of the boxes (was, were) dented.
8. Few of the children (remember, remembers) Brother Martin.
9. Not one of them (is, are) more than ten years old.
10. Each of those girls (sew, sews) her own dresses.
11. (Do, Does) each help her mother?
12. Nobody (want, wants) to have a low grade.

◇ Written Practice ◇

A. Write ten indefinite pronouns that are singular.

B. Write four indefinite pronouns that are plural.

C. Write the correct verbs.
1. Everyone (have, has) instructions now.
2. One of the helpers (is, are) enough.
3. Both of the boys (do, does) good work.
4. Everyone (know, knows) the answer.
5. Nobody (tell, tells) me where it is.
6. Everyone (sing, sings) heartily in music class.
7. Several of the teachers (give, gives) ideas for the art classes.
8. Each one of us (enjoy, enjoys) the classes.
9. Many of us (learn, learns) new skills quickly.

10. Somebody (teach, teaches) the art class.
11. Everybody (bring, brings) a notebook.
12. Few of us (complain, complains) about the work.

> **Review and Practice** >

A. Write the correct words for the definitions below.

concrete noun   indefinite pronoun
abstract noun   personal pronoun
direct object   demonstrative pronoun
predicate nominative

1. A word that takes the place of a noun and refers mainly to persons.
2. A word that names something which can be touched.
3. A word that receives the action of a verb.
4. A word that points out something.
5. A word that names an idea.
6. A word that renames the subject.
7. A word that refers to a person, place, thing, or idea without meaning a definite one.

B. Write correctly each word that needs a capital letter.
1. the amazon river in south america is the largest river in the world.
2. mr. and mrs. brown were missionaries in peru.
3. egypt and ethiopia are countries in africa.
4. guatemala city is the capital of guatemala.
5. the philippines are islands in the pacific ocean.
6. the longest river in guatemala, the motagua, flows into the caribbean sea.

68. Interrogative Pronouns

The word **interrogative** has to do with questions. **Interrogative pronouns** are pronouns that we use to ask questions. **Who, whom, whose, which,** and **what** are interrogative pronouns.

The pronouns **who, whom,** and **whose** refer to persons. **Which** refers to persons or things, and **what** refers only to things.

Who is that man?	**Which** is your sister?
Whom did you see?	**Which** is her coat?
Whose is this puppy?	**What** was that noise?

Who is in the nominative case. It may be used as the subject of a sentence.

> **Who** is here?

Whom is in the objective case. It may be used as a direct object.

> John helped **whom**?

When you are not sure whether to use **who** or **whom** in a sentence, it is helpful to substitute **he** for **who,** and **him** for **whom.**

> You saw (**who** or **whom**?)?
> > **Think:** You saw him.
> > **Say:**   You saw **whom**?

> (**Who** or **Whom**?) is coming?
> > **Think: He** is coming.
> > **Say:**   Who is coming?

Be careful when a sentence has inverted order. Sometimes the direct object comes at the beginning of the sentence. Change it to normal order to help decide which pronoun is correct.

(**Who** or **Whom**?) did Paul see?
> **Think:** Paul did see (**who** or **whom**?)?
> > Paul did see **whom**? (direct object)
> **Say:**   **Whom** did Paul see?

Remember that a direct object receives the action of an action verb. A direct object must be in the objective case. So the correct form for direct objects is **whom,** not **who.**

> **Whom** will we visit?
> We will visit **whom**? (direct object)

Whose is in the possessive case. It does not have an apostrophe. Be careful not to confuse **whose** with the contraction **who's. Who's** means "who is."

> **Wrong:** Who's bicycle is this?
> **Right:** **Whose** bicycle is this?
> > **Who's** coming to the door?

Remember: The interrogative pronouns are **who, whom, whose, which,** and **what. Who** is a nominative case pronoun; it is used for the subject. **Whom** is an objective case pronoun; it is used for the direct object. Do not confuse **whose** with the contraction **who's.**

> ⟩ Oral Drill ⟩

A. Tell which words are interrogative pronouns.
1. Whom shall we send? Who will go for us?
2. Which is the picture you drew?
3. What is he doing with those plants?
4. Whose flowerpot is this?
5. Whom did you see?

B. Tell whether each interrogative pronoun is used as a **subject** or a **direct object.** On the chalkboard, diagram the sentence skeletons and the direct objects.

1. Whom did you tell?
2. Who is there?
3. Whom should I help?
4. Which did you choose?
5. Whom shall we honor?

C. Tell which pronoun in parentheses is correct. (Remember to try substituting **he** for **who,** and **him** for **whom.**)

1. (Who, Whom) did you see out there?
2. (Who, Whom) was chosen to give the report?
3. Mark helped (who, whom)?
4. (Who, Whom) can see all things?
5. (Who, Whom) shall I call?
6. (Whose, Who's) car is that?
7. (Whose, Who's) coming tomorrow?
8. (Whose, Who's) hands have made our great world?

D. In Part C, numbers 1–5, tell whether each interrogative pronoun is used as a **subject** or a **direct object.**

E. Practice reading correctly each sentence in Part C above. For sentences with **whose** or **who's,** tell whether or not to use an apostrophe.

> Written Practice

A. Copy the interrogative pronoun in each sentence.

1. Whom did you help?
2. Which shall I choose?
3. Whose can this be?
4. What was that?
5. Who has seen my kitten?

B. Find each sentence in which the direct object comes first. Rewrite it so that the direct object comes last.

   1. Whom are we meeting?

   2. Who is in the car?

   3. Who said that?

   4. What has he said?

   5. Whom did you tell?

C. Diagram all the skeletons and direct objects in Part B.

D. Write the correct words. Be ready to tell in class why you chose the ones you did.

   1. (Who, Whom) is on the telephone?

   2. You invited (who, whom)?

   3. (Who, Whom) called Peter?

   4. (Who, Whom) did the angel encourage?

   5. (Who, Whom) did the apostle Paul help?

   6. (Who, Whom) was in the shipwreck?

   7. (Whose, Who's) out in the barn?

   8. (Whose, Who's) are these gloves?

   9. (Whose, Who's) going to read the story?

  10. In (whose, who's) name should we pray?

E. Use three interrogative pronouns in sentences of your own. Write questions you might ask a stranger your age who visits your church.

---

69. Addressing an Envelope

You may be able to write interesting friendly letters. Your letter may have excellent words of cheer or encouragement. But if your letter never reaches the person to whom it is sent, what good does it do? You must know how to address an envelope

correctly so that the letter can get to its destination.

The receiver's address should be written in about the center of the envelope. It usually contains three lines. The person's name is written in the first line, and the street address (or route and box number) in the second line. The third line has the city, state or province, and Zip Code or postal code. If the title **Mr., Mrs.,** or **Miss** is used, it should be written before the person's name.

The writer's address should be written in the upper left corner. This is the return address. The same arrangement is used for the return address as for the receiver's address.

The postal service has approved a two-letter abbreviation for each state. These abbreviations are written with all capital letters and no periods.

AL Alabama	LA Louisiana	OH Ohio
AK Alaska	ME Maine	OK Oklahoma
AZ Arizona	MD Maryland	OR Oregon
AR Arkansas	MA Massachusetts	PA Pennsylvania
CA California	MI Michigan	RI Rhode Island
CO Colorado	MN Minnesota	SC South Carolina
CT Connecticut	MS Mississippi	SD South Dakota
DE Delaware	MO Missouri	TN Tennessee
FL Florida	MT Montana	TX Texas
GA Georgia	NE Nebraska	UT Utah
HI Hawaii	NV Nevada	VT Vermont
ID Idaho	NH New Hampshire	VA Virginia
IL Illinois	NJ New Jersey	WA Washington
IN Indiana	NM New Mexico	WV West Virginia
IA Iowa	NY New York	WI Wisconsin
KS Kansas	NC North Carolina	WY Wyoming
KY Kentucky	ND North Dakota	

The following illustration shows an envelope properly addressed for mailing.

Luke Martin
72 Oak St.
Claysburg, PA 16625

MR ALVIN B YODER
214 HARRISON AVE
EASTON MD 21601

> Oral Drill >

Answer the following questions about addressing an envelope.

1. Why is it important to address an envelope clearly and correctly?
2. What are the abbreviations for **Street, Road,** and **Avenue**?
3. What is the postal service abbreviation for each of these states?

   a. Pennsylvania   e. Ohio
   b. Virginia   f. California
   c. Illinois   g. Maryland
   d. Georgia   h. Your own state

4. What is your own Zip Code? What punctuation separates the Zip Code from the name of the state in an address?
5. Whose address goes in the upper left corner? What is it called?

Written Practice

A. Make "envelopes" by drawing two rectangles about four inches by six inches each. Address them correctly for the following letters.

1. A letter from Lloyd Zook, 222 dawnlight trail, warren AR 71671, to Floyd R. Shenk, route 4, box 2234, athens, al 35611.

2. A letter from Mrs. Alma n. Kreider, route 1 box 414, frostburg, md 21532, to dr. Amos West, 3134 evergreen ave., danville, ky 40422

B. Write the postal service abbreviation for each of these states.

1. Tennessee	5. Indiana
2. Massachusetts	6. Florida
3. Texas	7. Michigan
4. Arizona	8. Your own state

C. Write a letter to a friend or relative, and address an envelope for it. After the teacher corrects and grades the letter, you may copy it again and mail it.

Review and Practice

List these phrases on your paper: **personal pronouns, demonstrative pronouns, indefinite pronouns,** and **interrogative pronouns.** After each one, write three pronouns from the following group which belong in that class.

him	few	you	anyone
what	some	these	those
this	whom	which	us

Write to someone about your age in a school in another state or country. Give your name, age, and grade in school. Tell something about your family, your father's occupation, and your home. Tell about your interests at home and at school. Tell anything else about yourself and your location that would be of interest to the receiver. This letter should be suitable for mailing.

---

70. Chapter 6 Review

A. Give the correct words for the definitions below.

pronoun	demonstrative pronoun
antecedent	indefinite pronoun
predicate nominative	interrogative pronoun
direct object	personal pronoun

1. The word for which a pronoun stands.
2. A word that receives action.
3. A word like **anyone, everybody,** or **both.**
4. A word that takes the place of a noun.
5. The word **this, that, these,** or **those.**
6. A word like **I, him, it,** or **them.**
7. A word in the predicate that renames the subject.
8. A word like **whose, whom, which,** or **what.**

B. Give each pronoun and its antecedent.

> When Moses and his people
>   From Egypt's land did flee—
> Their enemies behind them,
>   And in front of them the sea—
> God raised the waters like a wall,
>   And He opened up the way;
> And the God that lived in Moses' time
>   Is just the same today.
> —*Author unknown*

C. Give pronouns to replace the nouns in bold print.
1. **Mary and Martha** invited **Jesus** into their home.
2. **Lazarus** was **Mary and Martha's** brother.
3. **Mary** sat at **Jesus'** feet.
4. **Joann and you** were singing **the new song** while **Mother and I** read a story about the song.

D. Give each pronoun, and tell what case it is.
1. We should fear God and honor our leaders.
2. A tree is known by its fruit.
3. We love Him because He first loved us.
4. Keep your heart with all diligence.
5. She worketh willingly with her hands.
6. Our help is in the Lord. He made heaven and earth.
7. I will praise Thee forever because Thou hast done it, and I will wait on Thy Name, for it is good before Thy saints.
8. Thou openest Thine hand and satisfiest the desire of every living thing.

E. Give the archaic pronouns that mean the same as the following pronouns.
1. you (nominative)   3. your
2. you (objective)   4. yours

F. Name the five parts of a friendly letter.

G. Tell what kind of letter should be written for each occasion listed below. Choose from these: **sharing, invitation, answer to an invitation, thank-you letter, special request, apology.**
   1. You have three new calves in the barn.
   2. You forgot to send a card to your friend on her birthday.
   3. Aunt Martha has invited you to go along to a museum.
   4. You want to ask your cousin Mark to go with you to the museum.
   5. Jacob has broken his leg and must stay in bed a long time.
   6. You want Aunt Sarah's advice on how to take care of a poinsettia.
   7. Uncle Charles has given you a bicycle.

> Written Practice >

A. Write the correct word for each sentence. Be ready to tell in class why you chose the word you did.
   1. Sharon and (she, her) wrote letters.
   2. Please call Mark and (he, him).
   3. My daily helpers are (he, him) and (she, her).
   4. Arnold and (he, him) swept the basement.
   5. (Their, They're) bringing Joshua and (he, him).
   6. (Their, They're) children help (he, him) outside.
   7. Call (she, her) before (its, it's) too late.
   8. Mark and (he, him) have cleaned (its, it's) pen.
   9. The verses are long, but (your, you're) learning (they, them) well.
   10. One of the pupils (have, has) learned the whole chapter.
   11. Everyone (was, were) ready to learn the poem.
   12. Nobody (want, wants) to miss the train.
   13. Each of the girls (bring, brings) a dish.

14. Several of the children (was, were) eleven years old.
15. Only one of them (is, are) thirteen years old.
16. (Who, Whom) is at the door?
17. (Who, Whom) did you see at the meeting?
18. (Who, Whom) was tardy?
19. (Whose, Who's) baby are you holding?
20. (Whose, Who's) her mother?

B. Rewrite each sentence, using demonstrative pronouns correctly.
1. This here chair is comfortable.
2. That there stool is lighter than this one.
3. Them people are shopping for a new carpet.
4. Them who fear the Lord need not be afraid.

C. Diagram the skeletons, direct objects, and predicate nominatives.
1. Do you know him?
2. It was Grandmother and I.
3. Sharon and I helped Grandfather and her in the garden.
4. The tailor was measuring him for a suit.
5. The teacher called them inside.
6. Who reads the Bible?

D. Write these parts of a friendly letter correctly.
   1. nov 11 20—
   2. dear timothy
   3. yours truly
   4. john m keefer

E. Draw rectangles about four inches by six inches, and write
   the following addresses correctly in them.
   1. A letter from Carl Wise, Route 3, box 671, Barnett, MO
      65011, to Jerry R. Brown, 245 Village drive, Johnson, VT
      05656
   2. A letter from Amy w. Martin, Route 2, box 116, roseville,
      CA 95661, to wilma s wenger, route 1, box 73, Bedford, OH
      44146

F. Write the postal service abbreviation for each of these states.
   1. Kansas   5. West Virginia
   2. New York   6. Colorado
   3. Montana   7. Hawaii
   4. Oregon   8. Your own state

The Wind

I hear you blowing through the trees;
I like to feel the nice warm breeze.
Sometimes you howl, sometimes you roar
Or whistle through the keyhole . . . or
You blow with all your might and main
And turn into a hurricane.
You make my kite go sailing high;
You puff it up into the sky.
You make leaves dance across the lawn;
I see the path where you have gone.
Just yesterday you ran away,
But you came back again today.
You steal my hat, you blow my hair;
I see your mischief everywhere.
You're rough and noisy when you play,
But, Wind, I like you anyway.

See how many descriptive verbs you can find in this poem. Which words are adverbs? Which ones are adjectives?

Chapter 7
Adjectives and Adverbs

Adjectives

Descriptive Adjectives	Limiting Adjectives
What Kind of	***Which***
Color:	*Articles:*
red, green	a, an, the
brown, pink	*Demonstratives:*
Size:	this, that
tiny, huge	these, those
high, long	*Ordinal Numbers:*
Shape	first, second
round, oval	tenth, fiftieth
square, oblong	***Whose***
Taste	*Possessive Nouns*
bitter, salty	boy's lady's
spicy, sweet	Paul's, Mary's
Sound	bird's, men's
harsh, musical	*Possessive Pronouns*
shrill, loud	my, our, its
Touch	your, his
rough, sharp	her, their
cold, soft	***How Many***
Traits	*Cardinal Numbers*
kind, thoughtful	two, seven
lazy, angry	twelve, ninety
Others	*Indefinite Numbers*
late, swift	few, several
Scottish, French	some, many

Adjectives are words that describe, or modify, nouns and pronouns. Descriptive adjectives tell **what kind of.** *Limiting adjectives tell* **which, whose,** *and* **how many.**

71. What Are Adjectives?

Adjectives are words that describe, or modify, nouns and pronouns. They tell **which, whose, how many,** and **what kind of.** In the following phrases, all the adjectives are in bold print.

these small seeds   **the four green** frogs
a thin, timid kitten   **their ancient** tradition

Adjectives that tell **what kind of** are **descriptive** adjectives. There are hundreds of descriptive adjectives. Here are a few of them, listed in various groups.

color: red, orange, bronze, blue
size: tiny, wide, high, broad
shape: round, square, oval, triangular
taste: bitter, spicy, sweet, tart
sound: harsh, shrill, quiet, harmonious
touch: rough, cold, soft, fuzzy
traits: kind, considerate, lazy, stubborn

Some descriptive adjectives are made from nouns by adding adjective suffixes. Here are some examples. Can you give the nouns from which they are formed?

-ish: babyish, foolish, selfish, feverish
-like: childlike, lifelike, cloudlike, Godlike
-ic: historic, angelic, volcanic, Icelandic
-en: woolen, earthen, wooden, silken

Sometimes an adjective looks like another part of speech. Notice the boldface words in the sentences below.

Lois found a pretty **stone.**
   (noun; names a thing)

God said that the Israelites should **stone** Achan.
   (verb; shows action)

A high **stone** wall surrounded the castle.
(adjective; tells what kind of wall)

The janitor was **opening** the windows.
(verb; shows action)

Steam rose from an **opening** in the ground.
(noun; names a thing)

Brother Charles led the **opening** song.
(adjective; tells which song)

How can you be sure whether a word is an adjective or another part of speech? You can tell by the way the word is used in a sentence. Whenever a word modifies a noun by telling **which, whose, how many,** or **what kind of,** it is an adjective.

Adjectives are diagramed on slanted lines beneath the noun they modify. They may modify a subject, a predicate nominative, a direct object, or the object of a preposition.

Adjectives modifying a subject and a predicate nominative:

That black animal is **a mother** cat.

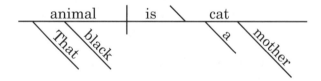

Adjectives modifying the object of a preposition and a direct object:

One of **the** boys caught **a big, lively** bass.

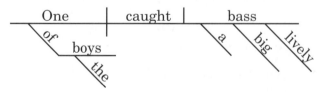

> **Remember:** An adjective is a word that modifies a noun or a pronoun. An adjective tells **which, whose, how many,** or **what kind of.**

> Oral Drill >

A. Supply descriptive adjectives for the blanks below.
1. four ——— ——— geese
2. my ——— ——— bicycle
3. a ——— ——— mountain
4. that ——— ——— animal
5. some ——— ——— children
6. the ——— ——— book

B. Tell which words are adjectives. On the chalkboard, diagram the sentences.
1. The beautiful stone wall was falling.
2. The clever insects built a secure shelter.
3. The tall dark-haired boy is a good batter.
4. The patchwork quilt is a beautiful one.
5. God hates a proud, deceitful look.

> Written Practice >

A. Write two descriptive adjectives to modify each noun.
1. traveler   3. clouds   5. hound
2. cabin   4. answer   6. flower

B. Write a synonym for each of these descriptive adjectives. Be sure your answers are descriptive adjectives.
1. big   3. hard
2. small   4. different

C. Diagram these sentences.
1. Righteous Noah was a faithful, godly man.
2. Mother served hot, tasty soup.
3. The thick black smoke covered the cloudless blue sky.
4. Jesus is a faithful Mediator.
5. Our great God is a merciful Father.

D. Write the definition of an adjective.

> Review and Practice >

A. Write the definition for each part of speech below.
1. noun   2. verb   3. pronoun

B. Write the correct word for each description.

     simple subject   direct object
     simple predicate   predicate nominative

1. It follows a linking verb and renames the subject.
2. It receives action.
3. It tells **who** or **what** the sentence is about.
4. It expresses action or being.

     concrete noun   forms of **be**
     abstract noun   linking verb
     action verb

5. It is a form of **be** or a verb like **taste, feel, smell, sound, look, appear.**
6. am, is, are, was, were, be, been, being
7. It names something that can be seen or touched.
8. It names something that cannot be seen or touched.
9. It tells what is happening.

C. In Chapter 6 you learned that some possessive pronouns are used as adjectives, and others are used only as pronouns. Two of them can be used as adjectives and as pronouns. Adjectives modify nouns, but pronouns stand alone.

Write two headings on your paper as follows, and write the possessive pronouns under the correct headings. The first two of each kind are done for you.

Possessive Pronouns Used as Adjectives:
> my, your

Possessive Pronouns Used as Pronouns:
> mine, yours

—————————————

72. Limiting Adjectives

Adjectives that tell **which, whose,** and **how many** are **limiting adjectives.** They limit the meaning of nouns or pronouns in certain ways. There are many kinds of limiting adjectives.

The articles **a, an,** and **the** are limiting adjectives that tell **which. A** is used before consonant sounds, and **an** is used before vowel sounds.

a hat	**an** apple
a uniform	**an** hour

The demonstrative words **this, that, these,** and **those** can be limiting adjectives. They tell **which** when they modify a noun or a pronoun.

this day	**that** one	**these** hills

Possessive nouns are used as limiting adjectives that tell **whose.** Remember that they always need apostrophes.

John's house	**lion's** den	**Carl's** work

Some possessive pronouns are also used as limiting adjectives that tell **whose.** They are the pronouns **my, your, his, her, its,**

our, and **their.** These pronouns are used as adjectives because they modify nouns. Remember that possessive pronouns never need apostrophes.

  my pen   **your** cat **his** pet   **its** food

The possessive pronouns **mine, yours, hers, ours,** and **theirs** are different. These words are not adjectives, because they do not modify nouns. They stand alone, and they refer to both the owner and the thing owned.

  Which are **your** boots? (adjective)
  Which boots are **yours**? (pronoun; means **your boots**)

  Her coat is on a hanger. (adjective)
  Hers is on a hanger. (pronoun; means **her coat**)

The possessive pronouns **his** and **its** may be used as adjectives and as pronouns.

  This is **his** Bible. (adjective)
  This Bible is **his.** (pronoun; means **his Bible**)

Many number words are limiting adjectives that tell **how many.** Some are exact **cardinal numbers,** such as **one, two, three,** and **ten.** Others are **indefinite numbers,** such as **some, many, every, each,** and **all. Ordinal numbers** like **first, sixth,** and **tenth** are also limiting adjectives. Ordinal numbers tell **which.**

  Jesus had **twelve** disciples. (cardinal number)
  Some wise men came to Bethlehem. (indefinite number)
  Jesus arose on the **third** day. (ordinal number)

Remember: Adjectives modify nouns and pronouns. Adjectives can be descriptive or limiting.

> Oral Drill >

A. Find the adjectives in these sentences. Tell whether they are **descriptive** or **limiting.**
 1. The first loud crash frightened the unprepared workers.
 2. Our old yellow cat has seven tiny new kittens.
 3. Those careful boys have saved every tender plant.

B. Tell whether each boldface word is a **pronoun** or an **adjective.** If it is an adjective, tell which word it modifies.
 1. **That** man bought **our** farm.
 2. **Their** house is not like **ours.**
 3. **Each** has **its** advantages.
 4. **Whose** coat is hanging on **this** hook?
 5. **Whose** is it?

C. Diagram these sentences on the chalkboard.
 1. Several loud blasts rocked the old boiler.
 2. Our little brother did a careful, tidy job.
 3. The last warm hamburger disappeared.
 4. My first teacher was a careful planner.
 5. The little airplane dipped its red wings.

> Written Practice >

A. Copy all the adjectives in these sentences. After each one, write **D** for descriptive or **L** for limiting.
 1. Every young child should learn the first great Bible commandment.
 2. One happy leper thanked his merciful Healer.
 3. Jesus' true friends obey Him.
 4. Those people serve the Lord.
 5. The five foolish virgins could not enter the closed door.
 6. The bold Jezebel was a wicked queen.

B. Copy each boldface word, and write **A** for adjective or **P** for pronoun after it. If it is an adjective, also write the word it modifies.

1. **Some** of these must be **your** pencils.
2. **Those** may be **hers.**
3. **Some** books are **yours.**
4. **These** are **our** papers.

C. Diagram these sentences.

1. Your little sister is a careful worker.
2. The two hungry boys ate several delicious hamburgers.
3. His loyal friend walked many miles.
4. Every interested pupil may read these fascinating books.
5. The hungry mice have eaten some yellow corn.

D. Write the first ten ordinal numbers.

Review and Practice

Write the correct words.

1. The elephant (raised, rose) the man with his trunk.
2. Then he (set, sat) the man on his back.
3. The elephants (lay, lie) the trees down easily.
4. The men will (let, leave) the elephants move the heavy logs.
5. They will not (let, leave) until the work is finished.
6. (Can, May) I touch an elephant?
7. (Can, May) an elephant pick up a peanut without crushing the shell?
8. (Can, May) he (teach, learn) to walk as quietly as a mouse?
9. No one needs to (teach, learn) an elephant how to do those things.
10. I (should have, should of) known.

> Challenge Exercise >

See if you can give all the possessive pronouns in seven pairs. The first word in each pair should be an adjective. (Two pairs will be "twins.")

Example: my—mine

●━●━●━●━●━●━●━●

73. Predicate Adjectives

Adjectives are words that modify nouns. They usually come before the nouns they modify.

Those **glossy green** fruits are avocados.
Many **discouraged, unsuccessful** students have turned their lives around.

An adjective may also come after a linking verb and modify the subject. This is a **predicate adjective.**

This boy is **honest.**
Honest tells what kind of boy.

The sky looked **dark.**
Dark tells what kind of sky.

The apple pie smelled **fresh** and **spicy.**
Fresh and **spicy** tell what kind of apple pie.

Review the list of linking verbs. Be sure you know them by memory.

Forms of *be*: am, is, are, was, were, be, been, being

"Sometimes linking verbs":
taste, feel, smell, sound, look, appear

To find a predicate adjective, first find the verb. It must be a linking verb, or the sentence cannot have a predicate adjective. If it is a linking verb, see if it is followed by an adjective that modifies the subject. (Try saying the adjective before the subject.) If the adjective modifies the subject, it is a predicate adjective.

> This boy is honest.
>> The verb **is** can be a linking verb. It is followed by the adjective **honest. Honest** describes the subject, for it is sensible to say **honest boy.** So **honest** is a predicate adjective.

> The sky looked dark.
>> The verb **looked** is a linking verb because it is sensible to say **the sky was dark.** The verb is followed by the adjective **dark. Dark** describes the subject, for it is sensible to say **dark sky.** So **dark** is a predicate adjective.

A predicate adjective modifies the subject. Adjectives in the predicate that do not modify the subject are not predicate adjectives. They are simply adjectives.

> The boy helped the **small** child.
>> **Small** is an adjective in the predicate. But it does not modify the subject, because the sentence is not talking about a **small boy.** Rather, **small** modifies **child** (the direct object). So **small** is not a predicate adjective.

The "sometimes linking verbs" may be used as either linking verbs or action verbs. To tell the difference, decide whether the subject is performing any action.

We **tasted** the lemon pie.
(subject doing the action; action verb)

The pie **tasted** delicious.
(subject not doing any action; linking verb)

Also remember that a "sometimes linking verb" can be replaced with a form of **be.** If the sentence still makes sense, it is a linking verb.

That feather pillow **looks** soft.
Think: That feather pillow **is** soft. (sensible)

We **looked** at the new book.
Think: We **were** at the new book. (not sensible)

Predicate adjectives are diagramed in the same way as predicate nominatives. A slanted line is used to show that the adjective in the predicate modifies the subject. If the predicate adjective is compound, the fork comes **after** the slanted line.

That feather pillow looks soft.

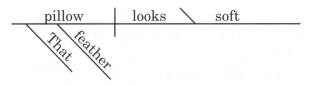

The apple pie smelled fresh and spicy.

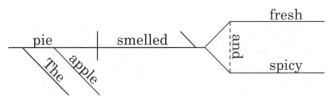

> **Remember:** A predicate adjective comes after a linking verb, and it modifies the subject. A predicate adjective is diagramed like a predicate nominative.

Oral Drill

A. Tell which words are predicate adjectives. Then give the other adjectives.
1. The cheery kitchen was clean and neat.
2. The sweet little bird sounded lovely.
3. Amy's warm, moist cupcakes tasted delicious.
4. The morning sun appeared dazzling and splendid.
5. The dark cellar smelled damp and musty.
6. These fresh peaches feel soft and fuzzy.

B. Diagram these sentences on the chalkboard.
1. King Solomon was wise.
2. Joshua was strong and courageous.
3. Several happy, excited children sang.
4. The potatoes tasted burnt.
5. I smell chocolate cupcakes.
6. They smell sweet and delicious.
7. Favor is deceitful, and beauty is vain.

Written Practice

A. Copy the adjectives in these sentences. Write **P** after each predicate adjective.
1. The old, winding path led up to an ancient castle.
2. Julia's friends were kind and thoughtful.
3. They made a beautiful scrapbook for her.
4. The mountain looked high and rugged.
5. All the pupils know the fifty states and their capitals.

6. They are studious and diligent.
7. The confused, terrified heifer jumped out the barn window.
8. My sister sounded cheerful and confident.
9. The clouds were low and dark.
10. The happy children played in the cool shade.

B. Diagram these sentences.
1. The obedient children looked happy and content.
2. Good friends are faithful.
3. A wise son heeds his father's instructions.
4. God's Word is quick and powerful.
5. The beautiful crystal vase was blue.
6. Jesus is a true friend.

Review and Practice

Correct numbers 1–4 by writing them properly as compound sentences. Correct numbers 5–8 by joining each set of sentences, using as few words as possible.

1. The pyramids in Egypt were built before Joseph's time some are still standing.
2. Monuments have been well preserved in Egypt men study them today.
3. The writing on the monuments was a mystery for hundreds of years, men have now learned to read it.

4. A black stone was found with a message written in three languages, it was named the Rosetta Stone.
5. The Rosetta Stone became the key to unlocking the language. The language was ancient. It was the Egyptian language.
6. Men then rushed to read the mysterious writing. The writing was on the walls of the tombs. It was on the walls of the pyramids.
7. Egyptian history is interesting. It is worthwhile because a number of Bible events took place there.
8. The Bible record of ancient history is perfectly true. It is perfectly accurate.

74. Poetry

Poetry is different from other kinds of writing. It is not written in sentences and paragraphs, but in lines and stanzas. Each line begins with a capital letter. Poetry is a special form of writing that is pleasing to hear.

In most poems, rhyme and rhythm work together to produce a certain feeling. Rhyming words have endings that sound alike, such as **light—bright, believe—receive,** and **carefully— prayerfully.**

Rhythm is a regular pattern of accented and unaccented syllables, with a certain number of syllables in each line. The following examples show the difference between lines with rhythm and lines without rhythm. The number after each line shows the number of syllables.

Rhythm: ´ ˘ ´ ˘ ´
Who has seen the wind?   5

´ ˘ ´ ˘ ´
Nei-ther you nor I.   5

No rhythm: ´ ˘ ´ ˘ ´ ˘ ´
Has an-y-one seen the wind?   7

´ ˘ ´ ˘ ´ ˘ ˘ ´
You have not, and nei-ther have I.   8

Good poems use descriptive words. These words paint pictures in our minds. Descriptive words help to carry the message of the poem to the reader.

Bible poems do not have rhyme and rhythm as we know them. There are other things that make them poetry. They can be written in lines and stanzas, they are full of descriptive words, and they are rich in meaning.

Many Bible poems are in the Book of Psalms. In the following psalm, some of the descriptive words are in bold print.

Psalm 18:1, 2

I will love Thee,
   O Lord, my **strength.**
The Lord is my **rock,** and my **fortress,**
   And my **deliverer;**
My **God,** my **strength,**
   In whom I will trust;
My **buckler,** and the **horn of my salvation,**
   And my **high tower.**

Remember: Poetry is a special form of writing that is pleasing to hear. When writing poetry, remember to capitalize the first word of each line.

> Oral Drill >

A. Read the poem, and answer the questions below.

September

Small things I love about the fall:
The cricket by the cellar wall,
Playing his shrill and merry fiddle,
And grassy bugs with horns that twiddle.

I love the spider spinning still
Beneath the woodshed windowsill,
And caterpillars traveling places,
With striped brown fur and worried faces.

—*Francis Frost*

1. How is this poem different from a story?
2. Would the writing be as interesting if it were in paragraph form, without rhyme and rhythm?
3. Which words rhyme in the first stanza? Does the second stanza have the same rhyming pattern as the first?
4. Which syllables are accented in the first line?
5. What adjectives describe the sound that crickets make?
6. What words describe the bugs?
7. What descriptive verb tells what the horns do? What does this word mean?
8. Why does the poet say that caterpillars have worried faces?

B. Answer the following questions about the poem "September" in Written Practice, Part A.
1. How can asters by the brookside make asters in the brook?
2. What are sedges?
3. What are gentians?
4. Why did the poet write about sedges and gentians?

> **Written Practice** >

A. Copy correctly the title and the first and last stanzas of this poem.

september

the goldenrod is yellow,
  the corn is turning brown;
the trees in apple orchards
  with fruit are bending down.

The gentian's bluest fringes
  Are curling in the sun;
In dusky pods the milkweed
  Its hidden silk has spun.

The sedges flaunt their harvest
  In every meadow nook;
And asters by the brookside
  Make asters in the brook.

From dewy lanes at morning,
  The grapes' sweet odors rise;
At noon the roads all flutter
  With yellow butterflies.

by all these lovely tokens,
  september days are here,
with summer's best of weather,
  and autumn's best of cheer.
    —*Helen Hunt Jackson*

B. Write the numbers 1–5, one number for each stanza in the poem "September." Beside each number, write the rhyming words used in that stanza.

C. Read each stanza, and choose the feeling that it brings.

1. Who sat and watched my infant head,
   When sleeping in my cradle bed,
   And tears of sweet affection shed?
       My mother.
   Feeling: (thankfulness, excitement)

2. The little cares that fretted me,
       I lost them yesterday,
   Among the fields, above the sea,
       Among the winds at play.
   Feeling: (fear, peace)

3. "Dear Mary," said the poor blind boy,
       "That little bird sings very long.
   Say, do you see him in his joy,
       And is he pretty as his song?"
   "Yes, Edward, yes," replied the maid.
       "I see the bird in yonder tree."
   The poor boy sighed and gently said,
       "Sister, I wish that I could see."
   Feeling: (contentment, sadness)

Review and Practice

A. Fill in the blanks. Choose from the words or phrases below.

capital letters	Arabic numerals	inside address
topic	encyclopedia	unnecessary
single	dictionary	order
greeting	signature	proper
organized	unity	Roman numerals
common	disorder	important

1. A ———— is a good tool for finding exact words when writing.

2. When you write a story, do not add ———— details.

3. A paragraph is a group of sentences that develop a —— topic.

4. The —— sentence gives the main idea of the paragraph.

5. The sentences in a paragraph must have —— and ——.

6. The five parts of a friendly letter are the heading, ——, body, closing, and ——.

7. All —— nouns in a paragraph should be capitalized.

8. An outline shows how the ideas in a composition are ——.

9. On an outline, main topics are shown by ——, subtopics are shown by ——, and details are shown by ——.

B. Write the correct words in parentheses.

1. There (is, are) animals called sea otters that play in the cold waves of the ocean.

2. There (is, are) many sea otters out in the water.

3. Each of the otters (dive, dives) for shellfish to eat.

4. One of the otters (is, are) opening a shellfish with a rock!

5. There (is, are) one sleeping on his back while floating in the water.

6. Every one of the otters (like, likes) a good race.

7. Everybody (enjoy, enjoys) watching them.

8. Few of the children ever (see, sees) otters except at the zoo.

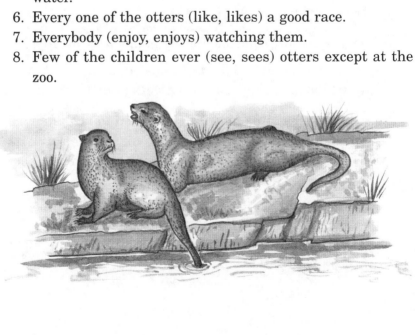

> **Challenge Exercise**

A. On art paper, copy one of the stanzas from the poem "September" in Oral Drill. Illustrate it with pictures that come to your mind from the descriptive words used in that stanza.

B. Write a four-line poem of your own that describes things you like about autumn. You may use the following phrases for ideas.

> refreshing breeze . . . colorful trees
> working together . . . clear, cool weather
> leaves so yellow . . . apples mellow
> caterpillars crawl . . . garden wall
> leaves fall . . . crow's call
> beautiful days . . . give God praise
> the One who made it all

75. Appositive Adjectives

Adjectives usually come before the nouns they modify.

> The **abandoned, neglected** house had fallen into ruin.
> My **friendly, curious** cow often gets herself into trouble.

For variety, adjectives may also be placed immediately after the noun they modify. Such adjectives are in the **appositive** position. Appositive adjectives usually come in pairs joined by **and.**

> The house, **abandoned** and **neglected,** had fallen into ruin.
> My cow, **friendly** and **curious,** often gets herself into trouble.

Appositive adjectives are usually set off by commas. A comma comes just before the first adjective and right after the second adjective.

The temple, huge and magnificent, was built by Solomon.
God's love, rich and pure, is beyond our understanding.

Adjectives in the appositive position are diagramed beneath the noun they modify, the same as other adjectives. The conjunction **and** is placed on a dotted line between the adjectives it joins.

The apples, red and juicy, were sold.

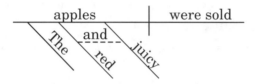

Remember: Appositive adjectives come immediately after the noun they modify. Appositive adjectives are usually set off by commas. They are diagramed like other adjectives.

> Oral Drill >

A. Change each sentence by placing two adjectives in the appositive position. Tell where commas are needed.

Example: Amy's warm, moist cupcakes tasted delicious.
Answer: Amy's cupcakes, warm and moist, tasted delicious.

1. These heavy, clumsy animals do not move rapidly.
2. The wet, shivering calf was found behind the barn.
3. The cold, satisfying lemonade quenched our thirst.

4. The lost, hungry little boy sat and cried.

5. The shy, frightened girl entered her new classroom.

B. On the chalkboard, write the sentences you made for numbers 3–5 in Part A. Then diagram the sentences.

C. Read each boldface adjective. Tell whether it is a **predicate** adjective or an **appositive** adjective.

1. The Philistine giant, **proud** and **boastful,** was **huge.**

2. All the Israelite soldiers were **afraid.**

3. David, **young** and **courageous,** was **fearless.**

4. Goliath, **bold** and **confident,** came to meet David.

5. David's stone struck Goliath, and soon he was **dead.**

6. King Saul was **happy** at first.

7. The women, **glad** and **joyful,** sang songs of praise and honor.

8. Saul, **disturbed** and **displeased,** was soon **jealous** and **spiteful.**

9. The king, **determined** and **desperate,** pursued David every day.

10. The Lord was **faithful,** and He kept David safe.

> Written Practice >

A. Rewrite each sentence, placing two adjectives in the appositive position. Use commas where they are needed.

1. The soft, white snow covered the countryside.

2. This thick, fuzzy blanket will be a welcome gift.

3. The deep, dark dungeon was muddy and cold.

4. Two wild, savage wolves attacked the sheep.

5. The helpless, fearful sheep were protected by the brave shepherd.

6. The bright, warm sunshine helped the flowers to grow rapidly.

B. Diagram sentences 1–4 that you wrote for Part A.

C. Copy each boldface adjective. After it write **P** for predicate adjective or **A** for appositive adjective.
1. Hundreds of people, **eager** and **interested,** formed a crowd around Jesus.
2. One man, **anxious** and **concerned,** fell at Jesus' feet.
3. His young daughter was very **sick.**
4. Jesus, **kind** and **compassionate,** followed the man.
5. Then the little girl was **dead.**
6. The sounds in the ruler's house were **loud** and **mournful.**
7. The mourners, **faithless** and **scornful,** were dismissed by Jesus.
8. The girl, **dead** and **silent,** was soon **alive** and **well.**

> Review and Practice

Copy each word that should have a comma after it, and add the missing comma.
1. Erma who was the first judge of Israel?
2. The first judge of Israel was Othniel, wasn't it Eleanor?
3. Othniel Caleb's nephew delivered the children of Israel from the king of Mesopotamia.
4. Shamgar the third judge of Israel fought with an oxgoad.
5. Gideon mighty and brave delivered Israel from the Midianites.

> **Challenge Exercise**

Sometimes sentences can be combined by putting predicate adjectives in the appositive position. Combine the sentences below in this way. Remember to set off the appositives with commas.

Example: The little boy sat down and cried. He was lost and hungry.

Answer: The little boy, lost and hungry, sat down and cried.

1. My sister often helps me. She is cheerful and confident.
2. The morning was windy and bitter cold. It was not fit for building.
3. The tea was cold and minty. It quenched our thirst.
4. Sharon finally found the poor kitten. It was wet and cold.
5. The hardworking boy sank into his bed. He was weary and sore.

◆━━━━━━━━━━◆

76. Adjectives That Compare

God is **powerful.** But how powerful is God? He is **more powerful** than any angel. He is the **most powerful** Being, for He alone is God. He is all-powerful!

Most descriptive adjectives have three forms or degrees of comparison. In the paragraph above, the adjective **powerful** is used in all three degrees. **Powerful** is the **positive degree.** It describes without making a comparison. **More powerful,** the **comparative degree,** compares God's power with the power of an angel. **Most powerful,** the **superlative degree,** compares His power with the power of all other beings. **Most powerful** tells us that God is above all other beings in power.

The comparative form of one-syllable adjectives and a few two-syllable adjectives is made by adding **-er.** If necessary, double the final consonant or change the **y** to **i** before adding **-er.**

The superlative form of one-syllable adjectives and a few two-syllable adjectives is made by adding **-est.** Again, it may be necessary to double the final consonant or change the final **y** to **i** before adding **-est.**

Positive	Comparative	Superlative
loud	louder	loudest
big	bigger	biggest
tiny	tinier	tiniest

For most adjectives with two or more syllables, the comparative and superlative forms are made by using **more** and **most** with the positive degree. This is done because words like **familiarer** and **wonderfullest** are awkward to pronounce.

Positive	Comparative	Superlative
pleasant	more pleasant	most pleasant
frightful	more frightful	most frightful
beautiful	more beautiful	most beautiful

Be sure to use comparative forms correctly. Use the positive degree to describe without comparing. Use the comparative degree to compare only two things. Use the superlative degree to compare more than two things.

Wrong: Of the two girls, Mary is tallest.
Right: Of the two girls, Mary is **taller.**

Wrong: Nathan is the faster runner in our class.
Right: Nathan is the **fastest** runner in our class.

Do not add **-er** to an adjective and also use **more,** or add **-est** and also use **most.**

> **Wrong:** John was a more faster worker than Gladys.
> **Right:**   John was a **faster** worker than Gladys.

> **Wrong:** James was the most fastest worker there.
> **Right:**   James was the **fastest** worker there.

A few adjectives have irregular forms of comparison. They are not made by adding **-er** and **-est** or by using **more** and **most.**

Positive	Comparative	Superlative
good	better	best
bad	worse	worst
much	more	most
many	more	most
little	less	least

Use a dictionary whenever you are not sure how the comparative and superlative degrees are formed. If no forms of comparison are shown, they are formed in the usual way. Add **-er** or **-est** if the adjective has one syllable, and use **more** or **most** if the adjective has two or more syllables.

Remember: The positive degree of an adjective is used to modify without comparing. The comparative degree is used to compare two things. It is formed by adding **-er** or by using the word **more.** The superlative degree is used to compare more than two things. It is formed by adding **-est** or by using the word **most.** Do not add **-er** to an adjective and also use **more** with it, or add **-est** and also use **most** with it.

A. Tell what is wrong with each sentence. Practice reading the sentences correctly several times.
1. Of the two kittens, the smallest one is mine.
2. Two melons were for sale, but the most expensive one was nearly spoiled.
3. This door is more heavier than that one.
4. It is best to trust in the Lord than to put confidence in man.
5. Of Jesse's eight sons, David was most brave.
6. God's love is more deep than the most deep sea.
7. Which of the two lights is palest?
8. Of all the girls, she seems to be thoughtfulest.
9. He was the most wisest boy of the two.
10. This apple is badder than that one.

B. On the chalkboard, write the comparative and superlative degrees of each adjective. Check a dictionary when you are not sure.

1. ugly	4. comfortable	7. good
2. bad	5. fast	8. much
3. sad	6. reverent	9. awesome

> Written Practice >

A. Write the correct form of each word in parentheses.
1. The Bereans were (noble) than those of Thessalonica.
2. God's Word is (precious) than gold.
3. To obey is (good) than sacrifice.
4. Jehu told the people to choose the (good) and most suitable son of Ahab.
5. Who is (great), the one who serves or the one who is seated?
6. We should give God the (high) praises of all.

7. His last state was (bad) than the first.

8. Balak sent princes (honorable) than the first.

9. Mary wants to be (kind) tomorrow than she was today.

10. God's Word should be (sweet) than honey to us.

11. We are (happy) when we help others than when we demand our own way.

12. Thankful people are (content) than complainers.

B. Write the comparative and superlative degrees of each adjective. Check a dictionary when you are not sure.

1. late
2. little
3. happy
4. bright
5. many
6. nervous
7. quiet
8. holy
9. busy

> **Review and Practice**

A. Write whether each sentence is a **statement, question, command,** or **exclamation.** (There are two exclamations.) Also give the correct end punctuation.

1. Are rocks a useful part of God's creation

2. Rocks in a field are a hindrance to a farmer

3. What a great variety of rocks there are

4. Go and pick up rocks in the north field

5. How would you like a house built of sandstone

6. What are rocks called if they are found in layers

7. Use an encyclopedia to find out what layered rocks are called

8. Shale is usually brown and crumbly

9. Shale is an example of stratified rock

10. How great and marvelous are Your works, O God

B. Copy each pronoun. After it write **N** for nominative, **O** for objective, or **P** for possessive.

1. I will sing a new song unto Thee, O God.

2. Hear my prayer, O Lord.

3. Hide not Thy face from me in the day when I am in trouble.
4. We are His people, and the sheep of His pasture.
5. Let them praise His Name.
6. Exalt the Lord our God.

———————————————

Adverbs

Adverbs modify verbs, adjectives, and other adverbs.

How	When	Where	To What Degree
well	now	here	very
loudly	yesterday	there	most
cheerfully	later	in	extremely
fast	soon	out	moderately
silently	usually	away	too
how	when	where	overly
briefly	often	around	rather
softly	then	outside	quite

77. What Are Adverbs?

Adverbs are words that modify verbs. Adverbs **add** to **verbs.** They tell **how, when,** and **where.**

> Birds fly **swiftly.** (**Swiftly** tells **how.**)
> We finished **early.** (**Early** tells **when.**)
> The airplane soared **high.** (**High** tells **where.**)

Many adverbs end with **-ly.** They are made by adding **-ly** to adjectives.

quietly   bitterly   rapidly   softly   happily

The words **not** and **never** are always adverbs. The words **ever, always,** and **seldom** are adverbs. These adverbs may come between the words of a verb phrase. But they are not part of the verb phrase. They only modify it.

God's Word <u>will</u> **never** <u>fail</u>.
Lauretta <u>is</u> **often** <u>singing</u> as she works.

An adverb may be at different places in a sentence. It may come just before or after the word it modifies. It may come at the beginning of a sentence or at the end.

Charles **slowly** <u>walked</u> to the house.
Charles <u>walked</u> **slowly** to the house.
Slowly Charles <u>walked</u> to the house.
Charles <u>walked</u> to the house **slowly.**

The words **how, when, where,** and **why** are also adverbs. When you answer questions that begin with these adverbs, you often use other adverbs.

When do bees gather nectar? Bees gather nectar **now.**
Where are my papers? My papers are **there.**

An adverb is diagramed beneath the verb it modifies. This is true no matter where the adverb is in the sentence. In a sentence with **cannot,** notice that the word **not** is an adverb and must be diagramed separately.

Birds fly swiftly.   God's Word will never fail.

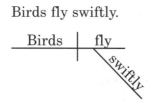

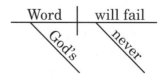

John came inside then.   Penguins cannot fly.
Then John came inside.

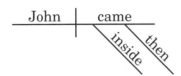   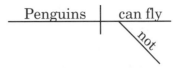

Remember: An adverb is a word that modifies a verb. Most adverbs tell **how, when,** or **where.**

> Oral Drill >

A. Which words are adverbs? Do they tell **how, when,** or **where**?
1. We will leave tomorrow.
2. The boys are working hard.
3. My brother lives there.
4. Nearby an owl hooted mournfully.
5. She never sleeps late.
6. The girls carefully counted the books yesterday.
7. When did you do it?
8. How can we do it faster?

B. Put the boldface adverb at the beginning of each sentence. Notice that it still modifies the verb.
1. The little brown bird **finally** saw us and flew off.
2. The boys may begin digging potatoes **today.**
3. The huge round tank rolled **slowly** onto its side.
4. The water will **soon** cover the bridge completely.

C. On the chalkboard, diagram the following sentences.
1. Peter's dog always comes along.
2. Crystal did not finish today.
3. An ostrich cannot fly.
4. Suddenly the rain was pouring down.
5. Carefully Roger chased the bull away.
6. Why do crickets sing?

> **Written Practice** >

A. Write an adverb that tells **how, when,** or **where** for each blank.
1. They —— work ——.
2. —— Mark will come ——.
3. We listened ——.
4. Mother —— writes ——.
5. You can stay ——.
6. —— the cat crept ——.

B. Diagram the following sentences.
1. Today we must do better.
2. Tomorrow these birds will fly away.
3. Howard carefully pushed the door open.
4. Clinton cannot come yet.
5. Uncle Melvin will arrive tomorrow.
6. The curious weasel gradually crept closer.
7. Where is your father working?

C. Copy each sentence, and add two adverbs. Underline the adverbs you write.
1. We shall see him.
2. The truck stopped.
3. The fish bite.
4. Bruce's brother arrived.
5. The bird whistled.
6. He was climbing.

> **Review and Practice**

A. Copy all the nouns in the following sentences, including the possessive nouns used as adjectives. After each one, write **S** for singular, **P** for plural, **SP** for singular possessive, or **PP** for plural possessive.
  1. Elijah hid by the brook that was called Cherith.
  2. The woman's meal and oil were very low.
  3. There had been no rain or dew for three years.
  4. Even the king's horses and mules were starving.
  5. The prophets' lives were in danger.
  6. Obadiah hid some of the Lord's prophets.

B. Copy the verbs in these sentences. Write whether each verb is in the **present, past,** or **future** tense.
  1. A poor widow was in debt.
  2. She went to Elisha.
  3. My boys will be sold into slavery!
  4. Borrow vessels from your neighbors.
  5. The woman filled all the vessels with oil.
  6. I will pay all my debts.
  7. God cares for you.

----

78. Rhyme and Rhythm in Poetry

You have learned that poetry is a special form of writing that is pleasing to hear, and that good poems use descriptive words. You have also learned that most poems have rhyme and rhythm patterns.

Various patterns of rhyme are used in poetry. Rhyme patterns are marked by placing the same letter after all the lines that rhyme with each other.

Amazing grace! How sweet the **sound**   a
That saved a wretch like **me!**   b
I once was lost, but now I'm **found;**   a
Was blind, but now I **see.**   b

He prayeth best, who loveth best   a
All creatures great and **small;**   b
For our dear God who loveth us,   c
He made and loveth **all.**   b

There are three green eggs in a small brown **pocket;**   a
And the breeze will swing, and the gale will **rock it,** a
Until three little birds on the thin edge **teeter,**   b
And our God will be glad, and the world be **sweeter!**   b

Rhythm is formed by a pattern of accented and unaccented syllables. There are various patterns of rhythm in poetry, depending on the arrangement of the accented syllables. In the following lines, the accented (′) and unaccented (˘) syllables are marked. These are the two most common rhythm patterns.

Pattern A:

Which-ev-er way the wind doth blow,

Some heart is glad to have it so;

Then blow it east or blow it west,

The wind that blows, that wind is best.

Pattern B:

If you hear a kind word spo-ken

Of some wor-thy soul you know,

It may fill his heart with sun-shine

If you on-ly tell him so.

Remember: Various patterns of rhyme and rhythm are used in poetry.

Oral Drill

On the chalkboard, mark the rhyme and rhythm patterns of the following stanzas. Tell which rhythm pattern in the lesson each one follows: **Pattern A** or **Pattern B.**

1. Lots of time for lots of things,
   Though it's said that time has wings;
   There is al-ways time to find
   Ways of be-ing sweet and kind.

2. I know not by what meth-ods rare,
   But this I know, God an-swers prayer.
   I know that He has giv'n His Word,
   Which tells me prayer is al-ways heard
   And will be an-swered, soon or late;
   And so I pray and calm-ly wait.

Written Practice

A. Copy each pair of rhyming words in these stanzas. Also write letters to show which rhyming pattern is followed: **aabb, abab,** or **abcb.**

1. Who taught the bird to build her nest
       Of softest wool, and hay, and moss?
   Who taught her how to weave it best
       And lay the tiny twigs across?

2. If a task is once begun,
   Never leave it till it's done.
   Be the labor great or small,
   Do it well or not at all.

B. Copy the following lines, and mark the accents. Write **A** or **B** to tell which rhythm pattern is followed (as given in the lesson).

1. No morn-ing dawns in gray or rose,
   But that I think of God.

   Pattern ———

2. We can on-ly do a lit-tle,
   But that lit-tle will be blest.

   Pattern ———

> Review and Practice

Copy the two pronouns in each sentence. After each one, write **personal, demonstrative, indefinite,** or **interrogative** to tell what kind it is.

1. Who built a navy of ships and put them on the shore of the Red Sea?
2. King Solomon did this, and King Hiram helped him.
3. Each of those was sent by King Hiram.
4. His servants fetched gold from Ophir and brought it to Solomon.
5. Everybody worked hard for him.
6. Which of the houses did they build first?
7. These are the cities he gave to King Hiram.

> Challenge Exercise

A. Copy the first stanza of each hymn, and mark the rhythm. Your lines should begin with the words in parentheses.

1. Praise to God, Immortal Praise (Praise, For, Bounteous, Let)
2. God Moves in a Mysterious Way (God, His, He, And)

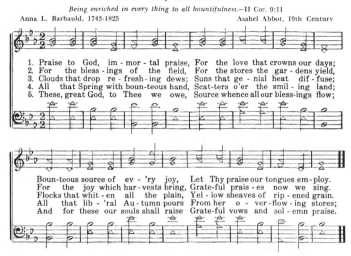

Praise to God, Immortal Praise

Being enriched in every thing to all bountifulness.—II Cor. 9:11

Anna L. Barbauld, 1743-1825   Asahel Abbot, 19th Century

1. Praise to God, im - mor - tal praise, For the love that crowns our days;
2. For the bless - ings of the field, For the stores the gar - dens yield,
3. Clouds that drop re - fresh - ing dews; Suns that ge - nial heat dif - fuse;
4. All that Spring with boun-teous hand, Scat-ters o'er the smil - ing land;
5. These, great God, to Thee we owe, Source whence all our bless-ings flow;

Boun-teous source of ev - 'ry joy, Let Thy praise our tongues em - ploy.
For the joy which har - vests bring, Grate-ful prais - es now we sing.
Flocks that whit - en all the plain, Yel - low sheaves of rip - ened grain.
All that lib - 'ral Au - tumn pours From her o - ver-flow - ing stores;
And for these our souls shall raise Grate-ful vows and sol - emn praise.

B. Use letters to mark the rhyming patterns of the stanzas you wrote in Part A.

---

79. Modifiers of Adjectives and Adverbs

You have learned that adverbs modify verbs. Adverbs can also modify adjectives or other adverbs. When they are used in this way, they usually tell **how** or **to what degree.** Words such as **well, swiftly,** and **carefully** tell **how.** Words such as **very, too, so, rather, quite,** and **extremely** tell **to what degree.**

To find an adverb that modifies an adjective or another adverb, find a word that tells **how** or **to what degree.** Then ask: Which word does this adverb modify? You can tell by saying the adverb with the word you think it may modify, and seeing if that is what the sentence really means.

The visitors entered the pleasantly lighted room.

> **Pleasantly** tells **how. Pleasantly entered** and **pleasantly room** are not what the sentence means. **Pleasantly lighted** is what the sentence means. **Pleasantly** modifies the adjective **lighted.**

The extremely hard job was finished yesterday.

> **Extremely** tells **to what degree. Extremely job** and **extremely finished** are not what the sentence means. **Extremely hard** is what the sentence means. **Extremely** modifies the adjective **hard.**

The sun will rise very early.

> **Very** tells **to what degree. Very rise** is not what the sentence means. **Very early** is what the sentence means. **Very** modifies the adverb **early.**

The door closed too swiftly.

> **Too** tells **to what degree. Too closed** is not what the sentence means. **Too swiftly** is what the sentence means. **Too** modifies the adverb **swiftly.**

An adverb that modifies an adjective or another adverb is diagramed beneath the word it modifies. Remember to say the adverb with the other word to be sure it fits the thought of the sentence. Study the following examples.

Adverb modifying an adjective:

> The painfully limping horse traveled slowly.
>
> > **Think: painfully limping,** not **painfully horse**
> > Painfully modifies the adjective limping.

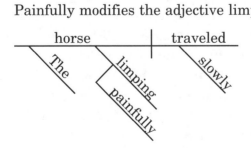

Adverb modifying another adverb:

The two ships passed quite closely.

Think: quite closely, not quite passed

Quite modifies the adverb **closely.**

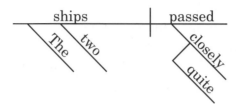

Remember: An adverb is a word that modifies a verb, an adjective, or another adverb. An adverb tells **how, when, where,** or **to what degree.**

> **Oral Drill**

A. Read each adverb that modifies an adjective, and tell which adjective it modifies.

1. Extremely loud noises are hard on your hearing.
2. Some animals died in the bitterly cold winter.
3. The rather difficult climb was exhilarating.
4. My petunias were washed out by an unusually heavy rain.
5. The exceedingly poor immigrants had just arrived.

B. Read each adverb that modifies another adverb, and tell which adverb it modifies.

1. Do not decide too quickly.
2. Why were the girls talking and laughing so loudly?
3. The job will most probably be finished by Monday.
4. Carla was trying especially hard that day.
5. The price of beef rose unusually high.

C. Diagram these sentences on the chalkboard.
   1. The very cold boy shivered constantly.
   2. Grandfather worked too hard yesterday.
   3. Sadie cleaned the extremely dirty room.
   4. Do not eat so fast.
   5. The ridiculously high-priced tool did not sell.
   6. Thomas draws quite well.
   7. Mr. Brown is an exceptionally good plumber.
   8. These are some especially fragrant roses.

> **Written Practice** >

A. Copy each adverb that modifies an adjective. After it write
   the word it modifies.
   1. It was a rather difficult test.
   2. Douglas heard a tremendously loud explosion.
   3. The bitterly disappointed boy wept unashamedly.
   4. The *Christian Pathway* is a widely distributed paper.

B. Copy each adverb that modifies another adverb. After it write
   the word it modifies.
   1. Luke finished his work quite hastily.
   2. Later he worked more slowly.
   3. Dora came in too soon.
   4. Why do bees work so busily?

C. Diagram the following sentences.
   1. An extremely hard hailstorm knocked the apples down.
   2. The magnificently beautiful temple was torn down.
   3. Brother Merle reviews these facts quite often.
   4. The unusually short meeting did help the farmers.
   5. The chocolate cake disappeared very rapidly.
   6. Do not talk too fast.
   7. Jewel learned her verses especially well.

D. Use the following adverbs in sentences of your own.
1. **quite** modifying an adverb
2. **unusually** modifying an adjective

> Review and Practice >

Find each word that should begin with a capital letter, and write it correctly.
1. king hiram of tyre sent servants to ophir to fetch gold for king solomon.
2. king solomon gave king hiram twenty cities in galilee.
3. king hiram named the land cabul, which means "worthless."
4. pharaoh came from egypt, captured gezer, burned it, and gave it to solomon's wife.
5. king solomon raised taxes to build the cities of millo, hazor, megiddo, and gezer.
6. king solomon's navy was built on the shore of the red sea, near eloth in edom.

80. More Practice With Adjectives and Adverbs

You have studied many things about adjectives and adverbs. In this lesson you can sharpen your knowledge by reviewing what you have learned.

Use the chart at the beginning of the chapter to review the different kinds of adjectives. Remember that possessive pronouns are often used as adjectives that tell **whose,** and demonstrative pronouns are often used as adjectives that tell **which.**

You know that adjectives modify nouns and pronouns. To find adjectives in a sentence, find the nouns and pronouns and then look for words that modify them. Can you tell which words are adjectives in the following sentences?

> The usually timid girl did surprisingly well with her first two reports.
> One noun is **girl.**
>> Adjectives that modify **girl** are **the** and **timid.**
>>> **Usually** does not modify **girl,** because it is not sensible to say **usually girl.**
> Another noun is **reports.**
>> Adjectives that modify **reports** are **her, first,** and **two.**

> My brother, excited and confused, threw the ball too high.
> One noun is **brother.**
>> An adjective that modifies **brother** is **my. Excited** and **confused** are adjectives in the appositive position that also modify **brother.**
> Another noun is **ball.**
>> The only adjective that modifies **ball** is **the.**

My little sister was happy with her gift.

> One noun is **sister.**
>> Adjectives that modify **sister** are **my** and **little.**
>>> **Happy** is a predicate adjective that also modifies **sister.**
>> Another noun is **gift.**
>>> **Her** is the only adjective that modifies **gift.**

You have learned that the words **taste, feel, smell, sound, look,** and **appear** are sometimes used as linking verbs. You should remember that when one of these verbs can be replaced with a form of **be,** then it is a linking verb. Look at the following sentences. Which one has a predicate adjective?

> Melvin tasted the apple.
> The apple tasted ripe.

Which makes sense: **Melvin was the apple** or **The apple was ripe**? The second sentence, of course. So you know that the second sentence has a predicate adjective. **Ripe** modifies **apple** by telling what kind of apple.

You learned that adverbs usually modify verbs. Can you tell which words are adverbs in the following sentence?

> The usually timid girl did surprisingly well with her first two reports.
> The verb is **did.**
>> An adverb that modifies **did** is **well.** Two other adverbs are **usually** and **surprisingly.** But these adverbs do not modify **did,** because **did usually** and **did surprisingly** are not what the sentence means. **Usually timid** and **surprisingly well** are what the sentence means. So **usually** modifies the adjective **timid,** and **surprisingly** modifies the adverb **well.**

Review the chart before Lesson 77. Remember that the words **how, when, where,** and **why** are adverbs. Remember that adverbs can be almost anywhere in the sentence—at the beginning, the middle, or the end. Remember that sometimes verb phrases are interrupted by adverbs like **not, never, ever, always,** and **seldom.**

An adjective or an adverb is diagramed on a slanted line beneath the word it modifies. The only exception is a predicate adjective, which is diagramed on the base line after a linking verb. Study the following examples.

An unusually kind man helped us especially well today.

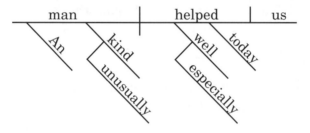

The rolls, warm and steaming, smelled delicious.

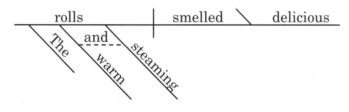

A. Do the following exercises about adjectives and adverbs.

1. What do descriptive adjectives tell? Give several different kinds of descriptive adjectives.

2. How can descriptive adjectives be made from nouns? Give some examples.

3. What do limiting adjectives tell? Name the different kinds of limiting adjectives.
4. What sentence parts can adjectives modify?
5. What do adverbs tell? Give some adverbs in each category.
6. Give some adverbs that can modify adjectives or other adverbs.

B. Diagram the following sentences on the chalkboard.
   1. Some large birds cannot fly.
   2. This wooden toy is not mine.
   3. Mine is green.
   4. I do not often wear boots.
   5. Yesterday two long trains went by.
   6. Did any trains pass today?
   7. The longest train moved rather slowly.
   8. When did you see it?
   9. Why do you go there so often?
  10. The extremely cold weather lasted awhile.
  11. The children, cold and shivering, came inside soon.
  12. The owl dived silently and caught the gray mouse.

▷ Written Practice ▷

A. Diagram these sentences.
   1. Daniel cannot sing loudly.
   2. He seldom speaks very loudly.
   3. Is this coat yours?
   4. That unusually small coat is not mine.
   5. Mine is not here.
   6. Doris carefully swept the floors.
   7. Visitors often come here.
   8. The clouds, puffy and white, floated lazily by.
   9. A kind friend sent this just lately.

10. The very grateful woman thanked him again.
11. A rather small boy moved this very heavy rock.
12. The frightened shepherds heard the angelic announcement.
13. The spoiled boy behaved quite childishly.
14. A tiny bird hovered nearby and sipped the sweet nectar.

B. Write sentences according to these descriptions.
1. A sentence with a demonstrative pronoun used as an adjective.
2. A sentence with a possessive pronoun used as an adjective.
3. A sentence with a cardinal number used as an adjective.
4. A sentence with an ordinal number used as an adjective.
5. A sentence with a possessive noun used as an adjective.
6. A sentence with an adverb that modifies an adjective.
7. A sentence with an adverb that modifies another adverb.
8. A sentence with a verb phrase interrupted by an adverb.
9. A sentence that begins with an adverb.
10. A sentence with **how, when, where,** or **why** used as an adverb.

81. Adverbs That Compare

Adverbs, like adjectives, can be used to make comparisons. Learn to use them correctly. Study the following adverbs that compare.

Positive	Comparative	Superlative
late	later	latest
low	lower	lowest
quickly	more quickly	most quickly

The positive degree modifies without comparing. The comparative degree is used to compare **two** actions. The superlative degree is used to compare **more than two** actions.

For comparing two actions, the word **more** is used with most adverbs. The suffix **-er** is added to a few of them.

> Which of the two animals can run **more swiftly**?
> A cheetah is smaller than an elephant, but it can run **faster.**

For comparing more than two actions, the word **most** is used with most adverbs. The suffix **-est** is added to a few of them.

> Which of the five boys can run **most swiftly**?
> Albert is the shortest boy in the class, but he runs **fastest** of all.

Be careful to use the correct degree of comparison. Use the comparative degree for comparing two actions. Use the superlative degree for comparing more than two actions.

> **Wrong:** This motor runs the most quietly of the two.
> **Right:** This motor runs the **more quietly** of the two.

> **Wrong:** Of all the flowers, yours grew better.
> **Right:** Of all the flowers, yours grew **best.**

Do not add **-er** to an adverb and also use **more** with it, or add **-est** and also use **most** with it.

> **Wrong:** Bruce can throw the ball more higher than I.
> **Right:** Bruce can throw the ball **higher** than I.

> **Wrong:** Herbert came to class the most latest of all.
> **Right:** Herbert came to class the **latest** of all.

Do not add the suffix **-er** or **-est** to most adverbs that end with **-ly.** Words like **swiftlier** or **carefulliest** would sound awkward. Check a dictionary if you are not sure whether **-er** and **-est** may be added.

Positive	Comparative	Superlative
easily	more easily	most easily
loudly	more loudly	most loudly

Exceptions:

early	earlier	earliest
lively	livelier	liveliest

Some adverbs have irregular forms of comparison.

Positive	Comparative	Superlative
well	better	best
badly	worse	worst
little	less	least
much	more	most
far	farther	farthest

Remember: The positive degree of adverbs is used to modify without comparing. The comparative degree is used to compare two actions. It is formed by adding **-er** or by using the word **more.** The superlative degree is used to compare more than two actions. It is formed by adding **-est** or by using the word **most.** Do not add **-er** to an adverb and also use **more** with it, or add **-est** and also use **most** with it.

> Oral Drill

A. Give the comparative and superlative degrees for each adverb. Use several of them in original sentences.

1. fast	4. early	7. fearlessly
2. late	5. much	8. quickly
3. badly	6. little	9. joyfully

B. Tell how to correct the following sentences.

1. You can write more better than I.
2. John ran swiftlier than Peter.
3. Of the two girls, Jane worked hardest.
4. You came most earliest of all.
5. This car rides smoothlier than the other one.
6. Of the two dogs, this one behaves best.
7. The jet flew the fastest of the two planes.
8. Of the two sisters, Mary cooks most.

> **Written Practice** >

A. Write the correct form of each adverb in parentheses.

1. We should love God (much) of all.
2. The second job went (badly) than the first one did.
3. The teacher came (early) than any student.
4. Of the twins, Laura works (fast).
5. Which jumped (far), the fox or the rabbit?
6. Margaret sews well, but Maria sews (well).
7. Lloyd is growing the (rapidly) of the two boys.
8. Of the four sisters, Marianne stitches (slowly).

B. Write the correct words in parentheses.

1. Of all the boys, the smallest one worked (more diligently, most diligently).

2. The meeting ended (sooner, more sooner) than I expected.
3. Anthony flew his kite on two days, and it flew (higher, highest) the second day.
4. Of the two girls, Arlene can bake cakes (better, best).
5. Arlin worked the (more happily, most happily) of the five boys.
6. The black telephone rings the (louder, loudest) of all the telephones.
7. Audrey spoke (kindlier, more kindly) than she had done before.
8. Lassie acted the (more friendly, most friendly) of all the dogs.

C. Use these words as adverbs in sentences of your own. Be sure to show what you are comparing.

Incomplete: Joe can run faster.
Complete: Joe can run faster than Tim.

1. superlative degree of **quickly**
2. comparative degree of **beautifully**
3. positive degree of **well**
4. superlative degree of **high**
5. comparative degree of **little**

> Review and Practice >

A. Diagram these sentences. (Number 6 is a challenge exercise.)
1. The puffer is a very unusual fish.
2. He uses air and inflates his body.
3. Now this big round fish looks scary.
4. Other fish will not eat him.
5. A few puffers do a strange thing sometimes.
6. They puff and puff, and suddenly they pop!

B. Write the correct form of each word in parentheses.

1. I (see) my grandfather in church last Sunday.
2. Marcus (do) not know that you are here.
3. Had you (know) that Jerry would be the song leader?
4. I (know) that Brother John had come.
5. We had (give) the Smiths an invitation to the meeting.
6. Lisa had never (see) a prairie dog before.
7. Kevin (catch) a cold last week.
8. He had not (catch) one all winter.
9. Maxine has (write) to me.
10. The ice on the lake has not (freeze) yet.
11. How much did your new stove (cost)?
12. It had (cost) more last week.
13. A bulldozer has (drag) the logs out of the woods.
14. The logs were (put) on a large truck.
15. Loren has (learn) to read well.
16. Have the boys (dig) enough holes for the fence posts?

82. More About Rhythm in Poetry

When you first learned about poetry, you probably thought rhyme was what made it special. Rhyme does help make poetry pleasing to hear. But rhythm is just as important, as you will see by reading the lines below.

To the First Robin

Welcome, little stranger;
You do not need to fear any harm or danger.
We are very glad to see you here,
Because you sing, "Spring is near."

These lines rhyme, but they do not have smooth rhythm. So they are not as enjoyable to read as lines with rhythm as well as rhyme.

In Lesson 78 you learned about the two most common rhythm patterns. Both patterns alternate between one accented syllable and one unaccented syllable. Pattern A begins with an unaccented syllable, and Pattern B begins with an accented syllable. These accent patterns are shown here.

Pattern A: ˘ / ˘ / ˘ / ˘ /
Pattern B: / ˘ / ˘ / ˘ / ˘

In this lesson you will meet two more rhythm patterns. Both of these patterns alternate between one accented syllable and **two** unaccented syllables. Pattern C begins with an unaccented syllable, and Pattern D begins with an accented syllable.

Pattern C:

˘ ˘ / ˘ ˘ / ˘ ˘ / ˘ ˘ /
To the work! to the work! We are ser-vants of God;

˘ ˘ / ˘ ˘ / ˘ ˘ / ˘ ˘ /
Let us fol-low the path that our Mas-ter has trod;

˘ ˘ / ˘ ˘ / ˘ ˘ / ˘ ˘ /
With the balm of His coun-sel our strength to re-new,

˘ ˘ / ˘ ˘ / ˘ ˘ / ˘ ˘ /
Let us do with our might what our hands find to do.

Pattern D:

$$\acute{/} \;\; \breve{} \;\; \breve{} \;\; \acute{/} \;\; \breve{} \;\; \breve{} \;\; \acute{/} \;\; \breve{} \;\; \breve{} \;\; \acute{/}$$
Oh, the un-search-a-ble rich-es of Christ!

$$\acute{/} \;\; \breve{} \;\; \acute{/} \;\; \breve{} \;\; \breve{} \;\; \acute{/} \;\; \breve{} \;\; \acute{/}$$
Wealth that can nev-er be told;

$$\acute{/} \;\; \breve{} \;\; \breve{} \;\; \acute{/} \;\; \breve{} \;\; \breve{} \;\; \acute{/} \;\; \breve{} \;\; \breve{} \;\; \acute{/}$$
Rich-es ex-haust-less of mer-cy and grace,

$$\acute{/} \;\; \breve{} \;\; \breve{} \;\; \acute{/} \;\; \breve{} \;\; \breve{} \;\; \acute{/}$$
Pre-cious, more pre-cious than gold!

These four rhythm patterns help to give different feelings to poems. Notice especially the feeling of Patterns C and D. The "galloping" rhythm helps to give a feeling of earnestness, excitement, or enthusiasm.

Remember: Both rhyme and rhythm make poetry pleasing to hear. Some rhythm patterns begin with an unaccented syllable, and some patterns begin with an accented syllable.

> Oral Drill >

On the chalkboard, mark the rhyme and rhythm patterns of the following stanzas. Tell which rhythm pattern in the lesson each one follows: **Pattern C** or **Pattern D.**

1. I know the song that the blue-bird is sing-ing
   Out in the ap-ple tree where he is swing-ing.
   Brave lit-tle fel-low! the skies may be drear-y—
   Noth-ing cares he while his heart is so cheer-y.

2. If you want to be hap-py, be-gin where you are,
   For God sets in each sky heav-en's joy-bring-ing star.

> **Written Practice** >

A. Copy the following lines, and mark the accents. Write **C** or **D** to tell which rhythm pattern is followed (as given in the lesson).

    1. More than the sil-ver and gold of the earth,
       More than all jew-els your spir-it is worth.
         Pattern ———

    2. Love the things that you see ev'-ry day all a-round.
       Earth's a mine where the rich-est of treas-ures are found.
         Pattern ———

B. Write letters to show which rhyming pattern is followed in each stanza: **aabb, abab,** or **abcb.**

    1. I have the finest mother
        That any boy could have;
      She cleanses all my scratches,
        And binds them up with salve.

    2. Good habits help us all through life;
      Bad habits bring us pain and strife.
      Our habits, whether right or wrong,
      Each day will grow more firm and strong.

    3. Back of the loaf is the snowy flour,
        And back of the flour, the mill,
      And back of the mill is the wheat and the shower,
        And the sun and the Father's will.

> **Review and Practice** >

Write the correct word for each sentence.

1. Jonathan and (he, him) read about the African catfish.
2. (This, This here) fish swims on its back just below the surface of the water instead of along the bottom like other catfish.
3. (Those, Them) catfish are sometimes called upside-down catfish.
4. (Your, You're) book says (there, their, they're) are more than two thousand kinds of catfish.
5. Mary and (I, me) are studying (they, them) and other unusual fish, and (its, it's) an interesting study.
6. Male catfish hold the eggs in (there, their, they're) mouth.
7. Then (they, them) release (there, their, they're) babies when they hatch.
8. For a while, (he, him) stays near the babies, and (they, them) swim back into his mouth for protection from enemies.

> **Challenge Exercise** >

A. Copy the first stanza of each hymn, and mark the rhythm. Your lines should begin with the words in parentheses.
   1. How Firm a Foundation (How, Is, What, Who)
   2. Cling to the Bible (Cling, Lose, Souls, Drink)

B. Use letters to mark the rhyming patterns of the stanzas you wrote in Part A.

83. Descriptive Language in Poetry

Good poetry has more than just rhyme and rhythm. It uses language that is colorful and powerful. Words and phrases are used that put clear pictures into our minds. Poems often bring feelings and impressions that other kinds of writing cannot give.

Words and expressions may be used in surprising ways. Read the following lines.

> The moon, like a flower
> In heaven's high bower,
> With silent delight
> Sits and smiles on the night.

> **September**
> Small things I love about the fall:
> The cricket by the cellar wall,
> Playing his shrill and merry fiddle,
> And grassy bugs with horns that twiddle.
> I love the spider spinning still
> Beneath the woodshed windowsill,
> And caterpillars traveling places,
> With striped brown fur and worried faces.
> —*Francis Frost*

The first stanza above says that the moon is like a flower happily smiling down on the world! The other two stanzas tell about bugs in the grass that twiddle their horns, and about caterpillars with worried faces!

Expressions like these are called **figurative language.** Figurative language often uses special comparisons. These comparisons may say two things are alike in a certain way, when they are quite different in most ways. Figurative language helps to make poems highly descriptive.

How is the moon like a flower? Of course, it does not have leaves and petals like a real flower. But it is round like a flower, and it looks lovely and cheerful as most flowers do. So we can easily understand the line "The moon, like a flower."

One kind of special comparison says that one thing is **like** or **as** something else. Jesus used a comparison like this when He said, "Be wise **as** serpents and harmless **as** doves." Of course, no one actually looks and acts like a serpent or a dove, but the comparison helps us to understand what Jesus meant. The first stanza in this lesson says that the moon is **like** a flower. The following poem says that a gentle word or kind deed is **like** a tiny seed.

One Gentle Word
One gentle word that we may speak,
    Or one kind, loving deed,
May, though a trifle, poor and weak,
    Prove like a tiny seed.
And who can tell what good may spring
From such a very little thing?
            —Anonymous

Another kind of special comparison does not use **like** or **as**. It says that one thing is something else.

Thy Word **is** a lamp unto my feet.
The lips of knowledge **are** a precious jewel.

Poems often compare nonliving things to living things. They may say that nonliving things act in ways that only living things can. The following poem says that the wind shouts, protests, and laughs. We know that the wind cannot really do these things, but these words give imaginative descriptions of the blowing wind.

The Wind

It screams, it howls, it whispers, it groans,
It roars, it shouts, it mutters, it moans;
Threatens, complains, protests, and whimpers,
Giggles and laughs, snickers and simpers.
It pushes, it tugs, it rushes, it heaves,
It squeaks, it squeals, it grinds, it grieves;
It tears, it rips, it chills, it burns,
It ruffles, it tosses, it twists and turns.
It streaks, it lashes, it batters, it hurries,
It glides and waves and weeps and worries;
It pierces, it jabs, it sails, it kites,
It cuts, it stabs, it bangs, it bites.
It flees, it flies, it flows, it glides,
It sweeps, it swells, it soars, it slides;
It plunges, it dives, it slaps, it stings,
It mounts and gallops, it cries and sings.
It flings, it flounces, it blasts, it blows,
What a relief when it finally goes!

—Robert Darrow

Another thing that makes this poem descriptive is the special sound of its words. Several lines have a number of words that begin with the same letter, as **sweeps, swells, soars,** and **slides.** Many words sound like the wind, as **screams, howls, ruffles,** and **lashes.** The reader can almost hear and feel the strong, noisy, continual blowing of the wind.

Remember: Good poetry uses language that is colorful and descriptive. One way it does this is by using comparisons. Another way is by using words that have special sounds.

 Oral Drill

Answer the questions about this poem.

Three Gates

If you are tempted to reveal
    A tale to you someone has told
About another, make it pass,
    Before you speak, three gates of gold.

These narrow gates: First, "Is it true?"
    Then, "Is it needful?" In your mind
Give truthful answer. And the next
    Is last and narrowest: "Is it kind?"

And if to reach your lips at last
    It passes through these gateways three,
Then you may tell the tale, nor fear
    What the result of speech may be.

                —Anonymous

1. This poem compares three gates to what three things?
2. In what two ways are the gates described?
3. What pairs of rhyming words are used in the poem?
4. What answer will let a tale pass through each gate? What answer will keep a tale from passing through?
5. Why does the poem say that the last gate is the narrowest?
6. Read the last stanza again. When **should** we fear "what the result of speech may be"?

> **Written Practice** >

A. Finish these lines with comparisons of your own.

> **Example:** The bulldozer crawled up the mound like . . .
> **Answer:**   a beetle going over a lump of dirt.

1. The white clouds drifted across the sky like . . .
2. His voice sounded like . . .
3. He was as slow as . . .
4. Your garden is as pretty as . . .

B. Read this poem, and do the exercises below.

Thy Word

Thy Word is like a garden, Lord,
  With flowers bright and fair;
And everyone who seeks may pluck
  A lovely cluster there.
Thy Word is like a deep, deep mine;
  And jewels rich and rare
Are hidden in its mighty depths
  For every searcher there.

Thy Word is like a starry host:
  A thousand rays of light
Are seen to guide the traveler
  And make his pathway bright.
Thy Word is like an armory,
  Where soldiers may repair,
And find, for life's long battle-day,
  All needful weapons there.

Oh, may I love Thy precious Word,
  May I explore the mine,
May I its fragrant flowers glean,
  May light upon me shine.
Oh, may I find my armor there,
  Thy Word my trusty sword;
I'll learn to fight with every foe
  The battle of the Lord.
                              —*Edwin Hodder*

1. The first stanza compares God's Word
   to the following things. Copy a descriptive phrase that tells
   what lovely things are found in each place.
   a. a garden   b. a mine
2. The second stanza compares God's Word to the following
   things. How does it say that each thing is useful?
   a. a starry host   b. an armory
3. What adjectives in the third stanza describe the following
   nouns?
   a. Word   b. flowers   c. sword

NOTE: You will be studying book reports in Lesson 93. Choose
a book now, get it approved by your teacher, and read it in time
to give a report on it.

> Challenge Exercise >

Write a descriptive poem of four to six lines. Use the following
lines for ideas.
1. The snow is a blanket that . . .
2. The brook is like . . .
3. My Bible is my lamp . . . (*or* map, sword, and so on)

84. Using *Good, Well,* and Negative Words

The words **good** and **well** are easily confused. **Good** is always an adjective and modifies a noun. Do not use it to modify a verb.

> Brother Titus does **good** work.
> **Good** modifies **work.**

> Sister Ann read a **good** story.
> **Good** modifies **story.**

Well is usually an adverb that tells **how** something is done. **Well** is an adjective when it means "healthy."

> **Wrong:** Kay sings good.
> > **Good** cannot tell **how.**
> **Right:** Kay sings **well.**
> > **Well** is an adverb telling **how.**

> **Wrong:** Carla was sick, but she is good again.
> > **Good** cannot mean "healthy."
> **Right:** Carla was sick, but she is **well** again.
> > **Well** is a predicate adjective meaning "healthy."

Good may be used as a predicate adjective. Remember that a predicate adjective follows a linking verb and modifies the subject of a sentence. **Well** is never used as a predicate adjective unless it means "healthy."

> **Wrong:** Pie with ice cream tastes well.
> > Pie cannot taste. So **tastes** is not an action verb, and **well** is not an adverb telling **how.**
> **Right:** Pie with ice cream tastes **good.**
> > **Good** is a predicate adjective describing **pie.**

Negative words mean "not" or "almost not." Usually they change a sentence so that it has an opposite meaning. These are some common negative words.

no	never	hardly
not	nobody	barely
none	nothing	scarcely

The negative words **no, not, never, hardly, barely,** and **scarcely** are adverbs. **None, nobody,** and **nothing** are pronouns. **No** may also be an adjective.

Contractions with **not** are negative words.

isn't	couldn't	won't
haven't	can't	

The contraction **ain't** is not a standard English word. Do not use it.

Do not use a sentence with a **double negative.** Use only one negative word to express a negative thought.

> **Wrong:** He couldn't find no eraser.
> **Right:** He couldn't find any eraser.
>   He could find no eraser.

Words like the following are not negative words. Each may be used with a negative word.

any	someone
anything	ever

Often there are two ways to correct a sentence with a double negative. Study the examples below.

Wrong	**Right**
I hardly never go.	I hardly ever go.
	I never go.
He didn't see nothing.	He didn't see anything.
	He saw nothing.

> **Remember: Good** is always an adjective. **Well** is an adverb when
> it tells **how,** but an adjective when it means "healthy."
>
> Use only one negative word to express a negative thought.

▷ Oral Drill ▷

A. Tell how to correct the following sentences. Then read each
   sentence correctly several times.
   1. Carol was sick, but she is good again.
   2. It was well that we told him.
   3. Harold does quite good with his lessons.
   4. He pronounces his words good.
   5. My mother's voice sounded well.

B. Give two ways to correct each negative sentence.
   1. He can't hardly solve this problem.
   2. I don't have no dictionary to use.
   3. I don't see none on the shelf.
   4. He doesn't have no pencil.
   5. The book isn't nowhere in sight.
   6. Hardly nobody has visited school this month.
   7. She wouldn't tell us nothing about it.
   8. Haven't you had nothing to eat?
   9. She ain't got nothing to do.
   10. They won't never see her again.

▷ Written Practice ▷

A. Write the correct words in parentheses.
   1. Our crops are growing (good, well).
   2. Today the singing sounded (good, well).
   3. The old car still looks (good, well).

4. It also runs (good, well).
5. How (good, well) do you follow directions?
6. We should be (good, well) neighbors to other people.
7. The doctor said that Grandmother was (good, well) enough to come home.
8. The Lord has done all things (good, well).
9. The earth is (good, well), but people have not always used it (good, well).
10. The fresh bread smells (good, well).

B. Rewrite each sentence correctly two ways.
   1. I can't see nothing.
   2. Daniel couldn't find none of his pens.
   3. Ain't the eggs never going to hatch?
   4. Isn't nobody going to mow the lawn?
   5. We won't find no shoes in this store.
   6. Haven't you never made a snowman?

C. Write these sentences correctly, using **hardly, barely,** and **scarcely.**
   1. That ship isn't hardly moving.
   2. We didn't barely arrive in time.
   3. There are scarcely no stars out tonight.

> **Review and Practice** >

A. Write **adj.** or **adv.** to tell whether each boldface word is used as an adjective or an adverb.
1. The children worked **hard.**
2. The **hard** work made them strong.
3. Jacob's pillow was **hard.**
4. This **fast** train will take us home in two hours.
5. The dolphins swam **fast.**
6. How can you work so **fast**?
7. These prices are too **high.**
8. The **high** water blocked the road.
9. He leadeth me beside the **still** waters.
10. Please sit **still.**
11. Our classroom was so **still** that we could hear the clock running.
12. The eagles build their nests **high.**

B. Choose and write the correct verbs in parentheses.
1. You may (set, sit) the lawn chairs in the shade.
2. Our friends will (set, sit) here to visit.
3. The chairs (set, sat) outside overnight.
4. Has this board (laid, lain) here all week?
5. Who (laid, lay) it there?
6. The tired boy went inside and (laid, lay) down to rest.
7. The hot air has (raised, risen) the balloon.
8. Jesus has (raised, risen) from the dead, and He is alive forevermore.

9. Please (raise, rise) the windows a little higher.

10. (Let, Leave) me help you carry that heavy load.

11. (Can, May) we (let, leave) our dog and cat with you?

12. Will you (teach, learn) me how to weave a rug?

13. I could (of, have) showed you last night if I would (of, have) brought the directions.

14. (Let, Leave) me supply the materials.

◆━◆━◆━◆━◆━◆━◆━◆━◆━◆

85. Chapter 7 Review

A. Give the answers.

1. What is the definition of an adjective? an adverb?

2. What do descriptive adjectives tell?

3. What three things do limiting adjectives tell?

4. Describe the different kinds of limiting adjectives.

5. What are the three little words called that are adjectives? Name them. Are they descriptive or limiting adjectives?

6. Give some negative words. Then give some words that may be used with negative words to express negative thoughts.

7. Give some adverbs that may be used between the words in a verb phrase.

B. Tell which words in these sentences are adjectives and which words are adverbs.

1. My black pen never writes well.

2. I might throw this old pen away soon.

3. That was a really delicious apple pie.

4. The older girl ate unusually slowly.

5. Thomas Edison was a dedicated inventor.
6. Some quite small tomato plants had sprung up.
7. How could David face Goliath so fearlessly?
8. Doris is not feeling well today.
9. We drove on a very straight road.
10. The big red strawberries made an especially delicious pie.

C. On the chalkboard, diagram sentences 1–6 in Part B.

D. Tell whether each boldface word is a pronoun or an adjective. If it is an adjective, tell which word it modifies.
1. **My** help cometh from the Lord.
2. **He** is **mine,** and **I** am **His.**
3. **Our** basket is here, and **yours** is over there.
4. **Their** stories were better than **ours.**

E. Give the rhyme and rhythm patterns of this poem.

Dear God

Dear God, I've had a hap-py day;　　———
　I tried to do my best.　　　　　　　———
And now I thank You for the night　　———
　When chil-dren all can rest.　　　　———

F. Answer the questions about the following poem.

Nighttime

Like a blanket,
Black and cozy,
　Nighttime puts
　The world to bed.
But dawn wakes it
In the morning
　With a sky
　Of rosy red.

God sends night to
Rest our bodies—
　Rest them for
　The coming day.
He sends morning,
When the children
　All arise
　To work and play.

　　　　　　—*Edith Witmer*

1. To what does this poem compare nighttime?
2. What does the poem say that nighttime does to the world?
3. What lines mean **God made the night so that we can sleep**?
4. What vivid adjectives are used to describe nighttime?
5. What colorful adjectives are used to describe the morning sky?

> Written Practice >

A. Write these definitions.
1. The definition of an adjective.
2. The definition of an adverb.

B. Diagram these sentences.
1. Tornado winds blow extremely fast.
2. Our cousins spoke quite excitedly.
3. His Swiss cows, brown and white, milk well.
4. Actually, the rich, creamy milk is easily sold.
5. Yesterday we picked several exceptionally large red apples.
6. The usually green grass now looks brown.
7. A mountain is an extremely huge hill.

C. Write the correct form of comparison for each word in parentheses.
1. Stephen is (tall) than his brother.
2. Of the two kinds of juice, apple juice tastes (good).
3. Which holds (little) water, a teaspoon or a tablespoon?
4. The Bible is the (much) wonderful book in the world.
5. This is the (bad) flood we have ever had.
6. Saturn is much (big) than the earth, but Jupiter is the (large) of all the planets.
7. Of all the planets, Mercury revolves the (fast).

8. The peas grew (much) quickly than the carrots.
9. We drove (far) on Friday than on Thursday.
10. The blue pen writes (badly) than the black one.

D. Write the correct words in parentheses.
   1. Don't you feel (good, well)?
   2. It is (good, well) that you are early.
   3. Grandma cannot see (good, well) anymore.
   4. This is a (good, well) bicycle, even though it is old.
   5. Lois reads (good, well).
   6. The baby doesn't feel (good, well), so please be quiet.
   7. I don't see (any, no) cherries on this tree.
   8. (Aren't, Ain't) there (any, no) more apples to pick?
   9. Hasn't she (ever, never) seen it snow?
   10. A cheetah can run (more swiftly, swiftlier) than a horse.
   11. Who ran (farther, farthest, more farther), William or Joseph?
   12. Of all the students, you are the (later, latest, most late) one here.

E. Write **adj.** or **adv.** for each boldface word.
   1. It was a **hard** job.
   2. Hit it **hard** with this hammer.
   3. Do not drive too **fast** with your bike.
   4. The **fast** horse would not stand **still.**
   5. Mother was afraid we would fall off the **high** cliff.
   6. Jets can fly extremely **high.**

F. Copy this stanza. Mark the rhyme and rhythm patterns.

Helpfulness

Watch for ways to help an-oth-er—   ———
Fa-ther, Moth-er, Sis-ter, Broth-er;   ———
Loads that one can hard-ly bear   ———
Grow much light-er when we share.   ———
—*Ada L. Wine*

G. Finish these lines with comparisons of your own.
    1. Larry runs like . . . and swims like . . .
    2. Kathy was as quiet as . . .
    3. The greasy container was as slippery as . . .

Periods:

Dr. Johnson and Mr. and Mrs. Brown live
on Riverside Street.

Commas:

Yes, Ronald, people's lives have been greatly changed
by cars, buses, trucks, and planes.

Chapter 8
Punctuation

Quotation Marks:
"Father," Henry said, "I will pick up the potatoes for you."

86. Punctuating Sentences and Abbreviations

When we speak to someone, we do much more than simply repeat words. We pause or speed up. We raise or lower the pitch of our voice. We may even make motions with our head or hands to make the meaning plain. When we write, we cannot do these things to help the reader understand what we mean. But we can use punctuation marks. So it is important to learn the correct use of punctuation in order to write clearly.

Remember the correct end punctuation for the four types of sentences. Use periods at the end of statements and commands. Use question marks with questions, and exclamation marks with exclamations.

An abbreviation is a short form that stands for one or more longer words. Many abbreviations are followed by a period.

doz.—dozen   P.O.—Post Office
gal.—gallon   qt.—quart

Abbreviations for well-known phrases or for the names of various organizations are often spelled with capital letters and no periods. The dictionary will often help you when you are not sure about the form of an abbreviation.

CIA—Central Intelligence Agency
TVA—Tennessee Valley Authority
KJV—King James Version
UN—United Nations
WW II—World War II
POW—prisoner of war

Abbreviations help us take notes faster when we write. They save time and space when certain words or phrases are used often. They are used mainly for informal writing, such as taking notes. Your teacher may also let you use them in math problems and English assignments. But most abbreviations should be spelled out in formal writing, such as stories and reports. The following abbreviations are exceptions. They may be used in all writing.

Abbreviations used with proper names:

Mr.—Mister	Sr.—Senior
Mrs.—Mistress	Jr.—Junior
Dr.—Doctor	

Abbreviations used in writing a time or date:

A.M.—before noon	B.C.—before Christ's birth
P.M.—after noon	A.D.—after Christ's birth
	("in the year of the Lord")

Use periods when you write initials with names.

R. Lynn Groff	Dr. M. M. Weikle
Gladys S. Martin	

Study the following common abbreviations.

Months of the year:

Jan.—January	Aug.—August
Feb.—February	Sept.—September
Mar.—March	Oct.—October
Apr.—April	Nov.—November
	Dec.—December

(May, June, and July are not usually abbreviated.)

Days of the week:

Sun.—Sunday	Thur.—Thursday
Mon.—Monday	Fri.—Friday
Tues.—Tuesday	Sat.—Saturday
Wed.—Wednesday	

The following list of abbreviations is in alphabetical order for easy reference. It does not include abbreviations already shown in the lesson.

Miscellaneous abbreviations:

amt.—amount	Mt.—Mount, Mountain
Ave.—Avenue	no.—number
Bldg.—Building	oz.—ounce
c.—cup	p.—page
Can.—Canada	pp.—pages
chap.—chapter	Pres.—President
Co.—Company	pt.—pint
c/o—care of	Rd.—Road
e.g.—for example	R.R.—Railroad
etc.—and so forth	St.—Street, Saint
ft.—foot	Supt.—Superintendent
Gov.—Governor	U.S.—United States
ht.—height	v.—verse
in.—inch	vv.—verses
Inc.—Incorporated	vol.—volume
lb.—pound	wk.—week
mi.—mile	yd.—yard
mo.—month	yr.—year

Remember: Use a period at the end of a statement or command. Use a question mark with a question, and an exclamation mark with an exclamation. Many abbreviations are followed by a period.

Oral Drill

A. Give the correct end punctuation for each sentence.
1. Blessed are the pure in heart
2. Adam, where are you
3. Please close the door
4. How great God is

B. Give the word or words for which each abbreviation stands.
1. doz.   5. vol.   9. St.
2. lb.   6. ht.   10. A.D.
3. gal.   7. Mrs.   11. Mar.
4. Can.   8. Dr.   12. Sun.

C. Say **yes** or **no** to tell whether each abbreviation may be used in formal writing.
1. Mr.   4. Jan.   7. Sr.
2. lb.   5. mi.   8. B.C.
3. Dr.   6. A.M.   9. no.

Written Practice

A. Divide each group of words into sentences with proper capitalization and end punctuation.
1. do you see that animal how strange it looks I have never seen anything like it do you know what it is called
2. oh, it is already 4:30 the meeting is at 5:00 I have twelve miles to drive do you think I can make it should I telephone before I leave

B. Copy each sentence, and add the missing punctuation.
1. Mr E B Myer lives in the US with his married son
2. Did Mr and Mrs Harlow arrive at 1:00 PM
3. The King James Version was finished in AD 1611
4. Go and see Dr James E Norris on Apple Street

C. List the names of the nine months that are commonly abbreviated, and write the correct abbreviation after each. Also list the days of the week, and write the abbreviation after each.

D. Write the correct abbreviations for these words.

1. before noon
2. for example
3. September
4. ounce
5. pages

6. and so forth
7. in the year of the Lord
8. President
9. Junior
10. Street

E. Write one of each of the four types of sentences, using the correct end punctuation.

---

87. Using Commas Correctly

When we speak, the look on our face and the tone of our voice help explain what we mean. But in writing we cannot use our face or voice to make the meaning clear. We need to use punctuation marks instead.

Commas help us to write clearly. They also help us understand what others write. A period calls for a full stop and a drop in the voice pitch. But a comma calls for only a pause, sometimes with a rise in voice pitch. Study the following rules for using commas.

1. **Use commas to separate three or more items in a series.** The items may be words or phrases. A comma is placed after each item except the last one, which comes after the word **and.**

Cars, buses, trucks, and **planes** have greatly changed people's lives.

A minister **comforts, encourages, teaches,** and **warns** his congregation.

The skunk paraded **across the floor, out the door,** and **around the corner.**

2. **Use a comma to separate two descriptive adjectives before a noun if the adjectives could be joined by *and.*** Remember that descriptive adjectives tell **what kind of.** Do not place a comma after a limiting adjective or after the last adjective, which comes just before the noun that is modified.

> **Wrong:** Two, long, objects lay in the grass.
> > (**Two** is a limiting adjective. **Long** is the last adjective.)
>
> **Right:**   Two long, shiny objects lay in the grass.
> > (It would be correct to say **long and shiny.**)

3. **Use a comma after *oh, well, yes,* and *no* when these words come at the beginning of a sentence.**

> **Oh,** I think so.   **Yes,** you are right.
> **Well,** go ahead.   **No,** it is too late.

4. **Use a comma to set off a noun of direct address.** A noun of direct address names the person to whom we are speaking. A comma must be placed before and after the name if it comes in the middle of a sentence.

> **Sharon,** please come here.
> Did you read this, **Lucy,** about the storm in 1913?
> Over here is the lighthouse, **Frederick.**

5. **Use commas to separate items in dates and addresses, and to set off dates and addresses from the rest of the sentence.** A comma is placed after the last item in a date or address in a sentence.

> On **Wednesday, January 5, 1950,** my grandparents moved to **Norfolk, Virginia.**
>
> My birthday is **February 2, 1961.**
>
> My aunt lived at **383 Lincoln Drive, Dalton, Ohio,** for three years.

Remember: Use commas to separate items in a series. Use a comma to separate two descriptive adjectives that could be joined by **and.** Use a comma after **oh, well, yes,** and **no** when these words come at the beginning of a sentence. Use a comma to set off a noun of direct address. Use commas to separate items in dates and addresses, and to set off dates and addresses from the rest of the sentence.

> **Oral Drill**

Read these sentences, saying **comma** at each place where a comma is needed.

Example: Martha please put on the plates glasses and silverware.

Answer: Martha (comma) please put on the plates (comma) glasses (comma) and silverware.

1. No the boys have not sold many cabbages carrots onions or beans.
2. The test was given to Dudley Duncan Franklin Oswald and his brother Glenn.

3. We stopped looked and listened before crossing.
4. The tall stately trees were beautiful.
5. The huge rolling waves tossed the boat up and down.
6. People will come from the north from the south from the east and from the west.
7. David gave thanks made requests and made intercession.
8. No man has condemned me Lord.
9. No not one person is righteous in himself.
10. Apple Drive Nashville Tennessee is her address Nancy.
11. Daniel that happened on May 12 1967.
12. Come here Naomi and look at this!

> **Written Practice**

A. Copy these sentences, and add the missing commas. They are in groups according to the rules in the lesson.

Rules 1 and 2:
1. We sang prayed and meditated.
2. We need four cheerful diligent girls to help with this job.
3. Moses kept the flock of Jethro led the flock to the back side of the desert and came to the mountain of God.
4. The neglected tumble-down barn burned last night.

Rules 3, 4, and 5:
5. No Sarah I have not memorized John 14.
6. When will you study it Marie?
7. Oh I will study it tomorrow.
8. Yes I will study it when Mother comes home.
9. Akron Ohio is called the Rubber Capital of the World.
10. The last time that volcano erupted was May 12 1967.

All five rules:
11. Jacob's sons took their families their cattle and their goods to Egypt.
12. That first tall thin man is our teacher.
13. Yes he was also our teacher last year.
14. Louise is your address Clinton New York since you moved?

B. Write an original sentence
   1. with a series of four nouns in the subject.
   2. with two descriptive adjectives before a noun.
   3. with a series of three verbs in the predicate.
   4. with a series of phrases.
   5. with a date or an address.
   6. with **oh, well, yes,** or **no** at the beginning.

Review and Practice

Diagram the following sentences.
1. The proud King Belshazzar had been feasting quite extravagantly.
2. The Jews' beautiful, golden vessels were being profaned.
3. Belshazzar and his people were praising several different idols.
4. Some fingers mysteriously wrote strange words.
5. Belshazzar's merry countenance changed then.
6. The great, unholy king feared exceedingly.
7. His trembling knees smote together.
8. The wise Babylonian astrologers could not interpret the mysterious words.
9. Daniel was a godly man.
10. Daniel correctly interpreted the perplexing message.
11. God is holy and just.
12. God is also merciful.

> Challenge Exercise >

Find and write the correct meaning for each abbreviation. Use your dictionary.

1. psi
2. km
3. amp
4. fps

5. AWOL
6. C
7. MP
8. N.D.

—◆—◆—◆—◆—◆—◆—

88. More About Commas

Commas help us to write clearly. In this lesson you will study a few more ways that commas are used in sentences. You will also review the use of commas in friendly letters.

1. **Use commas to set off words that interrupt the main thought of a sentence.** The sentence would mean the same without the interrupting words.

   The box, **as you see,** is empty.
   (**Compare:** The box is empty.)

   Our only hope, **I tell you,** is our faith in God.
   (**Compare:** Our only hope is our faith in God.)

2. **Use commas to set off some appositives.** If the appositive has adjectives modifying the noun, it is set off by commas. If the appositive is a noun without adjectives, no comma is needed.

   Brother Laban, **our minister,** preaches good sermons.
   God made Adam, **the first man.**

3. **Use a comma before the conjunction in a compound sentence.** Study the following sentences.

> A bird landed near the porch, but it saw the cat.
> My little brother was sick, and his friends came to visit him.
> Bow down thine ear, and hear the words of the wise.
> > (The subject **you** is understood in each part of this command.)

In Chapter 2 you learned that a compound sentence has a skeleton on **each side** of the conjunction. A simple sentence may have a compound subject or a compound predicate, but it has only one skeleton.

Do not put a comma between the subject and the verb. Do not use a comma before a conjunction if it only joins two subjects or two verbs.

> **Wrong:** Our cat, has hidden her kittens.
> **Right:** Our cat has hidden her kittens.

> **Wrong:** Thomas opened the book, and began to read aloud.
> **Right:** Thomas opened the book and began to read aloud.

> **Wrong:** Martha, and Jacob pulled weeds, and hoed.
> **Right:** Martha and Jacob pulled weeds and hoed.

4. **Use commas correctly in a friendly letter.**

   a. *Separate items in the address and the date in the heading.* Use a comma to separate the route number from the box number. Separate the city from the state or province, and the day from the year. Do not place a comma between a street number and street name. Do not place a comma between the state (or province) name and the Zip Code (or postal code).

333 Fulton View Road	Route 2, Box 259
Onego, WV 26886	Dover, OH 44622
May 22, 20—	April 2, 20—

   b. *Use a comma after the greeting.*

Dear Grandfather,	Dear Kenneth,

   c. *Use a comma after the closing.*

With love,	Sincerely,	Your loving son,

Remember: Use commas to set off words that interrupt the main thought of a sentence and to set off some appositives. Use a comma before the conjunction in a compound sentence. Use commas correctly in a friendly letter.

> Oral Drill >

Tell which words should have commas after them, and why the commas are needed.

1. Mary and Joseph Jesus' parents found Him in the temple.
2. The doctors Jewish leaders were talking to Him.
3. Solomon a wise king was the last to rule Israel and Judah.

4. It snowed yesterday but today it is raining.
5. Jonathan had not heard his father's command and he ate some honey.
6. Michal let David down through a window and he escaped.
7. You I hope have done your best.
8. Each student of course must do his own work.
9. a. 54 Pleasant Valley Road
   Fairfax VA 22021
   March 4 20—
   b. Route 2 Box 80
   Riverside CA 92503
   Oct. 6 20—
10. a. Dear John   b. Dear Aunt Susan
11. a. Dear Sister Mary   b. Dear Cousin Melanie
12. a. Lovingly yours   b. Sincerely yours

> Written Practice >

A. Copy each sentence or letter part, and add the missing commas.
   1. Esther the Jewish queen saved her people.
   2. Ahimelech gave hallowed bread to David Saul's son-in-law.
   3. Many praise psalms were written by David a shepherd.
   4. Saul asked counsel of God but He did not answer.
   5. Saul had rejected the word of the Lord and the Lord rejected him from being king.
   6. Man looks on the outward appearance but the Lord looks on the heart.
   7. Asia in fact is the largest continent in the world.
   8. The Atlantic Ocean by the way separates North America from Europe.
   9. Will you thank God or will you complain?

10. a. Route 4 Box 292
Tucson AZ 85741
Feb. 7 20—
b. 127 West Garden Road
Vineland NJ 08360
December 15 20—

11. a. My dear mother   b. Dear Grandmother
12. a. Dear Nancy   b. Dear Wayne
13. a. Yours truly   b. Sincerely yours
14. a. With love   b. Your loving granddaughter

B. Write a short friendly letter to thank Aunt Ruth for the book she sent you on your birthday. Include a correctly punctuated heading, greeting, and closing. In the body, include one sentence with an appositive and one sentence with words that interrupt the main thought.

> Review and Practice >

A. Write the correct words in parentheses. Sentences 10–14 should express negative thoughts.
1. Brian and (he, him) wrote on the chalkboard.
2. Grandfather will bring Lillian and (she, her).
3. The teacher helped Francis and (they, them).
4. Who answered the door? It was (he, him).
5. (Them, Those) pencils are mine.
6. Keith is feeling (better, weller) today than yesterday.
7. This chair is (more comfortable, comfortabler) than that one.
8. Of the twins, Lisa draws (better, best).
9. Loretta sings (good, well).
10. I saw (anything, nothing) strange outside.
11. He doesn't have (any, no) new books.
12. The coat was (nowhere, anywhere) in sight.

13. Hardly (nobody, anybody) ever fails a spelling test.

14. He can scarcely find (any, none).

B. Rewrite each sentence correctly.

1. These here gloves belong to the fourth graders.
2. Everyone are here now.
3. Nobody have finished on time.
4. Each have brought some.
5. This here dog followed my brother and I.
6. Who did you see out there?
7. These here are sweeter than them.
8. Alma and me need another broom.
9. I ain't buying no stamps.
10. I couldn't hardly catch that fly ball.

89. Telling a Story About a Personal Experience

What story about a personal experience could you tell to your class? Think about something that has happened to you. Perhaps there was a storm, fire, trip, sickness, accident, or flood. Or you may tell about a common event like a time when you made and flew a kite, or when you found baby squirrels in the attic. Stories about common things can be just as interesting as stories about unusual things.

Before you tell a story, be sure you remember the facts well. Who was there? What happened? Where did it happen? When did it happen? How did it happen? Why did it happen? Write brief notes of the details in proper order. Begin with what happened first; then tell what happened second, and so on. Do not add unnecessary details.

Sometimes we cannot think of a good idea for a story because it seems that few interesting things happen to us. But the trouble is not usually a lack of interesting experiences. It is rather that we have not been watching for things that would make interesting stories!

Even when something unusual does happen to a person, he may not tell a very good story about it. The following story is one example.

> **When I was eight years old, I broke my arm. It hurt a lot, but after a while it got better.**

Many more interesting details could be added to this story. Not everyone breaks an arm! Tell how it happened. What were you doing? Who was with you? Did you know right away that it was broken? Did your father take you to the hospital, or did an ambulance come? What happened at the hospital? Were any x-rays taken? Did you have to stay in bed for a time? Did you get cards, letters, or gifts? How long did you have to wear a cast? How did you spend the time while your arm healed? Do you still have any problems because of the fracture? Do you recommend that other people avoid breaking their arms?

Here is the beginning of the same story, with more details added. Notice how much more interesting the details make it.

> When I was eight years old, I broke my arm. It happened one evening when we were doing chores. My father asked me to bring a bucket from the upper story of the barn. I knew where the bucket was, so I thought I could get it without turning on the light. But I forgot about the hay hole up there.
>
> As I hurried through the dark, suddenly I stepped into empty space. Thud! I fell through the hay hole and landed on the concrete floor below, right on my left arm. The pain was terrible. I didn't know anything could hurt so much! My father heard me crying and came running to see what had happened.

Here is a list of notes for the first part of the story above.

1. Were doing chores
2. Father asked me to bring bucket
3. Didn't turn on light
4. Fell down hay hole and broke arm

When you tell a story to a small group, remember to speak clearly and at a natural, relaxed speed. Speak loudly enough so that everyone can understand you. Look at your listeners as you speak. You may glance at your notes when you need them, but you should not read your story. Use good posture. Both of your feet should be flat on the floor, your back straight, and your hands in front of you. You may use your hands to make meaningful gestures, but you should avoid awkward and distracting motions.

If you are nervous, quietly take a deep breath, and let it all out before you begin. Remember that your nervousness can actually give you energy to do a better job!

Remember: When you tell a story to a small group, include enough details to make your story interesting, and give them in the right order. Look at the listeners, and speak clearly enough so that everyone can understand you. Stand with a relaxed, natural posture. Do not make awkward and distracting motions.

Oral Drill

A. Answer these questions about telling a story to a small group.
1. How loudly should you speak?
2. Should you speak more slowly or more rapidly than when you are visiting with your friends?
3. Where should you look?
4. What should you avoid?
5. What kind of notes should you use?

B. Tell how you could add more details to the following story to make it more interesting.

I made a wagon last year, but it wasn't very strong. It broke when we rode it down a hill.

Written Practice

A. Think of an interesting event in your life to tell about. Write a list of brief notes to use when you tell the story. Put them in proper order. Let your teacher check the list.

B. Practice telling your story to others before you come to class. Prepare to talk for one or two minutes.

C. Tell your story to the class. Remember the rules for speaking before a group.

> **Review and Practice** >

Write the correct word or phrase for each blank. You will not use all the answers.

paragraph	outline	friendly letter
details	rhythm	good
stanzas	order	poetry
topic sentence	attractive	accent
unity	rhyme	

1. When you tell about a personal experience, you must include interesting ———.
2. A paragraph has ——— when all the sentences tell about the same topic.
3. The ——— of a composition shows how its ideas are organized.
4. A ——— is a group of sentences that develop one topic.
5. The word ——— is more exact than **nice.**
6. A paragraph has ——— when the sentences tell how to do something step by step.
7. A ——— has five parts.
8. The words in ——— are arranged in a special way that is pleasing to the ear.
9. The ——— gives the main idea of a paragraph.
10. The ——— of poetry is made by a regular pattern of accented and unaccented syllables.

90. Using Apostrophes Correctly

Apostrophes are used to make the possessive forms of nouns. Remember that a possessive noun tells **whose** about another noun. A noun in the possessive case is used as an adjective when it comes before another noun.

Study the possessive forms on this chart. Then read the rules below.

Singular	Singular Possessive	Plural	Plural Possessive
man	man's	men	men's
lady	lady's	ladies	ladies'
cat	cat's	cats	cats'
octopus	octopus's	octopuses	octopuses'

a. For singular nouns, make the possessive form by adding **'s.** This is true even for most nouns ending with **s.**

　　　cat—cat's　　　　　　　octopus—octopus's
　　Charles's coat is on the floor.

b. For plural nouns ending with **-s,** make the possessive form by adding an apostrophe. If a plural noun does not end with **-s,** add **'s.**

　　　ladies—ladies'　　　　　men—men's
　　Is this the **Davises'** car?

Do not use apostrophes to make the plural forms of nouns.

　　Wrong: Some city's have traffic jam's because of the many car's and truck's on the street's.
　　Right:　Some **cities** have traffic **jams** because of the many **cars** and **trucks** on the **streets.**

Apostrophes are used to form contractions. The apostrophe marks the place where one or more letters have been left out.

it is—it's	can not—can't
he is—he's	I shall—I'll
do not—don't	they will—they'll
we have—we've	would not—wouldn't
you are--you're	

Do not confuse contractions with possessive pronouns. Possessive pronouns tell **whose,** and no apostrophes are used in them.

it's = it is	its = belonging to it
who's = who is	whose = belonging to whom
you're = you are	your = belonging to you
they're = they are	their = belonging to them

your paper	**its** collar
their house	**whose** book

Apostrophes are used to make the plural forms of numbers, letters, signs, and symbols.

4's   T's $'s   ?'s

His *o*'s look like *a*'s.

You missed all the $'s in your answers.

Remember: Apostrophes are used to form contractions and possessive nouns. Apostrophes are also used to make the plural forms of numbers, letters, signs, and symbols.

> Oral Drill >

A. Tell where apostrophes are needed in these phrases.

1. a deers tail
2. Elishas oxen
3. the childrens book
4. two robins nests
5. a kings order
6. the geeses pen
7. ten trouts heads
8. the Morrises house

B. Spell the contractions for the following words.
   1. can not   3. I shall   5. you are
   2. will not   4. you will   6. he is

C. Tell how to correct the following sentences.
   1. Bobs *es* and *rs* look like *is*.
   2. Whose running around upstairs?
   3. I heard that your leaving.
   4. The broom was in it's place.
   5. The Lord saw they're trouble.
   6. The two womens' cake's were delicious.
   7. The childrens' toy's should be brought inside.

D. Tell how to spell the missing words.

Singular	Singular Possessive	Plural	Plural Possessive
1. day	——	——	——
2. mouse	——	——	——
3. man	——	——	——
4. child	——	——	——

E. Give original sentences for each word in numbers 1 and 2 of Part D.

> Written Practice >

A. Write the possessive form of each word in parentheses.
   1. the (pupils) lessons   7. our (mothers) helpers
   2. my (brother) truck   8. the (family) secret
   3. (Anna) gift   9. (Titus) notebook
   4. her (sister) friend   10. the (women) purses
   5. the (rabbits) home   11. our (neighbors) houses
   6. (Father) tools   12. (Grandmother) Bible

B. Write the contractions for the following words.
   1. it is   4. you are   7. we shall
   2. I am   5. he will   8. should not
   3. must not   6. are not   9. who is

C. Write the following sentences correctly.
   1. Philips *t*s look like *l*s.
   2. Your *F*s shouldnt look like 7s.
   3. Weve been using Harolds ax, and now its dull.
   4. Denniss coat should be hung on it's hook.
   5. Who's sock's are these?
   6. Be sure you're sin will find you out.
   7. The four girl's purses' were missing.
   8. The mices' cheese is all gone.
   9. We did'nt mean to be so late, but we could'nt find you're house right away.
   10. We missed they're road because it wasnt marked.

D. Write the missing words correctly.

Singular	Singular Possessive	Plural	Plural Possessive
1. dog	———	———	———
2. deer	———	———	———
3. baby	———	———	———
4. wolf	———	———	———
5. platypus	———	———	———

E. Write original sentences for each word in numbers 1 and 2 of Part D.

> Review and Practice

A. Copy each noun in the sentences below, including the possessive nouns. After each one, write **S** for singular, **P** for plural, **SP** for singular possessive, or **PP** for plural possessive.

1. Frank's hogs are doing quite well on his father's farm.
2. The teacher checked the students' papers with Dawn's red pen.
3. Jean borrowed Linda's crayons.
4. Pour Jay's milk into the cats' dish.

B. Copy the verbs or verb phrases in these sentences. After each one, write **A** for action or **B** for being to label the main verb.
1. I have never been to the West Coast.
2. I will teach you the lesson.
3. After this visit, I will have been there six times.
4. The men are digging a well by hand.
5. The fifth grade students are good workers.
6. Have you written a letter to Grandmother?
7. Here is a stamp for you.
8. Run and catch the bus.

91. Direct and Indirect Quotations

When we tell what a speaker has said, we are using a **quotation.** It may be a **direct quotation** or an **indirect quotation.**

A direct quotation repeats the exact words of a speaker.

> Jesus said, "Follow Me."
> "Follow Me," said Jesus.

An indirect quotation tells what a person said without repeating his exact words. The following sentence has an indirect quotation.

> Jesus said that they should follow Him.

Here are four differences between direct and indirect quotations.

a. Quotation marks are used with a direct quotation, but not with an indirect quotation.

> **Direct:**   The lady asked, "May I help you?"
> **Indirect:** The lady asked if she may help me.

b. The word **that** often comes before an indirect quotation.

> **Direct:**   Anna said, "I am studying Spanish."
> **Indirect:** Anna said **that** she is studying Spanish.

c. Some pronouns may be different.

> **Direct:**   "**I** shall feed **your** cat," promised Leon.
> **Indirect:** Leon promised that **he** would feed **my** cat.

d. Some verb forms may be different.

> **Direct:**   Loyal said, "I **live** near here."
> **Indirect:** Loyal said that he **lives** near here.

> **Direct:**   Janice promised, "You **will get** a letter."
> **Indirect:** Janice promised that I **would get** a letter.

> **Direct:**   Mervin exclaimed, "I **saw** a bear!"
> **Indirect:** Mervin exclaimed that he **had seen** a bear.

A speaker's exact words are the direct quotation. The other words in the sentence are called **explanatory words.** In the following sentence, the explanatory words are in bold print.

"I am the light of the world," **said Jesus.**

In this lesson you will work with sentences in which the direct quotation comes first. Use the following rules for these sentences.

a. Begin with quotation marks and a capital letter.

"<u>G</u>o, and sin no more," said Jesus.

b. Place the correct punctuation at the end of the quotation. Use a comma after a statement or command, a question mark after a question, and an exclamation mark after an exclamation. Add quotation marks **after** the punctuation at the end of the quotation.

> "What have you done<u>?"</u> asked Samuel.
> "I forced myself and offered the sacrifice<u>,"</u> Saul replied.

c. Put a period at the end of the sentence. A period is used because the explanatory words do not usually ask or exclaim, even though the quotation is a question or an exclamation.

> "Whom shall I send?" asked the Lord<u>.</u>
> "Oh, that my words were now written!" Job cried<u>.</u>

Remember: A direct quotation repeats the exact words of a speaker, but an indirect quotation does not. A direct quotation is enclosed in quotation marks, and a comma usually separates it from the explanatory words. Quotation marks usually come after other punctuation marks.

> Oral Drill >

A. Tell whether each sentence has a **direct quotation** or an **indirect quotation.**
1. Martha said that she would buy the book.
2. "My brother has a pet raccoon," Harold said.
3. They told us that the man drove a black car.
4. "We shall sew after supper," announced Betty.
5. Father told us, "George painted his car with a brush."
6. Paul declared that Frank had found the money.

B. Tell which words are the exact words of the speaker. Tell which are the explanatory words.
   1. A voice said, "This is My beloved Son."
   2. James and John asked, "Shall we command fire to come down from heaven?"
   3. "I will follow You wherever You go," a certain man said.
   4. "I have dreamed a dream," said Pharaoh.
   5. Jesus said, "Bring your son to Me."

C. Write these sentences correctly on the chalkboard.
   1. What shall I do to inherit eternal life a lawyer asked
   2. What does the Law say asked Jesus
   3. Who is my neighbor the lawyer questioned
   4. Which of the three was a neighbor to him Jesus asked
   5. Remember me requested Joseph
   6. I have dreamed a dream said Pharaoh
   7. Why is the decree so hasty from the king asked Daniel
   8. Oh, that I knew where I might find Him exclaimed Job

> Written Practice >

A. Write whether each sentence has a **direct** or an **indirect** quotation.
   1. "Let's take a hike," suggested the students.
   2. Susan said that she had seen a moose.
   3. Sharon said, "I'm willing to baby-sit."
   4. "You should do your lessons early tonight," Mother said.
   5. The teacher announced that we should have our reports ready by Monday.
   6. "I shall begin early," Joan told herself.
   7. Ronald said that he worked near here.
   8. John said, "I weeded the garden."

B. Copy each sentence, and add the correct punctuation and capital letters.
   1. Lord, do You not care that my sister has left me to serve alone asked Martha
   2. tell her to come and help me she continued
   3. you are careful and troubled about many things Jesus answered
   4. but one thing is needful, and Mary has chosen that good part He concluded
   5. woe unto you, scribes and Pharisees, hypocrites Jesus exclaimed
   6. there is nothing hidden that shall not be known Jesus taught

> Review and Practice >

A. Copy each verb or verb phrase. After each one, write the tense: **present, past,** or **future.**
   1. I cried unto the Lord.
   2. My yoke is easy, and My burden is light.
   3. They will sing for us.
   4. He sold his goods and bought the valuable pearl.
   5. The church will prosper.
   6. Peter saw the waves, and he was afraid.
   7. Jesus stretched forth His hand and caught him.
   8. God loves a cheerful giver.
   9. The wise virgins took oil in their vessels.
   10. God will bless the faithful.
   11. Jesus healed the lepers, the blind, and the lame.
   12. I shall not be moved.

B. Write the sentence type: **statement, question, command,**
   or **exclamation.** Also write the correct end punctuation.
   1. Oh, that men would praise the Lord
   2. The just shall walk in the ways of the Lord, but the trans-
      gressors shall fall
   3. Was Daniel's God able to deliver him from the lions
   4. Thank God for His mercy and love

92. More About Direct Quotations

There are different ways to write direct quotations. You have
learned about sentences in which a direct quotation comes first.

"Come unto Me, and I will give you rest," Jesus said.

Not all direct quotations are written this way. Sometimes the
quotation comes last in a sentence.

Jesus said, **"Come unto Me, and I will give you rest."**

Quotations are put at different places in sentences for variety.
Read the following conversations. Which sounds better?

"Oh, there's a bug on my dress!" squealed Rose.

"That's a ladybug. Don't hurt it," said Linda.

"Why? Are ladybugs special?" asked Rose.

"Yes, they are. They eat insect pests, such as aphids," said
Linda.

*   *   *   *   *

Rose squealed, "Oh, there's a bug on my dress!"

"That's a ladybug," said Linda. "Don't hurt it."

"Why? Are ladybugs special?" asked Rose.

"Yes, they are," Linda said. "They eat insect pests, such as
aphids."

In the second conversation, some direct quotations come after the explanatory words rather than before them. Variety in sentences makes writing more interesting to read.

In this lesson you will learn about sentences that begin with explanatory words. To write sentences like these, use the following rules.

a. Begin the first word with a capital letter, since it comes at the beginning of the sentence. Also begin the direct quotation with a capital letter. This is done because the speaker's words are a sentence within a longer sentence.

   A lawyer asked, "**W**hich is the greatest command?"

b. Place a comma at the end of the explanatory words, and a set of quotation marks just before the quotation. The quotation marks should come **after** the comma.

   Jesus said, "Thou shalt love the Lord thy God."

c. At the end of the quotation, place a period, a question mark, or an exclamation mark, depending on whether the quotation tells, asks, or exclaims. Place a set of quotation marks **after** the end punctuation.

   David said, "Oh, how love I Thy law!"
   The chief captain asked Paul, "Are you a Roman?"

> Oral Drill >

Write these sentences correctly on the chalkboard.
1. toads are big helpers to farmers said Father
2. why, what do they do asked the children
3. Father explained toads eat insects
4. toads help keep insects from hurting our garden added Mother
5. Mary asked may I touch the toad
6. oh, its skin is dry and bumpy Mary exclaimed
7. she said I thought it would be sticky.

> **Written Practice** >

Copy each sentence, and add the correct punctuation and capital letters.

1. Lisa said a toad's tongue is sticky
2. the toad shoots out its sticky tongue and catches insects Father told her.
3. Mary asked are toads and frogs the same
4. James said most toads live on land, but frogs like to live near water
5. toads are tadpoles when they are babies said Father
6. Mary asked don't tadpoles live in the water
7. toads live in water for part of their lives and on land for part of their lives said Mother
8. James added tadpoles have long tails and no legs
9. father said the toad's legs start to grow later
10. what happens to the tail asked James
11. it slowly disappears said Father
12. mother said I am glad God made such interesting creatures

> **Review and Practice** >

A. Write whether each sentence has a **direct** or an **indirect** quotation. (There are no quotation marks to help you.)

1. I wonder how milk snakes got their name said Glenn.
2. Father said that farmers used to think the snakes took milk from their cows!
3. Judy asked is a milk snake poisonous?
4. No, it is a helpful snake because it eats rats and mice said Glenn
5. The teacher said that a milk snake can also be called a king snake.

B. Copy each word that should have a comma after it, and add the comma.

1. The girls trimmed the weeds mowed the grass and swept the drive.
2. A large fierce dog chased the two frightened girls.
3. Yes Joshua June 6 1980 is David's birthday.
4. June 7 1980 is Kenneth's birthday Joshua.
5. Is Route 4 Box 283 Orwell New York your correct address Cora?
6. Brother John Kendall our minister came to visit us last evening.
7. Joseph Mary's husband took Jesus and His mother to Egypt.
8. Jethro the priest of Midian rejoiced with a thankful heart.
9. Michal Saul's daughter helped David.
10. Jehoshaphat king of Judah came down to Ahab king of Israel.
11. The children waited for Elizabeth but she did not come until morning.
12. The dog must keep quiet or he will be punished.
13. Harold collected all the pieces and we fastened them together with tape.
14. Mountain ranges of course kept people apart in the past.
15. The Pyrenees Mountains for example are a barrier between France and Spain.

Corel Corporation

93. Writing a Book Report

A book report tells what a book is about. If it is well written, a book report may help other people decide to read a certain book.

To write a book report, first choose a book and get it approved by your teacher or parents. Read the whole book before you begin writing your report.

The first paragraph of a book report should include the following information.

a. The title of the book. (The title should be underlined.)
b. The name of the author.
c. The copyright date of the book.
d. The place where the book can be found.

The second paragraph should name the main characters and give a brief description of each one. You may include what you think of them. This paragraph should also describe the setting of the book. The setting is the place and time of the story. In what country, city, or state did it happen? Did it happen in recent times, in the pioneer days of America, or when?

The third paragraph should give the plot of the book. The plot is the main problem that the characters face. Tell how the problem is handled, but do not give the outcome. A good way to do this is to ask questions about things that happened in the book. Leave your readers in suspense so that they will want to read the book too.

The fourth paragraph should give your opinion of the book. Tell what you enjoyed most about the story, and why you think others should read it too. Then sign your name.

Keep the report brief. You do not need to tell about everything that happened in the book.

Do not copy sentences from the book. You may copy key ideas, but you must put the ideas in your own words. Remember to use a variety of sentence patterns and descriptive words.

Study the following book report. It is written according to the pattern given in the lesson.

<u>Paula, the Waldensian</u> was written by Eva Lecomte of France. This book was written in French and later translated into English. It was first printed in 1942, and it has no copyright. The book is available from Rod and Staff Publishers.

Paula lived in France during the 1700s. She was an obedient, cheerful girl, and she loved the Lord with all her heart. Paula won many friends with her charming, gracious manners.

Paula went to live with her cousins after both of her parents died. But religion was a forbidden subject in her cousins' home. The family did not serve the Lord, and they were quite selfish in their ways. What happened when Paula was determined to pray before meals? What did her uncle do with her Bible? How did Paula bring great joy to her cousins? To find out, read <u>Paula, the Waldensian</u>.

I enjoyed reading about Paula's experiences as she stood for the right. Read this book, and let it challenge you to be faithful and live unselfishly for others. Above all, let it help you love God with all your heart as Paula did.

—*Rita Wells*

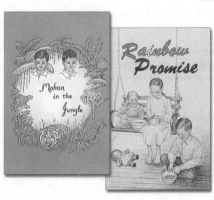

Oral Drill

Answer the following questions about book reports.
1. How do book reports help other people?
2. How much of the book should you read before you write a report about it?
3. What information should the first paragraph contain?
4. What information should the second paragraph contain?
5. What is the setting?
6. What information should the third paragraph contain?
7. What information should the fourth paragraph contain?
8. What is the plot of the book?
9. What parts of the story should you tell? What parts should you not tell?
10. Should you copy sentences from the book?
11. What should you write at the end of the book report?
12. What kind of sentences should you use in your report?

Written Practice

Write a report on a book you have read recently. Follow the directions given in the lesson.

Review and Practice

Write the correct abbreviation for each word or phrase.

1. Mister	5. before noon	9. gallon
2. Doctor	6. January	10. quart
3. Senior	7. Wednesday	11. Post Office
4. Junior	8. dozen	12. World War II

94. Divided Quotations

Some direct quotations are divided. The explanatory words separate the quotation into two parts.

> "Our Labrador retriever," announced William, "had thirteen puppies!"
>
> "Yesterday," began the teacher, "we had an interesting science lesson."

To write a sentence that has a divided quotation, use the following rules.

1. **Use a capital letter at the beginning of the sentence.** The beginning of the sentence and the beginning of the quotation are at the same place.

   > "**W**hen I go to school this fall," said Dennis, "Brother Marvin will be my teacher."

2. **Do not capitalize the second part of a divided quotation.** Of course, if the second part begins with a word that is capitalized for another reason, that word should still be capitalized.

   > "When you get there," instructed the teacher, "**s**it quietly and wait."
   >
   > "In the morning," said Martha, "**I** will work on it."

3. **Use commas to separate the explanatory words from the quotation.** Remember that quotation marks come **after** commas.

   > "Last night," said June, "we caught twenty fireflies."

4. **End the sentence with correct punctuation.** The end of the sentence and the end of the quotation are at the same place.

> "When we were picking berries," continued Jane, "we saw a bear<u>!</u>"
> "When you saw it coming," asked Mark, "did you run away<u>?</u>"

5. **Be sure the whole quotation is within quotation marks.** Quotation marks must be used at the beginning and the end of both the first part and the second part.

> <u>"</u>I'm sure that when the bear saw us,<u>"</u> added Sally, <u>"</u>he ran away faster than we did!<u>"</u>

6. **Place the end punctuation mark before the quotation marks.**

> "Next year, when it's berry-picking time," Mark asked, "will you go along<u>?</u>"
> "If you chase the bears away first," laughed Sally, "I will go."

Remember: In a sentence with a divided quotation, each part of the quotation is enclosed in quotation marks. The second part usually does not begin with a capital letter.

> **Oral Drill**

Write these sentences on the chalkboard, adding the needed punctuation.

1. Young man said the stranger where is Route 70
2. Nevertheless warned the preacher God is not mocked

3. This little part the mechanic explained will be very expensive

4. Last night exclaimed Kevin I saw a raccoon in the garden

5. No answered Maureen we did not see it

6. Can you tell asked Mervin which is which

> **Written Practice** >

Copy these sentences, and add the correct punctuation.

1. In the morning said Dennis we shall find it

2. Yes she agreed they are growing quite rapidly

3. Do you know asked the stranger how I can get there

4. In the meantime suggested the teacher you may study your spelling words

5. While we are waiting announced the leader we will sing a few songs

6. Excuse me said Kathy but I'll have to leave

7. After we eat said Uncle Kenneth I will tell you the story

8. Did you hear asked Marilyn just how it happened

9. All of a sudden exclaimed Marlin we saw that it was going to fall

10. Move away shouted Father before it falls on you

11. The falling tree continued Marlin fell onto the roof of the house

12. We surely were thankful added Margaret that no one was hurt

> Review and Practice >

A. Write the correct past form of each verb in parentheses.
   1. Fred (wind) the thread onto the spool.
   2. We (swing) a long time yesterday.
   3. The sun (shine) through the north window.
   4. The wheat was (grind) very fine.
   5. I (do) the dishes alone yesterday.
   6. Where has he (go)?
   7. Aunt Faith has (do) some scenery painting for the bulletin boards at school.
   8. I (run) nearly all the way to Grandmother's house.
   9. I have often (run) there.
   10. Have you (eat) your cereal yet?
   11. We (eat) the watermelon yesterday.
   12. We all (creep) softly to our beds after the lights were out.
   13. We all (sleep) well last night.
   14. Have you ever (feel) a caterpillar?
   15. The postage (cost) more than I thought it would.

B. Choose and write the correct verbs in parentheses.
   1. When I was sick, I (laid, lay) in bed all day long.
   2. The masons are (laying, lying) blocks for a wall.
   3. The flowerpot was (laying, lying) on its side.
   4. The men (laid, lain) a cable under the ground.
   5. The branches have (laid, lain) on the ground since the storm.
   6. (Set, Sit) down at the table for a while.
   7. (Set, Sit) the fruit dishes on the table.
   8. Gilbert (set, sat) the basket at the end of the row.
   9. The cow (raised, rose) her head.
   10. The ship (raised, rose) and fell constantly in the high waves.

11. Jesus said, "(Raise, Rise), take up your bed, and walk."
12. We (let, left) the dog run loose.
13. Do not (let, leave) the baby alone in the house.
14. The careless boy (let, left) his book in the rain.

◆━━◆━◆━◆━◆━◆━◆━◆

95. Writing Conversation

A story with conversation is more interesting than a story without it. Conversation helps to carry the action along, and it makes the characters in the story seem real.

When you write conversation, begin a new paragraph each time the speaker changes. Study this example from the story "To Market."

> "After we've taken the groceries home," suggested Manuel, "we can go back and show the birds to Angie."
>
> "Yes," agreed Nenet. "She'll love looking at them. She never has any fun."
>
> "It must be lonesome staying in the house all the time with no playmates," said Manuel.

When a speaker says more than one sentence in the same paragraph, quotation marks are placed before his first sentence and after his last one. Quotation marks are not needed before and after every sentence. Here is an example from the story "The Second Mile."

> "So far! Then let me carry your pack another mile. There is no one here to take it. Another mile will be nothing," said David.

If a quotation is divided by explanatory words, quotation marks must be placed at the end of the first part and before the beginning of the second part. Study the following example from the story "The Sacrifice."

"Our neighbor is a very unhappy person, and we should do what we can to help him. I must admit, though," Father went on, "that at times, it seems difficult to help people like Mr. Whitney. We will just have to continue to pray for him and show the love of Christ by our actions. Hopefully, we'll be able to keep the calf in our field."

Remember: Conversation helps to make stories interesting. A new paragraph is started every time the speaker changes. When a speaker says more than one sentence in the same paragraph, quotation marks are placed before his first sentence and after his last one.

Oral Drill

A. Look in your reading book for a story that uses conversation. Notice how a new paragraph begins every time the speaker changes. Find some quotations that are more than one sentence long.

B. Read a story from your reader that has much conversation. One student can be the "storyteller" and read all the parts that are not direct quotations. Another student can read all the words that a certain character said. A different student can read all the words another character said.

> Written Practice >

A. Copy this story. Start a new paragraph every time the speaker changes. Use correct capitalization and punctuation. The story should have four paragraphs when it is finished.

Jesus said to the man if you can believe, all things are possible. Lord I believe! cried the man. Please help my unbelief! After Jesus had healed the boy, His disciples asked why could we not cast it out? Jesus answered this kind does not go out except by prayer and fasting.

B. Write a conversation between two children your own age. They may be talking about something that happened at school, about their favorite chore or project at home, or about a trip or accident one of them was involved in. Have the speakers change several times. Proofread your work, make the necessary corrections, and recopy it neatly.

> Review and Practice >

A. Write whether each sentence has a **direct** or an **indirect** quotation. If it has a direct quotation, write correctly the word that should be capitalized.
1. Someone came and said to Jairus your daughter is dead.
2. He added that Jairus should not trouble Jesus.
3. Jesus said that he should not fear, but believe.
4. Jesus told Jairus she shall be made whole.
5. Jesus took the girl's hand and said maid, arise.
6. He commanded that they should give her food to eat.

B. Read each sentence. If it has a direct quotation, write the sentence correctly. If it has an indirect quotation, write **indirect quotation.**
1. The children said that they would enjoy a visit to the zoo.
2. Do your work well Father encouraged them.

3. Please help me clean the kitchen said Mother.
4. Henry said that he would help Father dig potatoes.
5. Martha exclaimed I liked watching the monkeys best.
6. Carrie said that she liked the lion house best.
7. I will pull down my barns and build greater the rich man said to himself.
8. But God told him that his soul would be required of him that night.
9. Do you think I came to bring peace on the earth asked Jesus.
10. Jesus asked what is the kingdom of God like.

> **Challenge Exercise**

Write the story in Ruth 1:6–18, using your own words. Use all three kinds of sentences with direct quotations: sentences that begin with direct quotations, sentences that end with direct quotations, and sentences with divided quotations.

96. Chapter 8 Review

> **Oral Drill**

A. Give the word or words for which each abbreviation stands. Tell which ones may be used in ordinary writing.

1. qt.	6. St.	11. oz.	16. A.M.
2. doz.	7. p.	12. wk.	17. A.D.
3. Mrs.	8. lb.	13. yd.	18. Jan.
4. Tues.	9. Dr.	14. chap.	19. Rd.
5. Ave.	10. R.R.	15. mi.	20. Sr.

B. Tell whether each sentence has a **direct quotation** or an **indirect quotation.**

1. "Did you know that the word **dollar** comes from England?" asked Kevin.
2. Kenneth asked, "But where did the English get it?"
3. Brother John said that **dollar** comes from the name of a coin minted in Joachimstal, a town in Europe.
4. "They called the coins **talers** for short," Kendall explained.
5. Karen added that in the Netherlands the name changed to **daler.**
6. "Of course," said Kevin, "the word then became **dollar** in English."

C. Tell whether each statement is **true** or **false.**

1. You should know your story well before you tell it.
2. You should tell your story with as few details as possible.
3. It is better to look somewhere other than at your listeners.
4. Nervousness can help you be a good storyteller.
5. Gestures should be natural and meaningful.
6. The copyright date of a book is of little importance.
7. In a book report, you should name the characters and tell what they are like.
8. A book report should give a summary of the whole story.
9. The plot of a story is the main problem that the characters face.
10. When you write a book report, you should leave your readers in suspense about the outcome of the story.

> Written Practice >

A. Write the correct abbreviations for these words.

1. amount
2. number
3. chapter
4. and so forth
5. Avenue
6. year
7. pages
8. President
9. Company
10. United States

B. Copy the words that should have commas after them, and add the missing commas.

1. Edith come and see this valuable coin.
2. This coin in fact is made of gold.
3. In October 1737 a sailing ship arrived in Philadelphia Pennsylvania with a group of Anabaptists from Rotterdam Holland.
4. My teacher Brother John told us what it was like to travel on a ship in those days.
5. The ships were small but the owners loaded them with many passengers.
6. Many fearful raging storms beat on the frail wooden ships.
7. Sometimes the passengers received poor food and many of them died.
8. Early Mennonite pioneers raised hogs sheep chickens and cows.

C. Copy these letter parts, and add the correct punctuation.

1. 598 Chestnut Street
   Chicago IL 60610
   Apr 6 20—
2. Dear Dwight
3. Your friend
4. Route 3 Box 22
   Northport MI 49670
   March 2 20—
5. Dear Grandmother
6. Your loving granddaughter

D. Find each word that has a mistake, and write it correctly.
1. I could'nt get any stamp's, because the post office wasnt open.
2. You're 5s look like Ss.
3. Have you seen they're stamp collection?
4. Its quite a large collection.
5. His' book has over one hundred stamp's.
6. Who's collection is this? Is it Marys?
7. I didnt bring our's. Their packed away.
8. Whose making that noise? Its Johns whistle.

E. Fill in the missing words on this chart.

Singular	Singular Possessive	Plural	Plural Possessive
1. girl	———	———	———
2. woman	———	———	———
3. goose	———	———	———
4. fox	———	———	———
5. mouse	———	———	———

F. Copy and add the correct capitalization and punctuation.
1. Gloria asked do you know how to make stickers
2. No replied Gwen I do not
3. Well said Gloria you use gelatin and corn syrup
4. Does it really work asked Gwen
5. I have found replied Gloria that it works quite well. Use four tablespoons water and one tablespoon gelatin. Add one-half teaspoon corn syrup. Stir it up, and spread it on the back of a pretty picture.
6. How do you dissolve the gelatin asked Gwen. Do you soften it first? Should the water be hot?
7. Gloria replied use one tablespoon cold water to soften the gelatin
8. Then you must use three tablespoons hot water to dissolve the gelatin Gloria continued

9. Let your stickers dry added Gloria until you are ready to use them

10. You can make your own designs Gwen exclaimed. Then you can lick them like stickers

G. Write whether each sentence has a **direct** or an **indirect** quotation.

1. Mabel said, "I saw the men shearing the sheep."
2. Ruth said that the men would sell the wool.
3. "Most sheep's wool is tannish white," said George.
4. Mary Lou said, "I knit afghans."
5. Rachel said that she had seen one of Mary Lou's afghans.
6. Gail said that she would like to have an afghan herself.

H. Copy and punctuate this conversation correctly. Divide it into paragraphs.

What is a martyr Emily wanted to know. A martyr is a person who gives his life because he will not give up his faith Mother explained. Was Stephen a martyr asked Emily. Yes Stephen was the first Christian martyr on record said Mother.

I. Write the numbers in the correct order for telling a story to
   your class.
1. Look at your listeners, and speak slowly and clearly enough
   so that everyone can understand you. Avoid awkward and
   distracting motions.
2. Decide what story you will tell, and write brief notes.
3. Take a deep breath to help you relax before you begin to
   speak.
4. Practice telling your story to someone at home before you
   give it at school.

Prepositions:
The marbles rolled across the floor, under the chair, behind the flowerpot, and down the stairs.

Conjunctions:
Mary picked snapdragons, but Rosa picked marigolds and petunias.

Chapter 9
Prepositions, Conjunctions, and Interjections

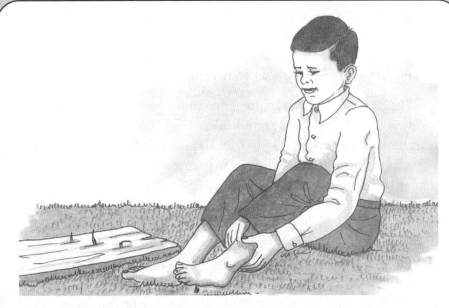

Interjections:
    Ouch! Oh, I stepped on a nail!

97. Writing a Story

We all like to hear or read a story. There are many good stories in the Bible, and from them we can learn many things about writing stories of our own.

To write a good story, you must know the facts. You must know who, what, when, where, why, and how. Put things in proper order—first things first and last things last. See how this is done in the following story.

> Elijah was staying with a widow in Zarephath because there was a famine in Israel. One day the widow's son became seriously ill, and soon he died. The widow was brokenhearted. What had she done that she should lose her son? Elijah carried the boy to his room and laid him on the bed. He prayed earnestly that God would let the child wake up again. Elijah stretched himself upon the child three times, and then he prayed again. God heard Elijah's prayer and restored the boy to life. How glad his mother was! She said, "Now I know that you are a man of God and that you speak the words of God."

When you write a story, be sure to include all the important information. Stick to the main idea, and do not stray away to unrelated details. If you leave out important facts, the story will not make sense. And if you add unrelated details, the story will be cluttered and hard to understand.

Write in complete sentences. Have variety in the length and kinds of sentences. Use words that say exactly what you mean, and spell them correctly. These things will help to make your story interesting and enjoyable for other people to read.

End with a sentence which tells the reader that the story is finished. But do not write, "That is the end of the story." One good way to end is by telling how people felt after the last thing happened. The story above has this kind of ending. You could also tell what lesson can be learned from the story. A story should not stop without a good ending.

> Oral Drill >

A. Read the story of the fiery serpents in Numbers 21:4–9.
   Answer these questions about the story.
   1. Who were the people, and where were they?
   2. Why were they discouraged?
   3. How did they anger the Lord?
   4. What did He do in response?
   5. What did the people tell Moses?
   6. What did the people ask Moses to do?
   7. What did God tell Moses to do?
   8. What happened when the people looked at the serpent of
      brass?

B. Tell what the people learned.

> Written Practice >

A. Write answers to the questions in Oral Drill.

B. Take your sentences from Part A, and put them in paragraph
   form. Make any changes that are needed so that they fit
   together smoothly. Check your paragraph to make sure it
   follows the rules in the lesson for a good story.

C. End your story with a sentence telling what lesson the people
   learned.

D. Proofread your story, and make corrections. Recopy it neatly.

Review and Practice

A. Write the numbers 1–5, one number for each stanza of the poem below. Beside each number, write the two pairs of rhymes in that stanza. Some rhymes are in two words, such as **done it—won it.**

Forget and Remember

Forget each kindness that you do,
    As soon as you have done it;
Forget the praise that falls to you,
    The moment you have won it.

Forget the slander that you hear,
    Before you can repeat it;
Forget each slight, each spite, each sneer,
    Wherever you may meet it.

Remember every kindness done
    To you, whate'er its measure;
Remember praise by others won,
    And pass it on with pleasure.

Remember all the happiness
    That comes your way in living;
Forget each worry and distress,
    Be hopeful and forgiving.

Remember good, remember truth,
    Remember heaven's above you;
And you will find through age and youth
    True joy and hearts to love you!
                —*Author unknown*

B. Copy this stanza, and mark the rhythm pattern. Write the letters **a** and **b** after the lines to show the rhyme pattern.

To God be the glo-ry—great things He hath done;
So loved He the world that He gave us His Son,
Who yield-ed His life an a-tone-ment for sin,
And o-pened the life gate that all may go in.

—*Fanny Crosby*

Common Prepositions

aboard	before	except	on	until
about	behind	for	over	up
above	below	from	past	upon
across	beneath	in	since	with
after	beside	inside	through	within
against	between	into	throughout	without
along	beyond	like	to	
among	by	near	toward	
around	down	of	under	
at	during	off	underneath	

There are other words besides these that may be preposi-tions. Check a dictionary if you are not sure whether a word can be used as a preposition.

98. Prepositions

A **preposition** is a part of speech. It is a connecting word that begins a **prepositional phrase.** Every preposition has an **object,** which is a noun or pronoun that the preposition connects to another word in the sentence. In the following sentence, the prepositional phrase is in bold print.

preposition   object
↓   ↓
Abel was the son **of Adam. (Of** connects **son** and **Adam.)**

In grade 4 you met the following prepositions.

across	**behind**	**in**	**to**
after	**down**	**near**	**under**
around	**for**	**on**	**up**
before	**from**	**over**	**with**

Now you are ready to learn more about prepositions.

Most prepositions are small, simple words. Study the chart before this lesson. You do not need to memorize the list, but you should become thoroughly familiar with the common prepositions.

Read the list several times. Refer to it often at first. Get a feel for the common prepositions. This will help you to find prepositional phrases in sentences.

There are other prepositions that are not on the list. You can easily recognize those if you are familiar with the most common prepositions. A dictionary will tell you whether a word can be used as a preposition.

A preposition is always the first word of a prepositional phrase. A prepositional phrase includes the preposition, its object, and any adjectives that modify the object. The object of a preposition is a noun or pronoun at the end of the phrase.

> The cabin **near the creek** is new.
> The preposition is **near,** and the object is **creek.**

> The girl **beside me** is my sister.
> The preposition is **beside,** and the object is **me.**

Use the following steps to find a prepositional phrase in a sentence.

a. Find the preposition.
b. Find the object of the preposition by saying the preposition and asking **whom** or **what.** The object is always a noun or a pronoun.

c. The prepositional phrase includes all the words from the preposition to its object. Any words in between are adjectives that modify the object. Not all phrases have adjectives.

> The man with Elijah was Elisha.
>> The preposition is **with.**
>> With **whom**? Elijah.
>> The prepositional phrase is **with Elijah.**

> A fiery chariot separated Elijah from him.
>> The preposition is **from.**
>> From **whom**? Him.
>> The prepositional phrase is **from him.**

> In Naaman's house, a little maid served faithfully.
>> The preposition is **in.**
>> In **what**? House.
>> The prepositional phrase is **in Naaman's house.**

Prepositional phrases may be found at different places in a sentence. In the three examples above, prepositional phrases are found in the middle, at the end, and at the beginning of the sentences.

> The man **with Elijah** was Elisha.
> A fiery chariot separated Elijah **from him.**
> **In Naaman's house,** a little maid served faithfully.

Remember: A preposition is a connecting word that begins a prepositional phrase. The object of a preposition is a noun or a pronoun.

> **Oral Drill**

A. Read the prepositions on the chart at the beginning of the chapter several times.

B. On the chalkboard, write each prepositional phrase. Underline each preposition, and put parentheses around its object. Then read the whole phrase.
   1. Elisha went to Bethel after Elijah's departure.
   2. He was a godly prophet from the northern kingdom.
   3. From the city came some children.
   4. With disrespectful words, they mocked him.
   5. Two bears from the woods hurt forty-two children.
   6. Children should always speak with kind respect.
   7. The boy with the colorful coat was Joseph.
   8. Ezra read clearly from the Law.

> **Written Practice**

A. Copy each prepositional phrase. Underline the preposition, and put parentheses around its object.
   1. Jericho was a city of palm trees.
   2. Jericho was located in a pleasant place.
   3. Water from Jericho's spring had caused the death of some people.
   4. Elisha asked for a new cruse.
   5. The cruse was filled with salt.
   6. Into the spring he poured the salt from the cruse.
   7. On that day God healed the waters of Jericho.
   8. Pure, healthy water flows from God's Word.

B. Write original sentences, using these prepositional phrases.
   1. down the hill
   2. under a tree
   3. on the porch
   4. behind the box

> Review and Practice >

A. Copy each sentence. Add the missing capital letters and punctuation.

1. havent people always known about corn
2. no david Europeans didnt know about corn before christopher columbus discovered america
3. doesnt the Bible speak about corn
4. yes carla it speaks about corn but the word **corn** in fact means any kind of grain
5. in Bible times people raised wheat barley and millet
6. oh can you imagine what the seven thin ears of corn looked like in pharaohs dream
7. in pennsylvania before 1790 said brother william corn was not the main crop
8. what was the main crop asked benjamin
9. brother william said that farmers sold much wheat in philadelphia lancaster and reading
10. corn a favorite food is the most valuable crop of the united states today
11. hard work was done to improve corn and now it is one of the four most important food crops in the world
12. write to mr mack at 815 meade street minerva ohio 44657 for more information on Mennonite pioneers

B. Write the missing words.

Singular	Singular Possessive	Plural	Plural Possessive
1. wolf	———	———	———
2. ox	———	———	———
3. baby	———	———	———
4. dog	———	———	———

99. Prepositional Phrases Used as Adjectives

A phrase is a group of words used as one part of speech. A prepositional phrase is used in this way. When a prepositional phrase modifies a noun or a pronoun, it is an **adjective phrase.** Adjective phrases usually tell **which** or **what kind of.**

> The peaches **on the table** are yours.
> **On the table** tells **which** peaches.

> Those are peaches **with brown spots.**
> **With brown spots** tells **what kind of** peaches.

An adjective phrase must come right after the word it modifies.

> The picture **on the wall** is my brother's.
> **On the wall** tells **which** picture.

In the sentence above, **on the wall** comes right after the noun **picture.** It is not hard to tell which word the phrase modifies, because the phrase comes right after that word.

An adjective phrase is diagramed beneath the noun or the pronoun it modifies. The preposition is diagramed on a slanted line, and its object goes on a horizontal line connected to it. Any adjectives go on slanted lines below the object of the preposition.

Adjective phrase modifying a subject:
The girl **in the blue dress** came first.

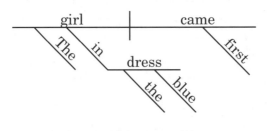

Adjective phrase modifying a direct object:
Yesterday we saw a flock **of wild geese.**

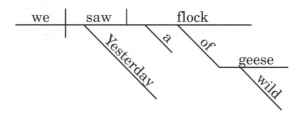

Adjective phrase modifying a predicate nominative:
This book is a collection **of poems.**

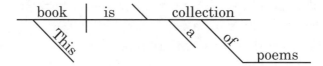

The object of a preposition is never the subject of a sentence. Make sure you choose the right word for the subject when it is followed by a prepositional phrase. Be especially careful when the subject is an indefinite pronoun, such as **each, one, some, more, all,** or **both.**

Some of my books are old.

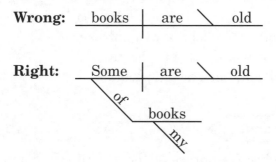

> **Remember:** A prepositional phrase may be used as an adjective. An adjective phrase modifies a noun or a pronoun.

> ⟩ Oral Drill ⟩

A. Read each adjective phrase. Tell which noun it modifies.
1. The fruit in that box looks delicious.
2. The car at the corner was hit.
3. The girl with the white cat has the new book.
4. The Israelites wanted freedom from Pharaoh.
5. He is a man with a good memory.
6. Some of these insects can bite.
7. None of the boys knows the answer.
8. A pen without ink is not very useful.

B. Use these prepositional phrases in sentences of your own. Be sure the phrase comes after a noun and tells **which** or **what kind of.**
1. from my grandmother
2. with red hair

C. On the chalkboard, diagram each sentence.
1. The pigeon with gray feathers came back then.
2. Moses' mother made an ark of bulrushes.
3. This book is a story about a horse.
4. Some of the oranges tasted peculiar.

> ⟩ Written Practice ⟩

A. Copy each adjective phrase. After it, write the noun that it modifies.
1. The book on that shelf has a story about the fire.
2. Hezekiah showed his house of treasures.

3. The only thing in my house is a pot of oil.
4. The falling tree hit the house with the tin roof.
5. The cat under the porch is mine.
6. Both of the girls made a cake with white icing.

B. Diagram the following sentences.
1. The vase on the windowsill broke.
2. Mother made the cookies with chocolate chips.
3. Spain is a country in Europe.
4. The picture on this page shows a buck with large antlers.
5. One of the boys fell down.

C. Add adjective phrases to these sentences. Write the new sentences.
1. Some are visitors.
2. That dog is mine.
3. That girl is my cousin.

D. Write sentences of your own, using these prepositional phrases. Be sure the phrase comes after a noun and tells **which** or **what kind of.**
1. with chocolate frosting
2. near the bridge

> Review and Practice >

A. Write the definition of a preposition. Write five prepositions from memory.

B. Write the correct form of each word in parentheses.
1. After Sue gave her report, she was (happy) than before.
2. James feels (well) today than he did yesterday.
3. Of all the children, Kevin has the (many) lessons to finish.
4. The Martins came (late) than the Benders.
5. The fourth graders have (little) work than the fifth graders do.

6. The tenth graders have the (much) work of all.
7. The new pump works (badly) than the old one did.
8. That was the (bad) storm I ever saw!
9. Of the two girls, Marilyn draws (well).
10. Of the twins, Jane is (tall).

◆━◆━◆━◆━◆━◆━◆━◆━◆

100. Prepositional Phrases Used as Adverbs

You have learned that prepositional phrases may be used as adjectives. They may also be used as adverbs to modify verbs. An **adverb phrase** may tell **how, when, where,** or **why.**

Connie reads **with expression.**
With expression tells **how** Connie reads.

The sun shone brightly **in the afternoon.**
In the afternoon tells **when** the sun shone.

A great storm arose **on the sea.**
On the sea tells **where** a storm arose.

Many Christians have died **for Jesus' sake.**
For Jesus' sake tells **why** Christians have died.

An adverb phrase may be at different places in a sentence.
a. It may come right after the verb.

Daniel prayed **to God** daily.

b. It may be at the beginning of the sentence.

To God Daniel prayed daily.

c. It may be at the end of the sentence.

Daniel prayed daily **to God.**

Although an adverb phrase can be put in different places, it still modifies the verb. This is true even if it follows a noun.

> **During the night** the wind blew **through the trees with great force.**
>> **Blew** is modified by three adverb phrases that tell **when, where,** and **how.**

> The stone struck Goliath **in the forehead.**
>> **In the forehead** modifies **struck,** not **Goliath.**

Adverb phrases may modify verb phrases. Be sure to get the whole verb phrase, not only part of the verb.

> Jesus was walking **on the water.**
>> **On the water** modifies the verb phrase **was walking.**

Adverb phrases can modify adjectives or other adverbs also. You will work with such phrases in a later grade.

An adverb phrase is diagramed beneath the word it modifies. The preposition is diagramed on a slanted line, and its object goes on a horizontal line connected to it. Any adjectives in the phrase go on slanted lines below the object of the preposition.

Father took the boy by the hand.

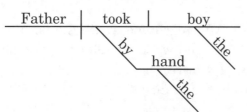

> **Remember:** A prepositional phrase may be used as an adverb. Most adverb phrases modify verbs.

> Oral Drill >

A. Give each adverb phrase and the verb or verb phrase that it modifies. Tell what question the adverb phrase answers.
1. Near the stream we stopped for our lunch.
2. The children were watching the fish for several minutes.
3. The cat climbed through the window.
4. Muddy water was pouring from the large hole.
5. Before the meeting the men talked in quiet voices.
6. Carl fastened the picture to the wall with thumbtacks.

B. In Part A, if an adverb phrase is at the beginning of a sentence, move it to the end. If an adverb phrase is at the end of a sentence, move it to the beginning. Say the new sentences that you make.

C. On the chalkboard, diagram the sentences in Part A.

> Written Practice >

A. Copy the adverb phrases. After each one, write the verb or verb phrase that it modifies, and write whether the adverb phrase tells **how, when,** or **where.**
1. Apples are hanging from the branches.
2. In a few days we will visit our uncle.
3. Gideon called an army with a trumpet.
4. God called Abraham to a new country.
5. I shall be leaving in two minutes.
6. In the barn we could smell fresh hay.
7. Can you act wisely in an emergency?

8. The empty jars were set neatly on the shelves.
9. May I go with you to the store?
10. The boys watched the strange bird with their binoculars.

B. Diagram the sentences in Part A.

C. Rewrite each sentence. Add an adverb phrase to the beginning of the sentence.
    1. He found the tracks.
    2. Marcia arrived.

D. Copy each sentence, and add an adverb phrase to the end.
    1. Flowers were blooming.
    2. He opened the envelope.

> Review and Practice >

A. Write the name of the part of speech described.
    1. It modifies a verb, an adjective, or an adverb. It tells **how, when, where, why,** or **to what degree.**
    2. It takes the place of a noun.
    3. It modifies a noun or a pronoun. It tells **which, whose, how many,** or **what kind of.**
    4. It is the name of a person, place, thing, or idea.
    5. It shows action or being.
    6. It is a connecting word that begins a prepositional phrase.

B. Copy each sentence, and label the parts of speech. Use these abbreviations: **n., pron., v., adj., adv., prep.**
    1. A large tree has fallen across the road.
    2. Does a rabbit usually drink water?
    3. When will Uncle Martin arrive?
    4. He has already arrived.

101. Using Conversation to Make Stories Interesting

Conversation in a story helps to make it interesting. It helps the reader to "see" the action, and it makes the characters seem real. Compare the two paragraphs below. Which one seems more real?

> John was hoeing beans one morning. It was warm, and he was getting tired of the job.
>
> *   *   *   *   *
>
> "Whew!" John exclaimed. He leaned on his hoe and wiped the sweat from his forehead. "It's really warm this morning, and I wish these beans were done."

The second paragraph is better because it **shows** the action instead of just telling what happened. We know John was hoeing because he leaned on his hoe. We know he was warm and tired because of his words and actions. The second paragraph puts a much clearer picture in our minds than the first one does.

Do not always use **said** in the explanatory words. Use other words that give more meaning to the story. Here are some words that are more descriptive than **said.**

shouted	whispered	complained
asked	demanded	asserted
exclaimed	suggested	admonished
countered	added	continued
agreed		

Remember, though, that **said** is often the best word to use. It does not sound natural to use a different word in every sentence. Use other words only when they add meaning.

Compare the following stories. The second one is better because it uses words other than **said.**

Carol **said,** "Do you know what the biggest animal is?"

Janet **said,** "Is it the elephant? I once saw an elephant that weighed five tons."

Carol **said,** "No, it is the blue whale. A full-grown blue whale may weigh one hundred tons."

Janet thought a little. Then she **said,** "That would be as heavy as twenty of the elephants I saw!"

Carol **said,** "A blue whale may be as much as one hundred feet long."

*   *   *   *   *

Carol **asked,** "Do you know what the biggest animal is?"

"Is it the elephant?" Janet **guessed.** "I once saw an elephant that weighed five tons."

"No, it is the blue whale," **said** Carol. "A full-grown blue whale may weigh one hundred tons."

Janet thought a little. Then she **exclaimed,** "That would be as heavy as twenty of the elephants I saw!"

"A blue whale may be as much as one hundred feet long," Carol **added.**

Use variety. Begin some sentences with explanatory words, and other sentences with direct quotations. Use divided quotations in some sentences. This kind of variety is another reason that the second story above is better than the first one.

Be careful to put quotation marks only where they belong. If a speaker says several sentences together, do not put quotation marks around every sentence. Put them only at the beginning and end of the whole quotation. Indirect quotations and the words that simply tell the story should not be inside quotation marks. Also remember to begin a new paragraph each time the speaker changes. Notice how these rules are followed in the stories above.

Natural conversation has some long sentences and some short ones. So when you write conversation, the sentences should vary in length. Do not write quotations that are too long, because they do not sound natural.

Contractions should not be used in formal writing, but you may use them in writing natural conversation. However, you should not use slang or crude expressions in writing conversation. Use correct English grammar.

> **Remember:** Conversation helps to make stories interesting. Conversation in stories should sound natural, and it should have good variety.

> Oral Drill

Tell how the following story could be changed to use conversation. Discuss what each speaker would say.

Edwin and Philip were studying their Sunday school lesson when Edwin asked why Haman hated Mordecai. Philip was not sure, but he wanted to find out. Edwin found the reason in Esther 3. Haman hated Mordecai because he refused to bow to him. Philip asked Edwin if he knew what the king commanded Haman to do to Mordecai. Edwin said that Haman had to put the king's royal clothing and crown on Mordecai and bring him on horseback through the street of the city. Philip added that that was a very great honor.

> **Written Practice** >

A. Rewrite the story in Oral Drill, using conversation. Divide it properly into paragraphs, and use correct capitalization and punctuation. Follow the rules for natural conversation and sentence variety.

B. Write a conversation between yourself and a man who is at your door. The man wonders where Jerry Funk lives. Jerry Funk is your neighbor, and he lives just beyond the trees down the road.

> **Review and Practice** >

A. Rewrite each sentence correctly in two ways.
   1. I can't hardly see you in the dark.
   2. Nanette don't like none of these pictures.
   3. Naomi didn't go nowhere without her.
   4. Gertrude didn't see nothing like it.
   5. Thelma doesn't have no flour for the cake.

B. Write the correct words in parentheses.
   1. Grace and (I, me) drew a picture of an elephant.
   2. Laura and (she, her) watched Grace and (I, me).
   3. Joann drew Linda and (I, me) sitting on a log.
   4. Karen saw Mother and (they, them) at the bus station.
   5. It was Wayne and (I, me) who cleaned the car.
   6. It was (good, well) that he saw the lion when he did.
   7. Is your arm (more good, better) by now?
   8. Gwen tells stories (good, well).
   9. Homer does (good, well) work on the farm.
   10. Howard recited his poetry quite (good, well).

102. Prepositions and Adverbs

Some words can be used as prepositions and as adverbs. It depends on the way they are used in a sentence.

An adverb never has an object. It does not begin a phrase, but it stands alone.

A preposition cannot stand alone. A preposition always begins a phrase, and it always has an object. The object of a preposition is a noun or a pronoun.

Notice the boldface words in the following examples.

The wind blew the tree **down.**
(adverb; stands alone)

The wind blew the box **down** the hill.
(preposition; object is **hill**)

A helicopter flew **over.**
(adverb; stands alone)

A helicopter flew **over** them.
(preposition; object is **them**)

Now look at the following sentence.

The pilot looked **below** and saw fluffy clouds.

Is **below** an adverb or a preposition? Think: Below **what**? **Clouds** comes after **below,** but the sentence does not say that the pilot looked below the clouds. Rather, this sentence has two verbs: **looked** and **saw.** The noun **clouds** is the direct object of **saw. Below** does not have an object, so it is an adverb.

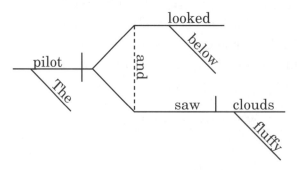

Here are several more examples.

The children went **along** gladly.
> **Think:** Along **what**? There is no word after **along** to tell **whom** or **what**. (**Gladly** tells **how,** not **what.**)
> So **along** is an adverb standing alone.

The children stood **along** the wall.
> **Think:** Along **what**? Wall.
> > **Along the wall** is a prepositional phrase.
> > **Along** is a preposition.

Please stand **by** and wait.
> **Think:** By **what**? There is no word that tells **whom** or **what**. (**And** and **wait** come after **by,** but they do not tell **whom** or **what.**)
> So **by** is an adverb standing alone.

Please stand **by** the gate.
> **Think:** By **what**? Gate.
> > **By the gate** is a prepositional phrase.
> > **By** is a preposition.

Remember: Some words may be either an adverb or a preposition. An adverb stands alone, but a preposition always has an object.

> **Oral Drill**

A. Tell whether the word in bold print is an **adverb** or a **preposition**. If it is a preposition, also give the whole phrase.
1. We read the story **about** Absalom.
2. Absalom traveled **about** and beguiled the people.
3. Absalom had made his plans **before.**

4. David left Jerusalem **before** their arrival.
5. David left the city **behind** and fled.
6. The people traveled **behind** their king.
7. Ittai walked **after** David.
8. Ittai's men also walked **after.**
9. David and his men passed **by.**
10. David was helped **by** his friends.
11. The sick man rose **up** and carried his bed.
12. The weary traveler plodded **up** the mountain.
13. The swine ran violently **down** a steep place.
14. Jericho's walls fell **down** suddenly.

B. Diagram these sentences on the chalkboard.
1. Before the house grew an enormous willow.
2. Where are we going for dinner?
3. Keep the dog inside today.
4. The blue bucket is behind the table.

> **Written Practice**

A. Label each boldface word by writing **adv.** for adverb or **prep.** for preposition. If it is a preposition, also write its object.
1. The new wall caved **in.**
2. The gloves were **in** the box.
3. He tore the cover **off** quickly.
4. He tore it **off** the can.
5. A marble rolled **down** the stairs.
6. Will you come **along** today?
7. Mother planted flowers **along** the fence.
8. I went **outside** while you were in the attic.
9. The cows are **outside** the barn.
10. The light was red, so we did not go **through.**
11. Two people drove **by** without helping the wounded man.
12. We walked **by** the empty house.
13. The smoke went **up** the chimney.

14. The wood was brought **in** soon.
15. The truck turned **off** the main road.
16. Please turn the light **off** now.
17. Margaret is **out** for a walk.
18. We drove **across** the Golden Gate Bridge.
19. The creek was narrow, and we jumped **across** easily.
20. The visitor soon came **in** again.

B. Diagram these sentences.
   1. Large, fleecy clouds floated above.
   2. A bird soared above the barn.
   3. His last battle is over now.
   4. On our vacation it rained for several days.

> **Review and Practice**

A. Copy each sentence, and label the parts of speech with these abbreviations: **n., pron., v., adj., adv., prep.** Use **conj.** to label the conjunction **and.**
   1. Jesus was born in Bethlehem.
   2. Wise men came from the East.
   3. They had seen His star.
   4. Herod inquired diligently from the wise men.
   5. The wise men left Jerusalem.
   6. The star went before them.
   7. It came and stood over the young child.

B. Name the class of pronouns in each set: **personal, demonstrative, indefinite,** or **interrogative.**
   1. someone, anybody, each, all
   2. I, she, us, them
   3. who, whom, which, what
   4. this, that, these, those

103. Using Prepositions Correctly

If there are too many carrots in a row, it is best to pull some of them out so that the others can grow bigger and better. The same is true of a sentence. If it has unnecessary words, it is best to take them out so that the sentence is clearer and easier to read.

Do not use unnecessary prepositions. Study the following examples.

When the word **where** is used in a sentence, the preposition **to** or **at** is often used at the end. These prepositions are unnecessary.

> **Wrong:** Where are you going to?
> **Right:** Where are you going?

> **Wrong:** I do not know where my books are at.
> **Right:** I do not know where my books are.

Do not use the preposition **of** unnecessarily. Do not say **off of, inside of,** or **outside of.**

> **Wrong:** Get the book off of the shelf.
> **Right:** Get the book off the shelf.

> **Wrong:** The paper is inside of the book.
> **Right:** The paper is inside the book.

> **Wrong:** The dog must stay outside of the house.
> **Right:** The dog must stay outside the house.

Some prepositions are similar in spelling or meaning. Be sure to use the right one. Study the meanings and uses of the following prepositions.

Use **into** when an entrance is being made. Use **in** to tell where a person or thing is located.

> **Wrong:** Joseph went in the house.
> **Right:** Joseph went **into** the house.
> **Right:** His grandfather was **in** the house.

Beside means "by the side of" or "next to." **Besides** means "in addition to."

> **Wrong:** Sit there besides her.
> **Right:**   Sit there **beside** her.
> **Right:**   We have more berries **besides** these.

Do not use a preposition where a verb should be used. Remember not to say **could of, should of,** and **would of** for **could have, should have,** and **would have.**

> **Wrong:** I would of helped you if I could of come.
> **Right:**   I **would have** helped you if I **could have** come.

Remember: Do not use unnecessary prepositions. Be sure to use the correct preposition when prepositions are similar in spelling or meaning. Do not use a preposition where a verb should be used.

> **Oral Drill**

A. Read these sentences, leaving out the unnecessary prepositions.
  1. What animals did Noah take inside of the ark?
  2. The waters returned off of the earth continually.
  3. Noah let a dove fly outside of the ark.
  4. Some people cut branches off of palm trees to lay on the road before Jesus.
  5. The angel asked Hagar where she would go to.
  6. Saul asked where Samuel and David were at.
  7. The sailors threw cargo off of the ship.
  8. Where is your brother at?

B. Read these sentences correctly.

1. Simon was casting a net in the sea.
2. Noah and his family went in the ark.
3. The bird dived in the water and caught a fish.
4. You may set that box here besides this one.
5. How many more trees do you have beside that one?
6. If I could of found your number, I would of called you.
7. I should of brought my tools; then I could of repaired that.
8. Please put the pencils in the box.

> Written Practice >

Rewrite these sentences. Leave out unnecessary prepositions, and change prepositions that are used incorrectly.

1. He fell off of the chair.
2. Where did he go to?
3. Do you know where he is at?
4. Mother is inside of the house.
5. Where did you take the scissors to?
6. The baby's ball rolled off of his highchair.
7. Where did you find the bucket at?
8. I should of gotten this tooth fixed before.
9. The dentist could of prevented my severe toothache.
10. If you want to play tag, please go outside of the building.
11. Curtis sits besides Daniel in school.
12. Don't you have any color beside green?
13. I heard a mouse run inside of the wall last night.
14. The three young men were cast in a fiery furnace.

> **Review and Practice** >

Write the correct words for these sentences.

1. The sun was (raising, rising) in the east.
2. "Don't (lay, lie) in bed too long," called Father.
3. The children (raised, rose) and dressed quickly.
4. Luke said, "I want to (teach, learn) how to tie my shoes."
5. "(Can, May) you please (teach, learn) me how to do it?" he asked.
6. Ellen replied, "I (taught, learned) how to do it myself just a few months ago."
7. "(Let, Leave) me show you how," she said.
8. Luke (set, sat) his shoes on the sofa.
9. He (set, sat) down (beside, besides) them.
10. The family (let, left) the house and went (in, into) the garden.
11. They were (raising, rising) strawberries to sell.
12. As the boxes were filled with berries, Susan carried them (inside, inside of) the house.
13. "(Can, May) I eat this big red berry?" asked Susan.
14. Father (let, left) her have it.
15. At noon Mother (laid, lay) a quilt on the grass.
16. The family (set, sat) down and ate a picnic lunch.

17. "You (can, may) rest awhile before we go back to work," said Father.
18. Everyone (laid, lay) down under the shady trees.

104. Conjunctions

A **conjunction** is a word that joins words or groups of words. A conjunction is sometimes called a **connector** because it connects words, phrases, or sentences.

The words **and, but,** and **or** are **coordinating conjunctions.** They connect like parts of equal importance. Words are joined to words, phrases to phrases, and sentences to sentences.

When two parts are joined by a coordinating conjunction, both parts must be used in the same way. For example, two nouns joined by a coordinating conjunction must both be used as subjects, or both be used as direct objects.

A conjunction that joins **words** may connect two nouns.

> Ann **or** Frances will stay overnight. (compound subject)
> Dale saw a turtle **and** a toad. (compound direct object)

It may connect two verbs.

> The little bird spied us **and** quickly escaped.

It may connect two adjectives.

> The house, old **and** neglected, had fallen into ruin.
> The next day was sunny **and** breezy.

A conjunction that joins **phrases** may connect two prepositional phrases.

> My English book is on my desk **or** on the shelf.

A conjunction may also connect two simple **sentences** to make a compound sentence. When two sentences are joined in this way, a comma usually comes before the conjunction. Remember to use both a comma and a conjunction, or the sentence will have a comma splice.

> We waited at the corner, **but** they did not come.
>
> **Incorrect:** Some apples were large, others were small.
>   (comma splice)

Different conjunctions show different relationships. The conjunction **and** is used to add one idea to another. The conjunction **but** shows a contrast between ideas. The conjunction **or** shows a choice between ideas.

The old bridge **and** the log cabin were washed away.
(adding ideas)

The little weasel was timid, **but** he was also curious.
(contrasting ideas)

Be careful, **or** you will get hit.
(showing a choice between ideas)

The following illustrations show how to diagram compound parts in sentences. You have studied all of these before.

Compound subject:

The peaches and the pears are ripe.

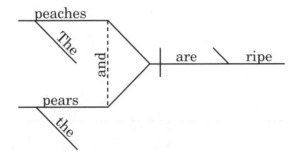

Compound predicate:

The baby cooed and gurgled.

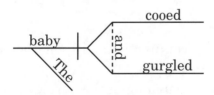

Compound direct object:
Ezra taught statutes and judgments.

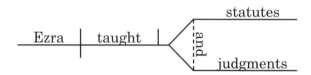

Compound predicate adjective:
The plums are sweet and juicy.

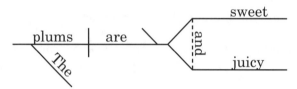

Compound sentence:
Fear God, and honor the king.

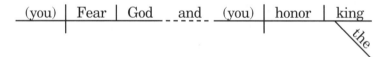

Remember: A conjunction is a word that joins words or groups of words. Three common conjunctions are **and, but,** and **or.**

> **Oral Drill**

A. Find each coordinating conjunction. Tell whether it joins **words, phrases,** or **sentences.**
 1. All the children were searching in the meadow and along the creek.
 2. Marigolds and pansies are common flowers.

3. You did well in English, but your math is not so good.

4. John or Mark will clean out the rabbit pen.

B. Find each coordinating conjunction. Tell whether it joins **nouns** or **verbs.**

1. Herman saw the flames and called his brothers.

2. Do you prefer pancakes or scrambled eggs?

3. Four boys and three girls were sick yesterday.

4. We looked for the kittens but could not find them.

C. On the chalkboard, diagram the sentences in Part B.

D. Combine the following sentences. Make the shortest possible sentence from each pair.

1. The boys enjoyed the forests. They enjoyed the mountains.

2. Are these little flowers pansies? Are they violets?

3. The truck rumbled across the bridge. The truck rumbled up the hill.

4. The wise man's house stood. The foolish man's house collapsed.

> Written Practice >

A. Write each coordinating conjunction. Write whether it joins **words, phrases,** or **sentences.**

1. Righteousness exalteth a nation, but sin is a reproach to any people.

2. Will you go inside or stay outside?

3. The cat sprang off the table and out the door.

B. Write each coordinating conjunction. Write whether it joins **nouns** or **verbs.**

1. We may leave Millie or Mary there.

2. The thirsty boy poured some cold lemonade and drank it eagerly.

3. Was Samuel a priest or a prophet?

4. The workers saw the truck and shouted at the children.

C. Diagram the sentences in Part B.

D. Make the shortest possible sentence from each pair.
1. Franklin picked some flowers. He gave them to his mother.
2. Cows were grazing in the meadow. Sheep were grazing there too.
3. The old house looked sad. It looked lonely.
4. We wanted to work outside. It rained.

> Review and Practice >

Write the correct form of each word in parentheses.
1. Marlin threw the ball the (far) of all the boys.
2. We go to church on Sunday (much) than on any other day.
3. Jupiter is the (large) planet in the solar system.
4. Spring came (late) this year than last year.
5. Of all the shoes I tried, this pair fits (well).
6. A microwave oven is the (fast) oven I know about.
7. It rained (little) today than yesterday.
8. Of all the song leaders, Brother Elmer leads songs (frequently).
9. The new light shines (brightly) than the old one.
10. Of the twins, Linda works (hard).

105. Writing a Good Title

A title often helps us to decide whether we want to read a story. A good title catches our interest. It gives a clue of what the paragraph or story is about, and it makes us want to find out more. Learn to write good titles so that others will want to read what you have written.

The following titles are written in a way that arouses curiosity. Would you like to read stories with these titles?

> The Students' Surprise
> When Fred Met a Bear in the Woods
> The Night of the Fire

A title should tell something about the main idea of the paragraph or story. It should not refer to only one detail in the story. On the other hand, a title should not include more than what the paragraph or story includes.

Good:
> Gideon and His Brave Three Hundred
> (It gives the main idea of a story.)

Too narrow:
> The Soldiers Who Broke Their Pitchers
> (It refers to only one detail in a story.)

Good:
> When Abram Rescued Lot
> (It gives the main idea of a story.)

Too broad:
> Abram and Lot
> (It would be impossible to tell everything about Abram and Lot in a short story.)

How can you decide what the main idea is? This is not as hard as you may think. Suppose someone should ask, "What story did you have in Sunday school?" You would not answer by telling the whole story. You would simply tell in a few words what the story was about. When you do this, you are giving the main idea.

Suppose the story was about the time Joseph's brothers sold him as a slave. To give the main idea of this story, you do not need to say that Joseph went first to Shechem and then to Dothan, or that his brothers threw him into a pit, or that they dipped his beautiful coat into blood. The main idea is that Joseph's brothers sold him as a slave. Compare the following titles for this story.

> **Too narrow:** When Joseph Was Thrown Into a Pit
> **Too broad:** Joseph and His Brothers
> **Good:**   When Joseph Was Sold by His Brothers

A title should not reveal the outcome of the story. It should keep the reader in suspense. Compare the following titles to see how this is done.

Good:

> A Surprise for Mother
>   (It makes the reader
>   wonder what the
>   surprise was.)

Poor:

> When We Surprised Mother by Cleaning the House
>   (It tells exactly what the surprise was.)

Good:

> Chicken Thief
>   (It makes the reader wonder what kind of thief it
>   was and whether he got away with any chick-
>   ens.)

Poor:

> The Night a Fox Stole Some Chickens
>   (The reader knows right away that the thief was a fox
>   and that he got away with some chickens.)

Good:
> Where Could Doris Be?
>> (It makes the reader wonder what happened to Doris.)

Poor:
> When Doris Got Lost in the Woods
>> (It tells exactly what happened to Doris.)

Follow the rules of capitalization when you write a title. Capitalize the first word, the last word, and all the main words. The following words are not usually capitalized unless they are the first or last word in a title.

Articles:
> a, an, the

Conjunctions:
> and, but, or

Prepositions of less than four letters:
> in, to, by, etc.

Notice how the rules of capitalization are followed in the titles above.

Take time to think of a good title when you write a story or paragraph. The best titles are usually short. They say a great deal with only a few words. Writing a good title is hard work, but it is important.

Remember: A title should give an interesting clue about the main idea so that the reader will want to read the paragraph or story. The first word, the last word, and all the main words of a title should be capitalized.

> ▷ Oral Drill ▷

A. Read the following titles and the story below them. Then answer the questions after the story.

Titles: a. Over a Twelve-Foot Fence
b. An Interesting Family Day
c. Locked in a Zoo
d. The Monkeys at the Zoo

It all started when Helen wanted to see the monkeys again. Father gave us permission to go and added, "Meet us here by the fountain when you come back."

We forgot everything else as we enjoyed the antics of the monkeys. Suddenly Helen exclaimed, "Daniel, we're the only ones here anymore!"

As we approached the fountain, we saw Father and Mother hurrying toward us. "The zoo has closed," Father announced. "We should have watched the time better."

"Now what do we do?" I wondered. "Stay here all night?" I eyed the twelve-foot fence that loomed above us, enclosing the huge Brookfield Zoo.

"Either that or climb the fence, I suppose," Mother said cheerfully.

"We could pray," Helen suggested. We bowed our heads and asked the Lord for help.

Helen and I could not imagine Mother climbing a twelve-foot fence. But we had prayed, hadn't we? Slowly Mother squirmed up the fence, puffing. I wiggled along beside her, gripping the fence with all my strength. Up over the top I went, then slowly, slowly down the other side. At last I stood on solid ground again.

I heard an awkward jump nearby. "Well, I made it," Mother laughed shakily. Father and Helen followed.

"Oh!" Helen gasped in dismay. "My purse—it's still on the other side!"

I groaned. Mother sighed, but Father burst into a hearty chuckle. I struggled up over the fence again. Minutes later I joined my family, panting triumphantly.

"Well, here we are," laughed Mother, "all over the top!"

"Let's thank the Lord," finished Father.

1. What is the main idea of this story? (**Think:** What is this story about?)
2. Which title is too broad, telling more than the main idea of the story?
3. Which title is too narrow, giving only one detail of the story?
4. Which title is the best one? Why?

B. Give the main idea of the following paragraph. Then suggest a good title for it. Of all the students' suggestions, decide which title is the best.

Seeing Eye dogs have very important work to do. They are German shepherd dogs that are trained at Morristown, New Jersey. Their work is to guide blind people. They watch traffic in the city and help blind people cross streets safely. They guide their masters around obstacles. They obey their masters well. But if a command is given that would be dangerous to obey, a good Seeing Eye dog will not obey it.

C. Tell how to write these titles correctly.
1. three big scratches
2. the doll on the roof
3. out of a blue sack
4. strange sounds in the dark
5. a promise to depend on

> **Written Practice**

A. Read these titles and the paragraph below them. Then do the exercises after the paragraph.

Titles: a. The Pilgrims' First Year
b. Wild Turkeys for a Thanksgiving Feast
c. The First Thanksgiving
d. The Pilgrims' and Indians' Thanksgiving of Feasting, Prayers, Sermons, and Songs

What was the first Thanksgiving like? In the autumn of 1621, a little band of Pilgrims observed three days of feasting and prayer. They wanted to show their gratitude to God for blessing them with a good harvest. Their Indian neighbors came to join the feast, bringing wild turkeys and venison from the forest. Pilgrims and Indians shared together in joyous feasting and in prayers, sermons, and songs of praise to God.

1. Write the main idea of this paragraph. The topic sentence will help you.
2. Write the title that is too broad. It includes more than what this paragraph is about.
3. Write the title that is too narrow. It gives only one detail of the paragraph rather than the main idea of the whole paragraph.
4. Write the title that is too long and detailed.
5. Write the best title for the paragraph.

B. Read this paragraph, and follow the directions below.

Forest fires are started in many different ways. Some fires are caused by lightning. Others are started by campers who leave the forest without properly putting out their campfire. Another cause of forest fires is people smoking. A few forest fires are lit purposely. But most forest fires are caused by carelessness or accident. We should never be guilty of starting fires through carelessness. "The earth is the Lord's, and the fulness thereof."

1. Write the letter of the main idea in the paragraph above.
   (**Think:** What is the paragraph about?)
   a. forest fires that are caused by lightning
   b. taking care of forests
   c. different ways that forest fires are started
   d. how campers may cause forest fires
2. Write a good title for the paragraph above.

C. Write these titles correctly.
   1. four surprised fishermen
   2. the bible on the road
   3. new kinds of seeds
   4. a cat in the cupboard
   5. words to live by

> Review and Practice >

Write correctly each word that should be capitalized.
1. in april we drove to new york city, the largest city in
   america.
2. conrad grebel was a church leader in the country of switzer-
   land.
3. on thursday, which was ascension day, we had four inches
   of rain.
4. the columbia river flows between washington and oregon
   on its way to the pacific ocean.
5. last year my brother joshua studied the book *european
   history.*
6. lois read *all on a mountain day* last wednesday.
7. mr. and mrs. irving invited mr. and mrs. boyd to come on
   sunday, may 27.
8. janice read *to a man with a lantern* last august.

106. Interjections

There are eight parts of speech altogether. So far you have learned about **nouns** (n.), **pronouns** (pron.), **verbs** (v.), **adjectives** (adj.), **adverbs** (adv.), **prepositions** (prep.), and **conjunctions** (conj.). Today you will study the eighth part of speech. It is the **interjection** (interj.).

An interjection is a word that expresses strong feeling. It is not used as a subject, predicate, object, modifier, or any other sentence part. So we say that an interjection is not related to the rest of the sentence. It is an independent word.

An interjection usually comes at the beginning of a sentence. Some common interjections are **oh, ouch, what, well,** and **whew.** There are many interjections, but not all of them are proper to use. We should use only those interjections that are suitable for God's people.

> **Oh!** That was a snake!
> **Well,** we shall do the best we can.
> **Ouch!** A bee stung me!

The Bible uses several interjections. The words **lo** and **behold** are interjections used to call attention to something or to express wonder or surprise. **Amen** expresses agreement or approval. **Alas** shows sorrow, pity, or concern. The interjection **ah** is a synonym for **oh.** It expresses feelings such as astonishment, grief, or desire.

A strong interjection is followed by an exclamation mark. The first word after the interjection is capitalized as the first word of a new sentence.

> **Ouch!** The hammer hit my thumb.

A mild interjection is followed by a comma. The word after the comma is not capitalized.

> **Well,** who is coming to see me?

Interjections are not related to the rest of the sentence. So they are diagramed on a separate line.

Whew! That box is heavy.

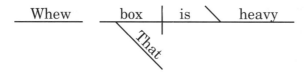

Well, we will still be on time.

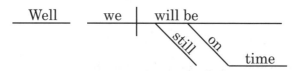

Remember: An interjection is a word that expresses strong feeling. It is not used as part of a sentence. A strong interjection is followed by an exclamation mark. A mild interjection is followed by a comma.

> Oral Drill >

A. Read each interjection, and tell whether it should be followed by a **comma** or an **exclamation mark.** Also tell whether the next word should begin with a **small letter** or a **capital letter.**
1. Well we will excuse you this time.
2. Oh let me hold the door for you.
3. Whew I thought that car was going to hit you.
4. Behold the eye of the Lord is upon them that fear Him.
5. The man exclaimed, "Oh the axhead fell into the water."
6. He cried, "Alas it was borrowed."

7. "Amen the Lord do so," said Jeremiah.
8. The Syrians said, "Lo the king of Israel hath hired against us the kings of the Hittites."

B. On the chalkboard, write the eight parts of speech and their abbreviations.

C. Write each sentence on the chalkboard, and label the parts of speech.
   1. Oh! God is good to us.
   2. The fruit, fresh and sweet, tasted delicious.
   3. Well, bring your books or your papers now.
   4. Lo, mine eye hath seen all this.

D. Diagram these sentences on the chalkboard.
   1. What! You should have started yesterday!
   2. Sh, the baby is sleeping on the couch.

> Written Practice >

A. Copy each interjection, and put a comma or an exclamation mark after it. Write **yes** or **no** to tell whether the next word should be capitalized. (Numbers 7–10 are from Bible verses.)
   1. Ouch you stepped on my toe.
   2. Oh a sunrise over the ocean is truly beautiful.

   3. Sh don't talk so loudly.
   4. What you have forgotten your book three times now.
   5. Whew it's really warm today.
   6. Well what brings you here so early?
   7. Alas that day is great, so that none is like it.
   8. Oh it is the time of Jacob's trouble, but he will be saved out of it.
   9. Behold it is coming, and it shall be brought to pass.
   10. Ah the sword is made bright.

B. Write the names of the eight parts of speech.

C. Copy each sentence, and label the parts of speech.
   1. Oh! I forgot my book again.
   2. Well, Ann and Beth are coming here.
   3. What! Is that the price?
   4. Oh! Look at those dashing waves.
   5. "Lo, I am with you always," Jesus said.

D. Diagram these sentences.
   1. Ouch! The dog bit my leg.
   2. Well, John and Elmer will chop the wood.
   3. Sh, the twins and the triplets are napping.
   4. Alas! What shall we do?

> Review and Practice >

Diagram the following sentences.
1. Sodom and Gomorrah were wicked cities.
2. God destroyed Sodom and Gomorrah.
3. God opened the rock, and the waters gushed out.
4. The Lord is gracious and righteous.
5. Grace and truth came by Jesus Christ.
6. Jacob's sons are these.
7. Lo, in her mouth was an olive leaf.
8. The God of heaven reigns over all.

9. All Thy works shall praise Thee.

10. Remember God now.

> **Challenge Exercise** >

Write one or two original sentences using all eight parts of speech. Label the parts of speech.

●━◆━◆━◆━◆━◆━◆●

107. Chapter 9 Review

> **Oral Drill** >

A. Name the eight parts of speech.

B. Give the definition of an adjective, an adverb, a preposition, a conjunction, and an interjection.

C. Find each prepositional phrase in these sentences. Tell whether it is an adjective phrase or an adverb phrase, and which word it modifies. Diagram number 3 on the chalkboard.

1. Raindrops on the window blurred my vision.
2. The pilot sits in the cockpit.
3. For devotions, the teacher read the parable of the sower.
4. The mother with small children needed help.
5. My teacher is the lady in the brown dress.

D. Diagram these sentences on the chalkboard.

1. Each of the boys brought a lunch.
2. Come along with me.
3. Scott mowed the lawn and weeded the garden.

4. The Mississippi River and the Mackenzie River are major rivers in North America.
5. Oh, bring my glasses and my Bible.
6. Your cake is moist and tasty.
7. What! Are we late, or is that clock fast?

E. Tell whether each boldface word is a preposition or an adverb.
1. We quickly went **outside** the house.
2. Take this bucket **outside** and empty it.
3. Peter stooped **down** and looked **inside** the sepulcher.
4. Jesus was not **inside.**

F. Read the following sentences. Leave out the unnecessary words, and change the words that are used incorrectly.
1. Where did you find the bucket at?
2. This morning I heard the fire crackling inside of the stove.
3. I wish the cats would keep off of the car.
4. The dog should stay outside of the house.
5. James ran in the barn wall with his bicycle.
6. Where is Jennifer going to?
7. Jerry is sitting besides Mark.
8. I wish I would of known you were there.

G. Answer these questions.
1. What must you know well to write a story?
2. What kind of sentences should be used in writing a story?
3. In what order should the facts of a story be given?
4. How does conversation help to make a story interesting?
5. What should a title do?
6. What should a title not do?

> Written Practice >

A. Diagram the following sentences.
1. None of the girls made their beds.
2. Oh! Look down and see the valley below.
3. Mr. Brown and Mr. White discussed the matter thoroughly.
4. Will you carry this jug and the basket?
5. The fragrant, spicy aroma filled the room.
6. Ah, this flannel comforter feels soft and warm.
7. Birds sing during the day, but crickets sing at night.
8. Is Father coming soon, or will he be late?
9. Our Father in heaven answers prayer.
10. In the evening the sun disappears behind the mountain.
11. Samuel bought the dog with pointed ears.
12. My grandfather is the man with the cane.

B. Copy each conjunction, and write whether it joins **words, phrases,** or **sentences.**
1. The plants looked small but healthy.
2. The rope broke, and Charles tumbled down.
3. Lilly mopped the floor under the table and around the sink.
4. We must go now, or we will be too late.

C. Combine each pair of sentences, making the shortest sentence possible. Be sure to avoid run-on sentences. Use the most suitable conjunction.
1. I can see the ball. I cannot reach it from here.
2. Did you finish the roof? Will you go back tomorrow?
3. They were digging. They were searching.
4. Papers flew about. Dust flew about.
5. My cousin is a teacher. My cousin is an artist.

D. Copy the sentences. Above each word, write the abbreviation for the part of speech.

1. Do your work well, or you may be sorry.
2. What! Did you spill all the paint?
3. Later the three brave men were thrown into a fiery furnace.

E. Read these titles and the paragraph below them. Then follow the directions after the paragraph.

Titles: a. Why Dutch Housekeepers Scrub Their Front Steps
b. Being Tidy
c. Tidiness in a Hard-won Land
d. The Neat Farms of the Dutch

The Dutch people are well known for their tidiness. They keep their homes, towns, and fields clean and neat. Farmers keep their small farms neatly arranged and as clean as possible. Many Dutch housekeepers scrub the steps and sidewalks in front of their homes every Saturday. The Dutch had to work hard to win their land from the sea, and they take good care of it.

1. Write the letter of the main idea in the paragraph above. (**Think:** What is the paragraph about?)
   a. the homes, towns, and fields of the Dutch
   b. the tidiness of the Dutch
   c. the Saturday work of Dutch housekeepers
   d. how the Dutch won their land from the sea
2. Write the title that is too broad. It includes more than this paragraph is about.
3. Write two titles that are too narrow. Each one gives only a detail of the paragraph rather than the main idea.
4. Write the best title for the paragraph.

F. Read this paragraph, and follow the directions below.

Airplanes come in many shapes and sizes, but they are all alike in certain ways. Every airplane has a body called a fuselage. It has wings that lift the airplane and a rudder for steering it left or right. Other parts that all airplanes have are ailerons and elevators. The ailerons are used to bank the plane, and the elevators are used for climbing or descending. Many airplanes also have flaps, which give the wings extra lifting power for taking off and landing. All these parts work together so that the airplane can do what it was made to do—fly.

1. Write the letter of the main idea in the paragraph above.
   a. things that fly
   b. the body and wings of an airplane
   c. how airplanes bank, climb, and descend
   d. some ways that all airplanes are alike
2. Write a good title for the paragraph above.

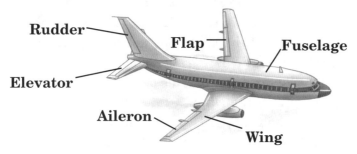

G. Write these titles correctly.
   1. the spider and the fly
   2. when the browns moved out
   3. a splinter in david's hand
   4. two surprises for ann

Titles

Habits

A habit is a sticky thing;
Much good or evil it can bring;
It binds a victim, holds him fast,
And keeps him in a vise-like grasp.

Bad habits grow with extra speed,
Much like a healthy, growing weed.
The roots grow deep, the stem grows stout;
How difficult to pull it out!

Good habits are a little slow;
They need a lot of care to grow;
If tended well, they grow more fair
Than any bloom a plant can bear.

Good habits help us all through life;
Bad habits bring us pain and strife;
Our habits, whether right or wrong,
Each day will grow more firm and strong.

Poetry

Names of People

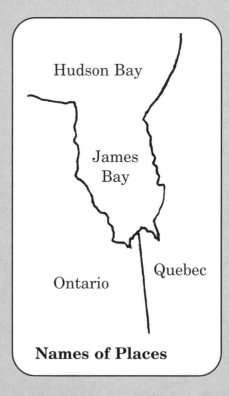

Names of Places

Chapter 10
Capitalization, Reference Books, and More Punctuation

108. Capitalization

Capital letters may not be used in just any way we please. They must be used according to the rules of grammar. Of course you know this. Now you must show that you know by faithfully following the rules.

Study the following rules for capitalization.

1. Capitalize the first word in every sentence.

> **A** soft answer turneth away wrath.
> **W**hat doth the Lord require of thee?

2. Capitalize the first word in a direct quotation.

> A Frenchman once said, "**T**here are some who speak one moment before they think."
> "**L**et your speech be always with grace, seasoned with salt," Paul wrote.

3. Capitalize the first word in every line of poetry.

> **W**hene'er a task is set for you,
> > **D**on't idly sit and view it
> **N**or be content to wish it done;
> > **B**egin at once, and do it.

4. Always capitalize the pronoun **I**.

> **What Am I?**
> **I**'m not a bird but **I** can fly;
> **I** like to sail up in the sky;
> Sometimes **I**'m low, sometimes **I**'m high.
> > What am **I**?

> **I** cannot whistle, chirp, or sing;
> **I** do not even have a wing;
> But **I**'m attached to a long string.
> > What am **I**?

I'm not an airplane or a jet,
But I can fly, do not forget.
I wonder, have you guessed it yet?
   What am I?

—*Ada Wine*

5. All names of God and all pronouns referring to God must be capitalized.

The true **G**od is three persons in one: the **F**ather, the **S**on, and the **H**oly **S**pirit.

After **J**esus fed the multitude, **H**e told **H**is disciples to sail across the sea.

"I believe that **Y**ou are the **C**hrist," said Martha.

People of the 1600s did not capitalize pronouns referring to God. For this reason, pronouns for God are not capitalized in the King James Version of the Bible. So it is correct to write pronouns for God in small letters when you copy verses from the Bible. But in other writing, capitalize all pronouns that refer to God.

Bible verse:
"The Lord is in **h**is holy temple" (Habakkuk 2:20).

Other writing:
God dwells among **H**is people today.

Remember: Capitalize the first word of every sentence, the first word in a direct quotation, the first word in every line of poetry, the pronoun **I,** and all nouns or pronouns that refer to God.

A. Tell which words need to be capitalized in this poem.

In the Morning

in the morning i go to my father;
i pray, and he hears my small prayer.
for christ said that he hears little children,
that he keeps them in his warm care!

—*Edith Witmer*

B. Tell which words need to be capitalized in these sentences.
1. regina asked, "did you know that stars have different colors?"
2. "no, i didn't," replied Robert.
3. the star Betelgeuse shines red. rigel twinkles in blue. capella appears yellow, and Vega looks white.
4. our great god created these beautiful jewels in the sky for our enjoyment and for his glory.

> Written Practice >

A. Copy the following sentences correctly. The verses are not exact quotations from the Bible.
1. god said to Moses, "i will send you to Pharaoh so that you may bring my people out of Egypt."
2. "the Israelites will serve me on this mountain," said the lord.
3. jesus said, "come to me, and i will give you rest."
4. "take my yoke, and learn of me," said jesus, "for i am meek and lowly."
5. jesus' yoke is easy, and his burden is light.
6. jesus commanded the disciples to baptize in the Name of the father, the son, and the holy ghost.

7. when the holy spirit came, he gave power to jesus' disciples and they were witnesses for him.
8. the minister said, "follow in the steps of christ."

B. Copy the following poem correctly.

Only a Minute

i have only just a minute,
only sixty seconds in it;
forced upon me, can't refuse it,
didn't seek it, didn't choose it;
but it's up to me to use it.
i must suffer if i lose it;
give account if i abuse it.
just a tiny little minute,
but eternity is in it.

> **Review and Practice**

Copy the following sentences, using correct capitalization and punctuation.

1. john said i didn't know the earth goes 66,600 miles an hour
2. that would be more than a thousand miles a minute he exclaimed
3. yes it goes that fast as it travels around the sun replied andy
4. is it true asked john that the earth is ninety-three thousand miles away from the sun
5. no john it is ninety-three million miles away andy corrected
6. god made the sun and all the planets stated john
7. andy replied yes he is a mighty god

109. Capitalizing Names and Titles

Every proper noun must be capitalized. Remember that a proper noun is the name of one particular person, place, thing, or idea.

Capitalize names and initials used with names.

Jane Parker	F. J. Crosby
Ernest Jones	F. W. Faber
Martin Luther	P. P. Bliss

Capitalize words used as titles before names.

Mr. Arthur Cleveland	Doctor Jones
Mrs. Sarah Adams	Brother Ray
Miss Katherine Brooks	Sister Dorothy
President Roosevelt	Uncle Elvin
Queen Elizabeth	Aunt Mary

A word used as a title is sometimes written after a name as an appositive. When this is done, the appositive is not capitalized.

Titles:

> In 1801, **J**ustice John Marshall was appointed to the Supreme Court by **P**resident John Adams.

Appositives:

> John Marshall, a **j**ustice of the Supreme Court, was appointed in 1801 by John Adams, the second **p**resident.

The name of a specific place or thing is a proper noun and must be capitalized. Study the list below.

a. Names of countries, states, cities, towns, continents, and some regions.

Peru	Centerville
Ohio	Asia
Akron	the Middle East

b. Names of oceans, seas, rivers, mountains, deserts, and islands.

Pacific Ocean	Appalachian Mountains
Black Sea	Syrian Desert
Thames River	Canary Islands

c. Names of parks, schools, buildings, and hospitals.

Yellowstone National Park	Green Hills Hotel
Bern Christian Day School	Bethesda Hospital

d. Names of historical times and events.

Middle Ages	Civil War
Victorian Age	Industrial Revolution

e. Names of holidays.

Labor Day	Thanksgiving Day
New Year's Day	Ascension Day

f. Names of groups and organizations.

Calvary Mennonite Church
Voices of Victory Chorus
American Red Cross
World Health Organization

g. Names of government offices and branches.

Internal Revenue Service
Secretary of State
Supreme Court
House of Representatives

h. Names of days and months.

Sunday	January
Wednesday	August

A common noun is capitalized when it is part of a proper noun.

Here is a picture of a snowcapped **m**ountain.
I think it is **M**ount **E**verest.

We crossed a wide **r**iver.
It was the **S**usquehanna **R**iver.

An abbreviation is capitalized if the full word would be capitalized. Some abbreviations are always written with capital letters.

Mr.—Mister	Dr.—Doctor
Jr.—Junior	Pa.—Pennsylvania
A.M. *and* P.M.	B.C. *and* A.D.

The names of seasons are not capitalized.

spring	fall (autumn)
summer	winter

Capitalize the first word, the last word, and all important words in the title of a book, magazine, newspaper, poem, song, or story. Do not capitalize an article (**a, an, the**), a conjunction (**and, but, or**), or a preposition with fewer than four letters, unless it is the first or last word in the title.

Hidden **R**ainbow	**A P**salm of **L**ife
Worth **D**ying **F**or	**A**bide **W**ith **M**e
The **T**imes **L**eader	**L**ost and **F**ound

Remember: Capitalize proper nouns, initials, and titles used before names. Capitalize an abbreviation if the full word would be capitalized. Capitalize the first word, the last word, and all important words in the title of a book, magazine, newspaper, poem, song, or story.

Tell which words should be capitalized.

1. maltbie d. babcock was born in syracuse, new york, in 1858.
2. he wrote the hymn "this is my father's world."
3. from a hill near lockport, new york, he often viewed lake ontario.
4. the hymn "now thank we all our god" was written by m. rinkart during the thirty years' war.
5. the quakers served in the pennsylvania assembly until the french and indian war.
6. mount mcKinley is the highest mountain peak in north america.
7. mount mcKinley was named after william mcKinley, the twenty-fifth president of the united states.
8. the amazon river in south america carries more water than any other river in the world.
9. on thanksgiving day, brother brown took his family to little rock park for lunch.
10. mennonites and amish in america suffered for their religious beliefs during the revolutionary war.

> Written Practice >

Copy each sentence, and capitalize properly.

1. the hymn "it came upon the midnight clear," which is often sung at christmas, was written by e. h. sears.
2. isaac watts was born at southampton, england.
3. i. watts wrote "joy to the world" and over seven hundred other hymns.
4. the supreme court can change the decision of any other court in the united states.
5. the peak of mount everest, the highest mountain in the world, is 29,028 feet above sea level.

6. mount everest is in the himalayas, a mountain range of asia.
7. the nile river, which flows through egypt on the continent of africa, is the world's longest river.
8. many redwood trees grow in sequoia national park.
9. the sunnyside chorus sang in the willow street retirement home one sunday last spring.
10. during the civil war, mennonites in the shenandoah valley of virginia suffered greatly for their faith.
11. ascension day comes in the spring, forty days after easter.
12. uncle ben's wedding will be at the salem mennonite church next fall.

Review and Practice

Write the correct words in parentheses.
1. (Set, Sit) here on the second bench.
2. (Let, Leave) the book on the table.
3. (Let, Leave) me help you.
4. Timothy (let, left) his coat and cap here.
5. Please (raise, rise) the windows a bit.
6. The stars (raise, rise) in the east and set in the west.
7. Jonathan (laid, lay) down to rest awhile.
8. He (laid, lay) his tools on the workbench.
9. (Lay, Lie) still so that the bed does not creak.
10. The sick man had (laid, lain) in bed for two weeks.
11. He is (good, well) again.
12. Are you feeling (gooder, better, more better) again?
13. This paper looks (worse, worser) than the first one.
14. I think this flowered wallpaper is (beautifuller, more beautiful) than that striped wallpaper.
15. A cheetah can run (swiftlier, more swiftly) than a horse.
16. "It is (I, me); be not afraid," said Jesus.

17. Ben and (I, me) fed the calves.
18. Janice and (she, her) fed the chickens.
19. Leonard (gave, given) the scraps to them.
20. Harold (saw, seen) a bear in the woods at the park.
21. The bear had (came, come) down from the north.
22. No one (brought, brung) him here.
23. Some workers (caught, catched) the bear and (took, taken) him to the zoo.
24. I (tagged, tug) you, and now (your, you're) out.
25. Joseph (dragged, drug) his feet when he walked, until his mother (taught, learned) him to walk right.
26. I didn't know you (brang, brought) ice cream.
27. Homer (began, begun) his homework early.
28. Jewel had (began, begun) before he did.
29. Who has (broke, broken) the new vase?
30. The veterinarian (came, come) at noon.

━━━━━━━━━━

110. Using Our Senses in Writing Descriptions

Good descriptive writing paints pictures in the mind of the reader. It tells what the writer could see, hear, taste, feel, or smell. By writing descriptions, we can help others to enjoy what we have enjoyed with our five senses.

The following paragraphs are two examples of good descriptions.

> The bakery was a busy, noisy place. Hundreds of pans clattered swiftly by on long conveyer belts. With a steady **slice, slice, slice,** machines above the pans cut off chunks of bread dough. The chunks fell one by one into the pans passing below— **thump, thump, thump.** Then the pans moved into long ovens, and

the bread was baked as it passed through. The air around the ovens felt very warm, but it was filled with the pleasant aroma of baking bread. Our guide gave us samples of the warm, fresh bread, and it tasted just as delicious as it smelled.

*   *   *   *   *

Before you open the rabbit hutch door, the eight chubby bundles of white fur are all nestled in a corner. Now as you open the door, one by one they turn to look at their strange visitor. Then one of the bravest of the bunch, taking one hop at a time, as if he doesn't trust you, comes toward you. His ears are held high in the air. His nose is twitching even faster than your heart is pumping. Now take a look at his sparkling pink eyes. Even though he can see behind him, above him, beside him, below him, and before him, his eyes hardly even move. His soft coat is as white as snow. Now if you think he is tame, jump or make a quick movement, and there are eight bundles of fur in the corner again.

—*A student*

These paragraphs tell about things that writers enjoyed with their senses. In describing the bakery, the writer used all five of his senses! Now read the following paragraph. Do you know why this description is not as good as the first one?

The bakery was a busy, noisy place. I saw hundreds of pans clattering swiftly by on long conveyer belts. I could hear the steady **slice, slice, slice** of machines above the pans, cutting off chunks of bread dough. I heard a **thump, thump, thump** as the chunks fell into the pans passing below. Then I saw the pans moving into long ovens, and I watched the bread baking as it passed through. I felt the warm air around the ovens, and I could smell the pleasant aroma of baking bread. I tasted a sample of warm, fresh bread that the guide gave me, and it was just as delicious as it smelled.

Expressions like "I saw," "I heard," and "I could smell" are usually not necessary in a description. You do not need to tell the reader that you **heard a clatter** or you **smelled an aroma.** He knows that a clatter is heard and an aroma is smelled. If you use exact words to describe what you see, hear, taste, feel, and smell, the reader can enjoy the same thing that you have enjoyed.

Remember: When you write a description, use exact words to tell what you can see, hear, taste, feel, and smell.

> Oral Drill >

Tell which senses the writers used in these paragraphs. Discuss the descriptive words that are used.

1. The temperature is down near zero tonight, and a winter breeze stirs in the tops of the pines. Long, clear icicles are fringing our house roof. Pure white snow thickly blankets the ground, the trees, the hills; and the evening sky is darkened overhead. Winter joys draw our minds to God, who has made everything beautiful.

2. He's fluffy and soft as a puff of cotton, and he's as cuddly as a teddy bear. He's black as midnight, and his black little eyes survey the world around him with a puppy's eagerness. Waddling around like a little stuffed bear, Fritz sniffs and investigates, getting acquainted with his new home.

Written Practice

Write a descriptive paragraph about one of the following topics.

1. a storm
2. an accident
3. a surprise visit
4. spring cleaning
5. inside a busy shop
6. making hay
7. children playing
8. baking day

Review and Practice

Write **true** or **false** for each sentence.

1. **Pleasant** is a more exact word than **nice.**
2. It is better to write "We should assist them" than to write "We should help them."
3. A description should tell about something step by step, such as from top to bottom, from left to right, or from near to far.
4. On an outline, Roman numerals come under capital letters, and capital letters come under Arabic numerals.
5. A good way to take notes is to write down every word.
6. The five parts of a friendly letter are the heading, greeting, body, closing, and signature.
7. Poetry is different from other writing because it usually has rhyme and rhythm.
8. Good poems use descriptive words.
9. Your own experiences will always give you many interesting topics for writing stories.
10. An indirect quotation repeats the exact words of a speaker.
11. Conversation makes a story more interesting and makes the characters seem real.
12. A title should catch the reader's interest and give a clue about the main idea of a paragraph or story.

111. Using the Dictionary

The dictionary is a valuable study tool. It shows the pronunciations, spellings, and meanings of words that we read and write. Learn to use this tool well.

The **entry words** in a dictionary are in bold print. They are listed in alphabetical order. When entry words begin with the same letter, they are alphabetized by the second letter.

a**n**chor   a**p**ple   a**x**e

When the first two letters are alike, words are alphabetized by the third letter, and so forth.

ba**b**oon   wind**m**ill
ba**c**teria   wind**p**ipe
ba**d**ger   wind**s**hield

Guide words are placed at the top of each page to help us find words quickly. The guide word at the left is the same as the first entry word on the page, and the guide word at the right is the same as the last word on the page. See the sample page from a dictionary below.

whom   zinnia

adj.	adjective	*n.*	noun
adv.	adverb	*prep.*	preposition
conj.	conjunction	*pron.*	pronoun
interj.	interjection	*v.*	verb

Three thirds make a whole. 1, 2 *adj.*, 3 *n.*

whom (hum), what person; which person. *pron.*

who's (huz), 1 who is. 2 who has.

whose (huz), of whom; of which. *pron.*

win (win), be successful over others. *v.*

wind' (wind), air in motion. *n.*

wind' (wind), move this way and that; go in a crooked way. *v.*, **wound, wind ing.**

wind mill (wind'mil'), a machine that works by letting the wind move the sails or vanes at the top. *n.*

windmill

wind y (win'dē), having much wind. *adj.*, **wind i er, wind i est.**

win ning (win'ing), that wins: *a winning team. adj.*

Wis con sin (wi skon'sən), one of the north central states of the United States.

Capital: Madison. *n.*

wis dom (wiz'dəm), knowledge and good judgment based on experience. *n.*

wom an (wum'ən), an adult female person. *n.*, *pl.* **wom en.**

worn (wôrn), 1 past participle of **wear.** 2 damaged by use. 3 tired; wearied. 1 *v.*, 2, 3 *adj.*

wor ry (wėr'ē), 1 feel anxious: *She will worry if we are late.* 2 trouble; care: *Worry kept me awake.* 1 *v.*, **wor ried, wor ry ing;** 2 *n.*, *pl.* **wor ries.**

worse (wers), 1 less well; more ill. 2 less good. *adj.*

wor ship (wèr'ship), 1 great honor paid to someone regarded as sacred: *the worship of God, idol worship.* 2 pay reverence to: *We worship God.* 3 religious services. 1, 3 *n.*, 2 *v.*

worst (werst), 1 least well; most ill. 2 least good. *adj.*

would n't (wud'nt), would not.

wound' (wünd), a hurt or injury. *n.*

wound' (wound), past tense and past participle of **wind'** *v.*

wrap (rap), to cover by winding or folding something around. *v.*, **wrapped, wrap ping.**

wrath (rath), very great anger. *n.*

wreck (rek), 1 destruction or serious injury. 2 destroy; ruin. 1 *n.*, 2 *v.*

wrist (rist), the joint connecting hand and arm. *n.*

write (rīt), make letters or words with pen, pencil, or chalk. *v.*, **wrote, writ ten, writ ing.**

writ ing (rī'ting), 1 act of making letters or words with pen, pencil, chalk, etc. 2 written form: *Put your ideas in writing. n.*

writ ten (rit'n), past participle of **write.** *v.*

wrong (rông *or* rong), not right; bad. *adj.*

Wy o ming (wī ō'ming), one of the western states of the United States. *Capital:* Cheyenne. *n.*

Y

yield (yēld), 1 produce: *This land yields good crops.* 2 amount yielded; product: *This year's yield from the silver mine was very large.* 1 *v.*, 2 *n.*

you'd (yud), 1 you had. 2 you would.

young (yung), not old. *adj.*, **young er** (yung'gər), **young est** (yung'gist).

you're (yur), you are.

you've (yuv), you have.

Z

zer o (zir'ō), 1 the figure or digit 0. 2 nothing. *n.*, *pl.* **zer os** *or* **zer oes.**

zin ni a (zin'ē ə), a garden plant grown for its showy flowers of many colors. *n.*, *pl.* **zin ni as.** (from Johann Zinn, 1727-1759, a German botanist)

The dictionary shows how to spell words correctly. It does not show plural forms such as **girls** and **foxes,** because they are formed by simply adding **-s** or **-es.** But it does show irregular plural forms such as **men** and **wolves.** To find an irregular plural form, look up the singular form. The plural form is shown after the entry word, usually with the abbreviation **pl.**

The dictionary also shows irregular verb forms. If two past forms are shown, the second form is the one to be used with a helping verb. If only one past form is shown, that form may be used with or without a helping verb.

For example, if you look up **give,** you will see **gave** and **given** as past forms. **Given** must be used with a helping verb. If you look up **find,** you will see only **found** as a past form. **Found** may be used with or without a helping verb.

The dictionary gives irregular forms of comparison for adjectives and adverbs. If you look up **smooth,** you may not see **smoother** and **smoothest,** because these are regular forms. But if you look up **good,** you will see **better** and **best** because these are irregular forms of comparison.

A few words have two correct spellings. If the two spellings are close together in alphabetical order, the more common spelling is usually shown as the entry word and the other one is shown as an alternate spelling. For example, in the entry for **neighbor,** you may find the alternate spelling **neighbour.** If the two spellings are not close together (such as **syrup** and **sirup**), each spelling is shown as a separate entry word. In this case, the entry for **sirup** will refer you to **syrup** because that is the more common spelling.

If you cannot find a word in the dictionary, you probably do not know how to spell it. Think of other ways the word might be spelled, and keep looking. If you still cannot find it, you may need to ask someone to help you.

The English language has one of the richest vocabularies in the world. It has descriptive words with many different shades of meaning. The reason is that English has borrowed thousands of words from many different languages. But this means that English words also have many different spelling patterns. Study English well so that you can make the best use of this interesting language.

> **Remember:** Use the dictionary to spell words correctly. Learn to find words quickly by using guide words.

> **Oral Drill**

A. Put these eight words in alphabetical order.

notation	purchase	prophecy
pronounce	pronunciation	phonics
routine	practice	

B. For each entry word, say **yes** or **no** to tell whether you would find it on a dictionary page with these guide words: **measure . . . mercy.**

1. men	4. merchant	7. mention
2. message	5. money	8. pity
3. bushel	6. medicine	9. memory

C. Use the dictionary to find the plural of each word.

1. ox	4. index
2. roof	5. scissors
3. father-in-law	

D. Use the dictionary to find the principal parts of these words. On the chalkboard, write all three principal parts. Write **have** with the forms that need helping verbs.

1. bear	4. look
2. cost	5. weave
3. blow	6. drag

E. Use the dictionary to find the forms of comparison for these adjectives.

1. ill
2. little
3. good
4. many
5. late

F. Find the other correct spelling for each word.

1. adviser
2. jailer
3. judgment
4. practice

G. Find the correct spelling of each word, and write it on the chalkboard.

1. sevarel
2. usally
3. suprise
4. enterance

> Written Practice >

A. Write these twelve words in alphabetical order.

pink	purple	push	purchase
purse	purity	pure	pyramid
orange	pursue	red	purge

B. For each entry word, write **yes** or **no** to tell whether you would find it on a dictionary page with these guide words: **hoarfrost . . . hollow.**

1. holiness
2. hint
3. holly
4. hobble
5. hoard
6. hoe
7. follow
8. homestead
9. hold

C. Write the plural of each word. Use the dictionary for help.

1. louse
2. newsman
3. trout
4. pliers

D. Write the three principal parts of each verb, using the dictionary for help. Write **have** with the forms that need helping verbs.

1. bring
2. cut
3. tag
4. set
5. swing

E. Find the forms of comparison for these adverbs, and write them correctly.
   1. well
   2. little
   3. far
   4. much

F. Write the other correct spelling for each word.
   1. ax
   2. likeable
   3. offense
   4. koodoo

G. Find and write the correct spelling of each word.
   1. seperate
   2. insterments
   3. recieved
   4. speical
   5. childern
   6. terrable

Review and Practice

Diagram the following sentences.
   1. Bananas grow on giant green plants.
   2. Banana plants are not trees.
   3. One plant can produce ten bunches of bananas.
   4. Each bunch may have fifteen bananas.
   5. A banana plant can add one inch to its size in one night.
   6. Bananas and oranges are tropical fruits.
   7. Brazil and India are important banana countries.
   8. The plantain is a kind of banana.
   9. The banana stem is cut down after one season, and a new stem grows in its place.
   10. Bananas are delicious and nutritious.

112. Pronunciation and Meaning

The dictionary shows how to pronounce words. After each entry word, there is a **phonetic spelling.** The phonetic spelling uses special symbols to show the correct pronunciation of the entry word.

If a word has more than one correct pronunciation, two or more pronunciations are given. If only one syllable of a word has two correct pronunciations, the rest of the word may not be repeated in the second pronunciation. Study the following example.

> **al·ka·line** (al′·kə·lin, -līn)

These phonetic spellings show that **alkaline** may be pronounced (al′·kə·lin) or (al′·kə·līn).

Because the English language has more sounds than letters, special symbols and **diacritical marks** are used to show word pronunciations. An upside-down **e** is called the **schwa** symbol. Diacritical marks include the bar or macron to show long vowels, and one or two dots to show various other vowel sounds. The **pronunciation key** in the front of the dictionary shows the meaning of each pronunciation symbol. Many dictionaries also have a short pronunciation key at the bottom of each page.

The dictionary also shows how to divide words into syllables. The entry word shows the syllables as they are divided when the word is written. The phonetic spelling shows the syllables as they are divided in speaking.

> **Written syllable divisions:** ex·pe·ri·ence
> **Spoken syllable divisions:** (ek·spir′·ē·əns)

Accent marks are used to show which syllables are stressed. Some words have a **primary** and a **secondary** accent. Usually a heavy accent mark shows that a syllable receives heavy stress. A lighter accent mark shows that a syllable receives medium stress. Unaccented syllables are not marked at all. Check your particular dictionary to see how it shows accent.

cab′·in   glad′·i·o′·lus   mon′·u·men′·tal

One of the main purposes of a dictionary is to give the meanings of words. Sometimes the same word has more than one meaning, but the meanings are related. In this case, only one entry word is listed and the different meanings are given. They are usually numbered. Read the definitions for the word **nickel** in the illustration below.

> **nick·el** (nik′·əl), *n.* 1. A silvery white metal. 2. A coin made of nickel and copper, worth five cents.

Sometimes two or more different words just happen to have the same spelling. Then each word has a separate entry because it is completely unrelated to the other word or words with that spelling. See the two entries for the word **pupil** in the illustration below.

> **pu·pil**₁ (pyü′·pəl), *n.* A person who is being taught by someone; student.
>
> **pu·pil**₂ (pyü′·pəl), *n.* A round opening that appears black, through which light passes into the eye.

Suppose you read the sentence **The pupil sat upright in his seat,** and you decide to look up the word **pupil.** You would know that this pupil is not the dark round center of the eye. You need to look until you find the definition that makes sense in the sentence.

Sometimes a dictionary entry includes a **run-on entry.** This is a phrase with a special meaning, in which the entry word is used. In the example below, **at the mercy of** is a run-on entry.

> **mer·cy** (mėr′·sē), *n. pl.* **mer·cies** 1. More kindness than what is deserved or expected; compassion. 2. Something to appreciate; a blessing.
>
> **at the mercy of.** Completely in the power of; unable to avoid punishment from.

Phrases may also be found as separate entries. The phrases **Indian corn, Indian paintbrush,** and **Indian summer** are included in alphabetical order among the other entries in a dictionary.

An abbreviation shows what part of speech an entry word is. If a word can be used as more than one part of speech, most dictionaries give the meanings in groups according to those parts of speech. What part of speech are the words **pupil** and **mercy** in the entries above? According to the entry below, what parts of speech can the word **express** be?

> **ex·press** (ek·spres′), *v.* 1. To put into words. 2. To squeeze out (a liquid). —*n.* 3. A fast way of sending something. —*adj.* 4. Fast; swift, as a way of travel.

Remember: A dictionary is useful for learning the pronunciations and meanings of words.

Oral Drill

A. Look up the following words in your dictionary. Pronounce them correctly according to the phonetic spellings.
   1. mischief   4. genuine   7. surprise
   2. ration   5. grievous   8. epitome
   3. covetous   6. question   9. official

B. Find two different meanings for each word. Give the part of speech for each meaning. Read the example sentence for each meaning if your dictionary gives one.
   1. hamper   4. baste   7. smelt
   2. rush   5. page   8. fuse
   3. till   6. pack   9. nip

Written Practice

A. Copy the following words. Beside each word, write the phonetic spelling. Include the syllable divisions and the accent marks.

1. chaos
2. animosity
3. idea
4. demonstration
5. interrogative
6. azure

B. Write the letter of the correct meaning for each boldface word in the sentences. Choose from the following meanings. (You will not write all the letters.)

a. *n.* A player whose turn it is to bat in baseball.
b. *v.* To beat with repeated blows.
c. *v.* To purchase by trading.
d. *n.* A liquid mixture as of flour, milk, and eggs, that thickens when cooked or baked.
e. *v.* To creep by growing over (a surface).
f. *v.* To keep going; operate.
g. *n.* A number of fish moving together.
h. *n.* A point in baseball, made by running safely around the bases and reaching home plate.
i. *v.* To move swiftly on foot.
j. *n.* A place where threads have become undone.

1. Jennifer will stir up a cake **batter.**
2. Who will be the next **batter** at recess?
3. We had to **batter** down the old door to get inside.
4. Can an ostrich **run** faster than a horse?
5. Ivy **runs** up the east wall of the mansion.
6. Does your car **run** better since it was at the garage?
7. Oh, no, my stocking has a **run**!
8. The children could hardly wait to help during the salmon **run.**

C. Write two different meanings for each of the following words. Give the part of speech for each meaning you write.

   1. punch   2. post   3. sage

D. Write the part of speech for each word in bold print, as it is used in that sentence.

   1. Please **staple** these papers together.

   2. Potatoes are a **staple** in our diet.

   3. Cotton is a **staple** crop in the South.

   4. A giant weeping willow **tree** stands in our back yard.

   5. Dogs can easily **tree** a gray fox.

   6. The squirrel sat on a **tree** stump in the woods.

113. Synonyms and Antonyms

The English language has a great variety of words. When we write, we can choose words that say exactly what we mean. In this lesson you will study words with similar meanings and words with opposite meanings.

Words with similar meanings are **synonyms.** Two synonyms may be very close in meaning, but they never have exactly the same meaning. They cannot always be used in the same way. For example, the words **broke** and **fractured** are synonyms. We might say that a man **broke** or **fractured** his leg, and we might also say that it happened when his ladder **broke.** But we would not say that his ladder **fractured**!

Another example is **fast. Swift, speedy, rapid,** and **quick** all mean **fast,** but each one has a little different shade of meaning.

Words with opposite meanings are **antonyms.** Sometimes we make our meaning the clearest by using an antonym to tell what something is **not.** Some antonyms are words like **happy** and

sad. Other antonyms are formed by adding a prefix such as **un-** or **dis-** to a word. In this way we can form antonyms like **happy—unhappy** and **obey—disobey.**

By continuing to read and write, and by using your dictionary, you will meet many new words and learn how to use them.

Remember: Synonyms are words with similar meanings. Antonyms are words with opposite meanings.

> **Oral Drill** >

A. Tell if the words in each pair are **synonyms** or **antonyms.**

1. deny—admit	6. round—circular
2. steward—servant	7. accept—reject
3. surplus—extra	8. poverty—wealth
4. rise—descend	9. bother—molest
5. pleasant—annoying	10. location—position

B. Match the synonyms. Write each pair on the chalkboard.

1. buy	fasten
2. total	purchase
3. couch	error
4. fault	proper
5. attach	sofa
6. correct	sum

C. Match the antonyms. Write each pair on the chalkboard.

1. conceal	union
2. proud	rise
3. dense	expose
4. separation	sparse
5. calm	humble
6. sink	anxious

> Written Practice >

A. Write each word and the matching synonym.

1. beneath	assist
2. neglect	under
3. almost	fierce
4. plot	overlook
5. help	nearly
6. violent	scheme

B. Write each word and the matching antonym.

1. sweet	follow
2. forward	last
3. first	sour
4. come	down
5. up	backward
6. lead	go

C. Write both a synonym and an antonym for each word. Use a dictionary to help you.

1. join	3. gentle	5. trust
2. help	4. sensible	6. bad

D. Copy this paragraph, using synonyms to express the same ideas as the words in bold print. You may use the synonyms you found in Part C.

Never **join** with a group of **bad** men. Instead, look for and **trust** those who will **help** your character. Listen to their **sensible** advice, and learn their **gentle** ways.

E. Correct this Bible story by writing an antonym for each bold-face word.

Two men went (1) **down** to the temple to pray. The one, a Pharisee, (2) **sat** and prayed, "God, I thank You that I am not (3) **righteous** as other men are." Then he told God about (4) **none** of the (5) **evil** things he had done.

The other man was a tax collector. He knew that he had done many (6) **good** things. He smote his breast and prayed, "God, be (7) **severe** to me a (8) **saint.**"

> **Review and Practice**

A. Copy the title and the stanza below, using correct capitalization.

> **october's bright blue weather**
> o suns and skies and clouds of june,
>   and flowers of june together,
> ye cannot rival for one hour
>   october's bright blue weather.
> —*Helen Hunt Jackson*

B. Copy each sentence, using correct capitalization.
1. "before abraham was, i am," said jesus.
2. the lord jehovah reigns, and he will judge the world.
3. king ahasuerus chose esther to be queen instead of queen vashti.
4. the amazon river begins in the andes mountains and flows into the atlantic ocean.
5. last april our church sang at the washington hospital on good friday.
6. the officer was mr. edward k. lewis, jr.
7. in december, january, and february, it is winter in north america but summer in most of south america.
8. philip p. bliss wrote "let the lower lights be burning" after he heard about a shipwreck on lake erie.

114. Making Introductions

An introduction helps people who are strangers to get acquainted. There is a proper way to make introductions. Knowing how to introduce people will help you to make friends better. The Bible says, "A man that hath friends must shew himself friendly" (Proverbs 18:24) and "Be ye kind one to another" (Ephesians 4:32).

Follow these rules when making introductions.

1. **To introduce a younger person and an older person, say the older person's name first.**

   "Brother Thomas, this is my neighbor Ronald Shenk.
   "Ronald, this is Brother Thomas, my teacher."

   "Sister Miriam, this is Regina Thorpe, my classmate and friend.
   "Regina, this is Sister Miriam, my Sunday school teacher."

2. **If a man and a woman or a boy and a girl are about the same age, introduce them by saying the woman's or girl's name first.**

   "Sister Nancy, this is Uncle Mark.
   "Uncle Mark, this is Sister Nancy, my teacher."

3. **If two boys, two girls, two men, or two women are about the same age, introduce them by saying either name first.**

   "Mark, this is my cousin Bruce Martin.
   "Bruce, this is my friend Mark Simmons."

4. **To introduce anyone to your mother, say "Mother" first.**

   "Mother, I want you to meet my teacher, Sister Beth.
   "Sister Beth, this is my mother."

5. **To introduce yourself to a stranger, say "Hello" and give your name.** Sometimes you will be alone with another person whom you do not know. A good thing to do then is to walk up, smile, and say "Hello. My name is —— ——. I don't think we have ever met before."

When you are introducing others, it is good to give some extra information about them. Tell about something you know both persons are interested in, to help them get started in conversation.

> "Carl, Raymond recently moved here from Ohio."
> "Karen, Lucy is one of our best artists."
> "Ruth, Sally enjoys writing poems."
> "Howard, Marcus just got six white rabbits."

When you are introduced to someone, it is a good idea to repeat his name at once. If you heard it wrong, your mistake can be corrected right away. Repeating the name will also help you to remember it.

> "Charles, this is my brother Edgar. Edgar has been to Guatemala."
> "I'm glad to meet you, Edgar! What did you do in Guatemala?"

Remember: Be courteous and respectful when you make an introduction. Say an older person's name before a younger person's, say a woman's name before a man's, and always say "Mother" first.

Oral Drill

A. Tell which rule in the lesson applies to each introduction.
1. Mother, this is Mr. Brown.
2. Father, this is my friend Arthur Wilson.
3. Louise, let me present Frank Martin, my helper.
4. James, I'd like you to meet Richard Krause, my neighbor.
5. Mother, this is Brother Nathan, the principal at our school.

B. Tell whose name should be said first in the following introductions.
1. Your classmate who is a boy, and your cousin who is a girl.
2. Your mother and your music teacher.
3. Your sister and a girl who is your age.
4. Yourself and a stranger.

C. Make an introduction in class, using real names. You may get ideas from Part B.

Written Practice

Write an introduction for each case.
1. You are introducing Ronald Morgan, a neighbor boy about your age, and your uncle Emory.
2. You are introducing your classmate Susan Albright and your cousin Harold Miller.
3. You are introducing your grandmother and your minister Brother Reuben Weaver.
4. You are with another person you have never met, and no one else introduces you.

> Review and Practice >

Copy this friendly letter correctly. Remember the rules for capitalization and for using commas in sentences and in letters.

5235 oak street

altoona alabama 35952

april 6 20—

dear louisa

greetings in the Name of jesus. "The lord is good to all: and his tender mercies are over all his works" (psalm 145:9).

I enjoyed our family trip to paraguay very much. paraguay you know is in south america. They were having summer of course while it was winter at home!

On january 11 we flew from miami florida. We landed in asunción the capital city. Then we took a bus and drove over two hundred miles to the city of encarnación in southern paraguay. Someone from the mission station came there to pick us up. Soon we were off the blacktop road. We drove on dirt roads for many more miles! I certainly hoped it wouldn't suddenly rain, as it often does in paraguay. The roads become slippery and muddy and vehicles get stuck. Sometimes they are stuck all night! But the lord was watching over us and we arrived safely at the mission point.

I enjoyed so much being with my friend lois esh. She was born in paraguay. Her parents moved there fifteen years ago.

I hope you can come soon louisa and see my pictures. "The lord watch between me and thee, when we are absent one from another" (genesis 31:49).

your friend

phoebe miller

115. Homophones

Homophones are words that are pronounced alike, but their spellings and meanings are different. It takes care and thought to spell homophones correctly, but this is important so that the reader gets the right thought. Read the following sentences. They sound very nearly the same, but there is a great difference in which one you write!

The doctor has no patients.
The doctor has no patience.

Of course, if a doctor has no patience, he is not likely to have patients either.

Study the following examples of homophones.

air—heir	flour—flower	load—lode
boy—buoy	great—grate	might—mite
chews—choose	heart—hart	not—knot
dear—deer	idle—idol	rose—rows

Some homophones come in sets of three.

sent—cent—scent	to—too—two
I—eye—aye	vain—vane—vein
right—write—rite	you—ewe—yew

In some sets of homophones, one word is a contraction. Be sure to use the correct word. Think of the words a contraction stands for when you use it.

your—you're
    Your means "belonging to you."
    You're means "you are."

its—it's
    Its means "belonging to it."
    It's means "it is."

whose—who's
> **Whose** means "belonging to whom."
> **Who's** means "who is."

aisle—isle—I'll
> An **aisle** is a walkway between seats.
> An **isle** is a small island.
> **I'll** means "I shall" or "I will."

there—their—they're
> **There** means "at that place."
> **Their** means "belonging to them."
> **They're** means "they are."

Remember: Homophones are words that are pronounced alike, but their spellings and meanings are different. Use homophones carefully. Check a dictionary when you are not sure of the correct spelling or meaning.

> **Oral Drill**

A. Give a homophone for each word. You may use a dictionary.

1. vale	4. whose	7. its
2. I'll	5. your	8. wood
3. there	6. made	9. ewe

B. Find the errors in these sentences. Tell how to spell the correct homophone.
1. She new the pale was leaking.
2. Hear is a pear of steal knives.
3. He blue his horn at the bare on the rode.
4. The peace of would was two large for hour stove.
5. You're pare tree wood yield more pairs if it were pruned.
6. The Lord saw awl there troubles.

7. The wild bore had hurt it's write front hoof.
8. Are these books your's, or who's are they?
9. When we rise to prey, we always stand in the isle to our left.
10. There is a gnu songbook in each desk.
11. The rows plants were set out in straight rose.
12. Can you make cents out of this problem about dollars and sense?
13. If you roe close, you can see a heart, a row, and some other dear.
14. Who through the bawl threw the window?
15. Jesus is the Sun of God.

> **Written Practice**

A. Write each word and the matching homophone.

1. some	prey
2. know	sealing
3. board	beet
4. beat	sum
5. ceiling	flower
6. pray	no
7. flour	bored
8. cellar	eight
9. moan	mown
10. ate	seller

B. Write the correct homophones.
1. (Its, It's) (to, too) bad (there, their) dog lost (its, it's) (tail, tale).
2. The (brakes, breaks) on the old truck gave out.
3. How much do you (way, weigh)?
4. What is the bus (fair, fare)?
5. You can (sea, see) the (sea, see) from this window.
6. (Some, Sum) people cannot (some, sum) up (there, their, they're) ideas in a few words.

7. The (use, ewes, yews) and their lambs are in the pasture.

8. The English (use, ewes, yews) wood from trees called (use, ewes, yews) to make fine bows.

9. The little bird (soared, sword) high above the (blew, blue) sea.

10. God's Word is like a sharp two-edged (soared, sword).

11. (Ant, Aunt) (Mary, Merry) gave me a recipe for a new (desert, dessert).

12. Who (knows, nose) if an insect has a (knows, nose)?

13. Will the teacher (lesson, lessen) the number of questions in this (lesson, lessen)?

14. Have you (heard, herd) that he (sold, soled) his (heard, herd) of cows?

15. The (made, maid) has (made, maid) some delicious (rolls, roles).

> **Review and Practice**

A. Write **S, A,** or **H** to tell whether the words in each pair are synonyms, antonyms, or homophones.

1. great—grate
2. plain—simple
3. berry—bury
4. honest—deceitful

5. cold—frigid
6. freedom—slavery
7. need—knead
8. discharge—release

B. Rewrite each sentence correctly in two ways.

1. Haven't you never been at the ocean?
2. Harlan doesn't want no popcorn.
3. Students shouldn't never use poor English.
4. We hadn't scarcely heard you come.
5. Nina hasn't no new dresses.

116. Using a Concordance and a Bible Dictionary

Two valuable books that can be helpful in Bible study are a concordance of the Bible and a Bible dictionary.

Bible helps such as these are not perfect as the Bible is. They may not always be accurate, so we must carefully compare them with the Scriptures. If we use them wisely, they can help us to understand the Bible better.

A concordance is useful for finding verses in the Bible that contain a certain word. You may have a concordance in the back of your Bible, but that is a very small, limited one. There are other concordances that are larger and more extensive. *Strong's Exhaustive Concordance* is a very good, complete concordance. It has an entry for every word in the Bible!

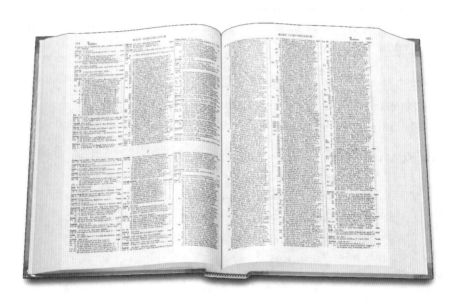

The words in a concordance are arranged in alphabetical order, as in a dictionary, with guide words at the top of each page. Under each entry word are references showing where the word is found, and beside each reference is the phrase that contains the word. The references are listed in the order of the books of the Bible. If you want to find references only from the Book of Psalms, you would find the section with verses from Psalms.

Suppose you are making a puzzle about Bible trees and you wonder if the elm tree is mentioned in the Bible. Look for **elm** in a concordance as you would in a dictionary, using the guide words. You will find **elms,** with the reference Hosea 4:13 and the phrase "under oaks and poplars and *e.*" The *e* stands for **elms** in this case.

A Bible dictionary gives interesting facts about Bible people, places, things, and customs. Entry words are arranged in alphabetical order, as in a dictionary, and information is given about each item.

Perhaps you need some information about elm trees in the Bible to help you make a good clue for your puzzle. You could look in a Bible dictionary for the information. Again find the word **elm** as you would in a dictionary, using the guide words. Under **Elm** your Bible dictionary may say "See **Plants**" or "See **Vegetable Kingdom**." If so, turn to that entry and find the alphabetized list of plant names. There you will find that the elm trees of the Bible are called turpentine trees today.

Remember: Use a concordance of the Bible to find verses that contain a certain word. Use a Bible dictionary to find information about people, places, things, and customs of the Bible.

```
> Oral Drill >
```

A. Look up **mountain** and **mountains** in a concordance. (You may use the small one in the back of your Bible if you have one.) Have at least one person use a larger concordance in case your small concordance does not give enough information.
   1. How many references from Isaiah does your concordance give?
   2. Where is the verse in Matthew that talks about removing mountains?
   3. In Exodus 3, Moses came to the mountain of ———.
   4. Scan the references under **mount,** and name some particular mountains of the Bible.

   Example: Mount Ephraim

B. Look up the name **John** in a Bible dictionary.
   1. How many different Johns are listed?
   2. Find the part about the apostle John, and give his father's name and his mother's name.
   3. Which book of the Bible tells about John Mark?

```
> Written Practice >
```

A. Look up **snow** in a concordance, and find the Bible verses that give answers for the following exercises. Write the answers in complete sentences, with the references.
   1. What brave deed was done in the midst of a pit in time of snow?
   2. What did Job speak of doing with snow water?
   3. What does God say to the snow?
   4. What kind of messenger is like the cold of snow?
   5. "He giveth snow like ———."
   6. Who says that our sins shall be as white as snow?
   7. Whose hair was as white as snow?

B. Look up the name **Anna** in a Bible dictionary.

1. How many women named **Anna** are mentioned in the Bible?
2. What Hebrew name means the same as **Anna**?
3. Where did Anna live?
4. What verses tell about Anna?
5. Name at least one other Bible character that lived at the same time as Anna.

> **Review and Practice**

Write the correct word or phrase for each sentence.

1. Do you have more apples (beside, besides) these?
2. Please set this basket (beside, besides) that one.
3. The runaway slaves went (in, into) the secret room.
4. They would hide (in, into) the room until they could travel on.
5. Where did you (go, go to)?
6. My book fell (off, off of) the table.
7. Rebecca and (she, her) picked the apples.
8. We gave some to Larry and (they, them).
9. Of all the apples we bought, the ones from Jason's orchard are (sweeter, sweetest).
10. Of the twins, Jeffrey is (taller, tallest).
11. Jerry runs (more faster, faster) than Joseph.
12. Apple pie is (gooder, better) than pumpkin pie.

117. Using Hyphens and Colons

Hyphens and colons are not used as often as commas and periods. But they are important punctuation marks, and you should learn to use them correctly.

Compound number words from twenty-one through ninety-nine are written with hyphens.

> twenty-one   one hundred forty-three
> thirty-two

All compound words that have **in-law** are written with hyphens. Hyphens are also used in all **great-** compounds that refer to relatives.

> brother-in-law   great-grandfather

Other compound words are also spelled with hyphens. There is no rule to tell which words have hyphens and which ones do not. We must simply learn them or check a dictionary.

Hyphens are used to show how words are divided into syllables.

> hy-phens   di-vid-ed   syl-la-bles

A hyphen is used to divide a word at the end of a line. The following paragraph has several examples of this.

> Sometimes a line in your para-
> graph becomes full before you fin-
> ish writing a word. You are permit-
> ted to divide the word by using a
> hyphen, separating the word into syl-
> lables, if you follow the rules!

A word should be divided at the end of a line only when necessary. When you must divide a word, remember the following rules.

a. Do not divide a one-syllable word.

Wrong: clo-uds, stren-gth

b. Divide only between syllables.

Wrong: batt-les, cou-rtesy
Right: bat-tles, cour-te-sy

A colon is used for writing the time with numbers. The colon is placed between the hour and the minute.

Mother plans to be back by **4:30.**
The plane will leave at **9:52.**

A colon is used in writing Scripture references. It is placed between the chapter and the verse.

Jesus said, "I am the bread of life" (John **6:35**).
John **3:16** has been translated into more than a thousand
languages.

A hyphen shows a series of connected verses. The hyphen means "through." A comma shows a break in a series of verses.

Brother John read 1 Corinthians 13:**1–10.**
We are memorizing Matthew **6:9–13, 19–21, 33.**

Remember: Hyphens are used in compound number words from twenty-one through ninety-nine and in other compound words like **father-in-law.** A hyphen is used when it is necessary to divide a word between syllables at the end of a line.

When time is written with numbers, a colon is placed between the hour and the minute. When a Scripture reference is written, a colon is placed between the chapter and the verse.

> Oral Drill >

A. Write the following words on the chalkboard, using hyphens between the syllables. Use the dictionary if you need help.
1. apostolic
2. intensely
3. reliability
4. apiary
5. inexpensive
6. disciplinary

B. Tell where hyphens are needed in the following sentences.
1. Elizabeth Anne's sister in law made seventy two dough nuts for the school picnic.
2. The science book says that an adult has about two hun dred bones.
3. Was Elias Martin the brother in law or father in law of your great aunt?
4. Was Fannie Martin the mother in law or sister in law of your great grandfather?

C. Write these times as numbers on the chalkboard.
1. three forty-five
2. ten twelve
3. six fifteen
4. twelve o'clock
5. eleven four
6. five fifty-two

D. Write these Scripture references on the chalkboard, using numbers.
1. Matthew five, verse one
2. Verses twelve through fifteen of Deuteronomy, chapter ten
3. Ephesians four, verses eleven through sixteen, twenty-two through twenty-four, and twenty-nine through thirty-two

> Written Practice >

A. Write these words, using hyphens to divide them into syllables. Use the dictionary if you need help.
1. heartily
2. purposefully
3. adapted
4. remarkable
5. abated
6. heroic

B. Write each word correctly that needs a hyphen.
   1. Aunt Maryann's father in law has sixty two grand children.
   2. Is your aunt Clara's mother in law the same person as my great aunt Sarah's sister in law?
   3. The family line of Uncle John's father in law has been traced back twenty four generations!
   4. Is the boiling point of water ninety nine or one hun dred degrees Celsius?

C. Write these times as numbers.
   1. two thirty
   2. six twenty
   3. twelve forty-five
   4. four forty-four
   5. seven thirty-two
   6. six o'clock

D. Write these Scripture references, using numbers.
   1. Isaiah, chapter fifty-three, verse one
   2. Ruth, chapter one, verse sixteen
   3. Psalm ninety, verse twelve
   4. Matthew, chapter five, verses one through twelve
   5. Proverbs thirty, verses ten, fourteen, and twenty

E. Write the following times. (Make up an exact time if you are not sure.)
   1. The time you usually get up in the morning.
   2. The time you usually go to bed in the evening.
   3. The time you have your first recess at school.
   4. The time you eat lunch at school.
   5. The time it is now as you do this assignment.

> Review and Practice >

Write the part of speech suggested by each clue.
1. It takes the place of a noun.
2. It is a connecting word that begins a prepositional phrase.
3. It names a person, place, thing, or idea.

4. It shows action or being.

5. It can be concrete or abstract.

6. It can be nominative, objective, or possessive.

7. It can be demonstrative, indefinite, or interrogative.

8. It tells **which, whose, how many,** or **what kind of.**

9. It modifies a noun or a pronoun.

10. It expresses strong feeling and is not related to the rest of the sentence.

11. It shows tense.

12. It modifies a verb, an adjective, or an adverb.

13. It joins words or groups of words.

14. It may be an article.

118. Using the Telephone

Using the telephone requires special courtesy. It is part of being kind to our neighbors and friends. "Let your speech be alway with grace, seasoned with salt, that ye may know how ye ought to answer every man" (Colossians 4:6).

When you make a call, be sure to dial the right number. Do your best to avoid disturbing others by calling a wrong number. If you do not know the number, find it in the telephone directory or ask someone to find it for you.

When you are calling and no one answers right away, let the telephone ring at least seven times. If the other person cannot get around well, it is good to let it ring even longer.

When someone answers the telephone, say "Hello." Then tell who you are and why you are calling. Keep your lips about an inch from the mouthpiece, and hold the earpiece lightly against your ear. Speak loudly enough so that your listener can easily hear you, but do not shout.

When you answer the telephone, say "Hello" and tell who you are. For example, say "Hello; this is the Martins' residence, Melanie speaking." If you answer a telephone away from home, tell where you are. For example, if you are working in a bookstore, you might say "Hello; Masters' Bookstore, Anita Price speaking."

If the call is for someone else, offer to get him or to take a message. When you take a message, listen carefully and write it down accurately. Ask questions if there is anything you do not understand.

Let the person who called you end the call. Then you will not end the conversation before he has finished everything he wanted to say. Unless for a good reason you must end the conversation, let the person who called say "Good-bye" first.

Remember: When using the telephone, be courteous and respectful.

> **Oral Drill**

Tell what you would say in the following situations. Use them for practice with telephone conversations in class. Use toy telephones if you have them.

1. Mr. Martin calls on the telephone and asks to speak to your father, who is not at home. (Let one student be Mr. Martin, and another student be the one who answers at home.)

2. Anna calls and asks for your older sister, Julie, who is not at home. She wants Julie to bring a certain address to school the next day.

3. You are helping Mrs. Rhoda Myer. While she is in the garden, her telephone rings and you answer it. The caller is Sister Mary, who wants to take Mrs. Myer to the store the next morning around 9:10.

4. You call to your father's work place at Agri's Grain and Feed Mill. You want to tell your father to bring home some rabbit pellets. A secretary named George Lowe answers the telephone and then calls your father to the telephone. (You will need three students to practice this one.)

Written Practice

A. List five things you should do to show courtesy when you use the telephone.

B. Suppose you need to answer the telephone while you are working in the Pattersons' home. In one or two sentences, write what you should say.

Review and Practice

A. Copy these sentences, using capital letters and punctuation marks where they are needed.
1. lester said when explorers arrived in brazil, they saw indians wearing rubbers on their feet
2. they dipped their feet in bowls of rubber explained lester
3. brother leon said well those waterproof shoes fit them perfectly
4. where did they get the rubber questioned leora
5. it was sap explained lester from rubber trees
6. oh come here exclaimed jean and look at these old dusty books i found

7. in 1 samuel 5 15, we read that the philistines took the ark of god from ebenezer to ashdod and set it in the house of dagon their fish god

8. does psalm 22 have thirty one verses

9. the mark bowman family will meet you at liberty square in philadelphia at 1 30 P M on labor day

10. i think that i shall never see
    a poem lovely as a tree.
    a tree that looks at god all day,
    and lifts her leafy arms to pray.

11. mr joyce kilmer a famous poet wrote the poem "trees"

12. the fruit of the spirit includes love joy peace and faith

13. mr elton's address is 115 springview avenue carlisle pennsylvania

14. on may 24 1991 we plan to visit mr and mrs kimball in chicago illinois and see their new greenhouse

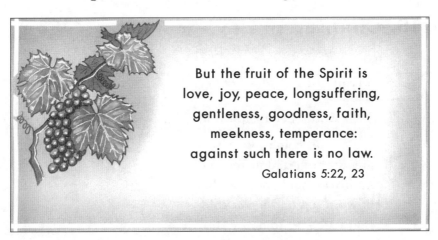

But the fruit of the Spirit is love, joy, peace, longsuffering, gentleness, goodness, faith, meekness, temperance: against such there is no law.
Galatians 5:22, 23

B. Write the correct verb for each sentence.
   1. My sister (brang, brought) apple cider for the treat.
   2. Our dog (swam, swum) the whole way across the lake.
   3. We were afraid our pet had (drowned, drownded), but soon he (come, came) home again.

4. I (saw, seen) several mallards by the water.
5. One of the balloons (busted, burst) with a loud pop.
6. Last week they (cost, costed) only five cents a pack.
7. The baby (sleeped, slept) soundly all afternoon.
8. There (is, are) several ways to do this job correctly.
9. I'm sure I (tug, tagged) you before you reached base.
10. I believe someone has (took, taken) my pencil.
11. Lillian often (borrow, borrows) my pen.
12. You (write, writes) interesting letters.
13. Yesterday I (tryed, tried) a new recipe.
14. The boys (likes, liked) the food so well that they have (ate, eaten) all of it.

119. Chapter 10 Review

A. Tell which words need capital letters.

no rainbow
if all were rain and never sun,
    no bow would span the hill;
if all were sun and never rain,
    there'd be no rainbow still.
                —*Christina Rossetti*

fame
fame is a bee.
it has a song—
it has a sting—
ah, too, it has a wing.
                —*Emily Dickenson*

B. Tell which words should be capitalized.
1. the song "god moves in a mysterious way" was written by william cowper.
2. mr. henry f. lyte wrote "abide with me."
3. sarah f. adams of london, england, wrote "nearer, my god, to thee," one of president mcKinley's favorite hymns.
4. the parliament of canada has two parts: the house of commons and the senate.
5. mount cook is the highest peak in the country of new zealand.
6. the rhine river is the most important inland waterway on the continent of europe.
7. brother glen and sister grace visited the st. louis botanical gardens on new year's day.
8. the mennonites will conduct services in the denver community hall next thursday.
9. during world war I, many mennonites whose ancestors were from germany suffered persecution.
10. easter day, ascension day, and memorial day all come in the spring.

C. Tell whether you would find each entry word on a dictionary page with these guide words: **locust** . . . **Lot.**

1. lodge	4. loss	7. love
2. Luz	5. Moab	8. lock
3. loft	6. Lois	9. long-suffering

D. Give a synonym, an antonym, and a homophone for each word.
1. great   2. pale   3. weak

E. Tell where you should look to find the following information.
1. How to spell the plural of **sister-in-law.**
2. Which verse in the Bible mentions ice.
3. Whether it is ever correct to use **littler** and **littlest** as forms of comparison for **little.**

4. The other correct spelling for **jailor.**
5. Whether this word is spelled right: **suprise.**
6. How many Jameses are mentioned in the Bible.
7. Where the land of Moab is.
8. How many verses in the Bible mention snow.
9. The principal parts of the verb **swim.**
10. How to pronounce the word **mischief.**
11. How many meanings the word **smelt** has.
12. What part of speech the word **scow** is.

F. Give answers to these questions.
1. Whose name should you say first when you introduce the following people?
   a. a younger person and an older person
   b. a visitor and your mother
   c. a man and a woman
2. If you are with a stranger and there is no one to introduce you, what should you do?
3. What should you do before you dial a telephone number?
4. How should you speak into a telephone?
5. When you call someone, how long should you let the telephone ring?
6. How should you answer the telephone when you are at home?
7. How should you answer the telephone when you are away from home?
8. What should you do when you take a message?
9. Who should end a telephone call?

> **Written Practice** >

A. Copy these poems, using correct capitalization.

there's a wideness in god's mercy
there's a wideness in god's mercy,
   like the wideness of the sea;
there's a kindness in his justice,
   which is more than liberty.
                    —*Frederick William Faber*

bed in summer
in winter i get up at night
and dress by yellow candlelight;
in summer quite the other way,
i have to go to bed by day.
                    —*Robert Louis Stevenson*

B. Copy each sentence, using correct capitalization.
   1. the hymn "nearer, my god, to thee" is based on jacob's experience at bethel.
   2. "let the lower lights be burning" was written by p. p. bliss.
   3. "blest be the tie that binds" was written by pastor j. fawcett.
   4. mr. a. c. coxe wrote the first stanza of a hymn while he was in the united states.
   5. later he crossed the atlantic ocean, and he finished the hymn in oxford, england.
   6. the senate and the house of representatives are the two parts of congress.
   7. mount fuji is a volcano on an island of japan.
   8. the volga river is the longest river in europe.
   9. christmas day comes on december 25 every year.
   10. yellowstone national park has many geysers and hot springs.
   11. the mennonites had a large meeting at the providence mennonite church one sunday last winter.
   12. the *martyrs mirror* was printed for the mennonites just before the french and indian war broke out.

13. the victorian age was during queen victoria's reign in england.
14. the lord is my shepherd; i shall not want.
15. then i answered, "i am willing, O lord."

C. Write **S, A,** or **H** to tell whether the words in each pair are synonyms, antonyms, or homophones.

1. ordinary—peculiar
2. ask—request
3. waste—waist
4. distant—far
5. arrive—depart
6. final—initial
7. answer—respond
8. danger—safety
9. pair—pare
10. ball—sphere
11. mist—missed
12. plan—scheme

D. Make a sentence by writing this list of words in alphabetical order. Punctuate it correctly.

Ernest winter Evans last Eric Kenton flew Kentucky from

E. Write the letter of the correct meaning for each word in bold print.

   a. *v.* To cover with ashes.
   b. *n.* A bench for rowers in a galley.
   c. *n.* A ridge of earth.
   d. *v.* To tilt or incline.
   e. *n.* A place for keeping money.

1. We planted ivy on the **bank** by the front yard.
2. The check was deposited in the **bank.**
3. The little airplane **banked** and turned.
4. **Bank** the fire before you leave.
5. The guide said, "Take seats on the **bank** while I tell you how the slaves rowed the ship."

F. Write the part of speech for each boldface word. You may use a dictionary.

1. Do not **jam** the typewriter keys.
2. I like a sandwich with peach **jam** and peanut butter.

3. The Millers were caught in a traffic **jam** for two hours.

4. Father had to **jam** on the brakes when a deer ran out in front of us.

5. The men worked hard to open the **jammed** door.

G. Write the correct homophones.

1. The (vale, veil) in the temple was torn in two.

2. When was the last (time, thyme) you used (time, thyme) for seasoning food?

3. (We, Wee) saw a (we, wee) black lamb in the meadow.

4. Did (you, ewe, yew) see the (you, ewe, yew) and her lamb under the (you, ewe, yew) tree?

H. Copy the words or numbers that are written incorrectly, and add the missing hyphens and colons.

1. Mrs. Brown's sister in law will be ninety eight years old tomorrow.

2. English class begins at 10 00 in the morning.

3. There are twenty two students in the class.

4. My great uncle will have a topic on Galatians 5 22 26 at 8 15 this evening.

5. Brother Matthew's father in law will speak on 2 Tim othy 2 15 at the patrons' meeting.

I. Which one of the five senses did the writer use in this description?

A newly released monarch butterfly slowly pumps his still-wet wings. Golden orange splashes contrast sharply with black bars on his wings. He waves his shiny black antennae like long, curved spears. Soon he will soar up and away into the crystal blue sky.

Index